Cleveland Garden Handbook

SECOND EDITION

Susan McClure

and 17 Other Cleveland Garden Experts

GRAY & COMPANY, PUBLISHERS

CLEVELAND

The first edition of this book was published in 1993 as
The Greater Cleveland Garden Guide.

Gray & Company, Publishers
11000 Cedar Avenue
Cleveland, Ohio 44106
(216) 721-2665

ISBN 1-886228-00-0

Thanks to the scores of Cleveland-area gardeners who make northeast Ohio so rich horticulturally—they provide the resources for this resource guide; to all the contributors; to the staffs of the Cleveland Botanical Garden, Holden Arboretum, and the Cooperative Extension Service; and to Anna McCormack for tracking down the facts, and Beth Spindler for her creative illustrations. Thanks also to my husband, Ted, who—once again—cooked some excellent dinners while I worked to finish this project!

In memory of Peter Brumbaugh, a great plantsman.

Contents

Contents (continued)

SECTION II • LOCAL GARDEN RESOURCES

6 Landscape Professionals and Suppliers

7 Horticultural Organizations

8 Garden Education, Information, and Events

9 Learning from Other Gardens

Contributors

Alexander Apanius is a landscape designer and horticulturist located in Hudson who designs residential, commercial, institutional, and municipal gardens and landscapes. He is on the board of the Association of Professional Landscape Designers, an international organization, and is the former director of the Cleveland Botanical Garden. He prefers low-maintenance, naturalistic landscaping featuring native plants.

Jeff Andrey, co-owner of Dugan's Garden Center, started working in garden centers in high school and later received his nursery management degree from the Agricultural Technical Institute. He enjoys growing bonsai, restoring a century home, and giving talks to gardening groups.

Peter Brumbaugh, who died in 1995, was owner of Wood and Company, a full-service garden center in Cleveland Heights. He grew up in the bulb business; Wood and Company, under the management of Peter's aunt in the late 1800s, was the first garden center in the Cleveland area to import bulbs from Holland.

Davey Tree Expert Company, headquartered in Kent, Ohio, specializes in caring for landscape plants and is especially well known for its work with trees. The company stays on the cutting edge of plant care technology because it has one of the largest corporate research facilities in the country.

Kathleen Gips is a herbarist who has been growing, using, studying, lecturing, and writing about herbs for 20 years. She operates the Village Herb Shop in Chagrin Falls and a mail-order catalog. She collects antique posy holders, has made thousands of gallons of potpourri, and has published *The Language of Flowers: A Book of Victorian Floral Sentiments*.

Suzanne Hively is garden editor and pets columnist for *The Plain Dealer*. She is also a former flight instructor and commercial artist. Her hobbies, in addition to gardening, include showing dogs and boating.

Bob Hobar, director of sales and marketing for Irrigation Supply, Inc., has been working with irrigation systems for 20 years. He is a certified Irrigation Association designer.

Contributors (continued)

Richard Kay, owner of Breezewood Gardens for almost 20 years, has a degree in biology from Denison University and one in horticulture from Ohio State University. He sells plants and gardening supplies and is an avid gardener.

Tom Krupa is manager of Gale's Garden Center in Willoughby Hills, where he has worked for 20 years. He has a degree from Ohio State University Agricultural Technical Institute. He especially enjoys flower gardening at home with his family.

Lake County Nursery, Inc., is one of Ohio's largest wholesale nurseries. They have more than 1,000 acres in cultivation and carry many of the newest and best woody plants. They also offer perennials, ground covers, and ornamental grasses, which they showcase in their own Mary Elizabeth Show Garden.

Rob McCartney, horticulturist for Sea World of Ohio, creates landscaping to entertain and educate. According to recent marketing surveys, his ideas are working; landscaping has been rated the number one feature of the park in various guest surveys. McCartney, who has a master's degree in horticulture, received the International Society of Arboriculture's Award for Academic Achievement.

Greg Payton is the horticultural technician of the Holden Arboretum Rhododendron Garden. He is a member of the Great Lakes Chapter of the American Rhododendron Society.

Bobbie Schwartz, garden designer and consultant, owns Bobbie's Green Thumb. Two of her designs—one residential and one industrial—have won design awards. She is also active in the Ohio Nursery and Landscape Association and especially enjoys growing perennials.

Robin Armstrong Siktberg, who has a degree in horticulture with a minor in journalism, is horticulturist for the Cleveland Botanical Garden. She is in charge of developing and maintaining the gardens and also teaches, writes, and answers garden questions. In her spare time she grows perennials at home.

Don Vanderbrook is a nationally known floral designer who has decorated for exciting events such as the 200th anniversary of Congress, President Bush's Inaugural party, and the British Embassy for Queen Elizabeth's visit. He has a charming formal flower garden at his rural home.

Mike Wells is field manager for Gali's Florist and Garden Center, which was started in 1945. A master gardener for over 25 years, he recently moved here from New York City, where he was active with the New York Botanical Garden. He had a tropical plant business in which he grew over 350 different African violets and over 100 orchid hybrids and 20 different orchid genera.

Ron Zayac, owner of Warren Road nursery, specializes in growing uncommon plants, such as new and better types of daylilies. He got started in horticulture by volunteering in community garden programs and helping teens plant vegetables for the food bank.

Introduction

Have you ever needed a solution to a particular gardening problem but not known where to look? Do you wonder what you need to keep your landscape beautiful? When you need help with a complicated task, such as pruning, tackling pests, or landscaping, do you know how to choose the right professional for the job? Do you sometimes think about taking classes in gardening or botany—or even toy with the idea of beginning a career in horticulture? Are you interested in meeting people with similar gardening interests to trade information and share secrets? Would you like to know more about the gardens in this area that you can tour for recreation and inspiration?

If any of the above apply to you, like most gardeners in this area you probably know that the answers you need exist. But they are sometimes hard to find.

Do you sometimes wonder why a friend has sandy soil while you have clay—and what you can do about it? Do Cleveland's droughts and downpours cause problems for your landscape and headaches for you? Have you ever wanted to make your garden or landscape more successful with less work? Does your garden ever get behind schedule because a few tasks have slipped your mind?

There are solutions to these problems, too, if you know whom to ask, where to look, and what too look for.

The greater Cleveland area has a wonderfully rich and diverse population of gardens and gardeners and a resulting wide range of gardening resources. This book is meant to bring together in a single handy guide the best and most useful of these many resources and to tell where, when, and how to find out more about them. In it are the answers to these questions and many more like them. It will help you:

- Learn how to take care of your yard;
- Find out how to handle your soil and choose the right plants for any landscape job;
- Navigate the vast network of gardening professionals and suppliers;
- Understand climate and soil and how they affect your garden and landscapes;
- Plan a calendar of necessary tasks for every month of the year;
- Get help for common problems and guidance for evaluating your landscape and making landscape improvements;
- Discover special gardens to tour;
- Learn about programs to further your garden education;
- Gain access to horticultural groups and plant societies;
- Find where to turn for more information.

This book is designed to help turn new homeowners into gardeners and good gardeners into great ones!

Using This Book

Plant Names

Whenever possible, I have called plants by their common names—for example, rose and daylily. On occasion, however, I must refer to the more specific botanical name in order to avoid confusion with other plants. Even if you don't care to use these botanical names when you are talking with friends, they can be useful when you want to order plants or review information on them in other texts.

Using Botanical Names

A botanical name consists of genus and species, which are written in italics. The genus name is always capitalized. For instance, rose in the genus *Rosa*. The species name is not capitalized, as with the old-fashioned species of fragrant French rose, *Rosa gallica*.

Often you also will find a variety name (indicating an improvement or variation on a species that has occurred naturally and been propagated for gardens) or cultivar name (indicating a plant that is known only in cultivation and was hybridized in a breeding program, cloned, or developed from a man-made mutation). Variety names are written in italics. Cultivars are capitalized and enclosed in apostrophes. For instance the creeping blue-green-leaved sargent juniper is *Juniperus chinensis* 'Glauca'. Although this cultivar may grow like other creeping junipers, 'Glauca' differs because it holds its blue-green color especially well in winter. If you like that look, look for this cultivar name on a nursery tag or in a catalog. Likewise, you can find cultivars with special characteristics for nearly every type of landscape or garden plant—just look for a cultivar name and explanation of the cultivar's special characteristics. (You may have to ask salespeople or check reference books to find out how a cultivar differs from the species and from other cultivars.)

Hybrid plants, the result of interbreeding two or more species, will be indicated by an "x" placed between the generic name and the species name. For instance, the old-fashioned alba rose is written *Rosa* x *alba*. This hybrid is also available in cultivars such as *Rosa* x *alba* 'Incarnata', which has white blooms tinged in pink.

Occasionally, when hybrid plants have many parents, we may leave out the species name and refer to the plant by genus and cultivar. One example is the Meidiland roses, new disease-resistant, extra hardy, hybrid shrub roses from France. The botanical name for a scarlet-flowered type with arching three-foot-long fronds is *Rosa* 'Scarlet Meidiland'. Occasionally, when cultivars come from overseas, you may also see the original, foreign name listed. For 'Scarlet Meidiland', the French cultivar name is 'Meikrotal' P.P. 6087.

You can find most species names listed in *Hortus Third* (1976, MacMillan, New York, NY), a massive dictionary of cultivated plants. For more information on the process and meaning of botanical nomenclature, look for the classic book *Botanical Latin* (by William Stern, 3rd Ed. 1983, David and Charles Publishing, North Pomfret, VT), or *Gardener's Latin* (by Bill Neal, 1992, Algonquin Books, Chapel Hill, NC), a fun, small book that will tell you what some of these botanical names mean.

Horticultural Terms

I may occasionally use horticultural terms that are not familiar to you. Some of these may prove valuable—for example, by helping you clearly explain a process or problem when talking to a landscaper or experienced gardener. Horticultural terms that may be uncommon are accompanied by a brief description.

References

Cross-references within the text indicate related entries in other sections and chapters.

You may want further information or details about some subjects discussed in this book. When an especially good book exists, I have referred you to it. Most of these can be obtained from local bookstores or libraries. There is also a list of some publishers that specialize in gardening books and a guide to area gardening libraries in chapter 8.

Disclaimer

Please note that addresses, dates, times, and other data were accurate when collected but are always subject to change. Use the phone numbers listed in this book to verify important information.

Cleveland Garden Handbook

SECOND EDITION

CHAPTER 1

Understanding Our Natural Resources

Whether you are an experienced gardener or a novice, it is important to understand the natural resources that affect your garden in so many ways. Any growing plant is intimately tied to soil and sun, rain and snow, wind, humidity, temperature—all of which together provide the substances it needs to grow. When you understand what to expect from weather and earth you can then make better decisions about what, how, when, and where to plant.

Certain generalizations can be made about our local natural resources that usually prove true. But climate and soil can also vary widely from site to site within this region, and for a lot of reasons. The following sections discuss the climate of greater Cleveland and the great variety of weather it brings, and the region's primary soil types and what they mean for gardeners.

Climate

Northeast Ohio Climate: Expect the Unexpected

Each time the weather does what we don't expect, many gardeners are surprised, However, history says we should be learning to expect the unexpected. An 1863 letter mentioned in *Western Reserve Magazine* describes weather fluctuations that fell upon an early Cleveland Shaker farming community: "Ever since the fore part of April way into June it was so wet and cold in these parts that nothing would grow, especially in this stiff clay." The same article also mentions "Droughts [no rain for months in 1851] and late frosts [ice a quarter inch thick on June 9, 1862]." Does some of this sound familiar?

As with any hobby that is tied to nature, conditions for gardening vary—from week to week, season to season, decade to decade. Compare any two recent summers and chances are good one was drenched with excessive rain and the other relatively dry. The last spring frost can come in April or at the end of May. Winters, too, can be been quite different, featuring sub-zero range temperatures (our usual) or warm stretches that rarely see a dip below the teens. January can bring heavy snowfall and also 60-degree days! Dealing effectively with climate can be one of the principal challenges for gardeners.

What Is Climate?

Climate is the prevailing set of natural conditions that affect a particular region—the noticeable and measurable features that make us (and our plants) hot or cold, soggy or dehydrated, and, in some cases, alive or dead. These features include temperature, precipitation (rain, sleet, hail, snow), humidity, sunlight, wind. In addition, climate includes the more or less consistent patterns of seasonal change that a region experiences. Local climate is largely a product of wider, even global, climate patterns interacting with regional variations in topography (the natural and manmade features of the landscape). Within even local climates there is room for further regional variation.

Local Climate

Ours is a region on the edge. The Greater Cleveland area straddles three different geographic sections: we are bounded on the north by Lake Erie, on the south and east by the western edge of the glaciated Allegheny Plateau, and on the west and northwest by the Eastern Lake and Till Plains.

Our terrain is generally level, with the exception of the east side's "heights," actually a single large ridge rising about five hundred feet above shore level. Other principal geographic features are the Cuyahoga, Chagrin, and Rocky rivers—the area's principal drainage into Lake Erie. These rivers create valleys 100 to 150 feet below the surrounding land surface.

Our climate has been described as generally "continental" in character—moderately warm summers and relatively cold winters with abundant, though varying, precipitation. But the strong modifying influence of Lake Erie gives our climate's character its own special twist.

On the U.S. Department of Agriculture's hardiness map, most of northeast Ohio is classified within zone 5, with sections fronting the lake included in zone 6. (You'll find hardiness zones listed in many gardening books and catalogs. It's good to remember your zone so you can choose plants accordingly.) Various factors, however, make the Greater Cleveland area different from even nearby areas classified in the same zones. For example, central Ohio is also in zone 5, but we tend to get more cloud cover in winter than they do; that cloudiness keeps our daytime high temperatures lower, because the sun doesn't get through to warm up the air below. Our zone 6 areas also tend to have cooler summers than southern Ohio's zone 6.

Proximity to Lake Erie, which moderates summer and winter temperatures for those within a couple of miles of its shore, is partly responsible for this difference. It also produces lake effect snows on the east and south sides that are unpredictable—and unusual, as well. In fact, according to TV8 weatherman Dick Goddard (as quoted in *The Plain Dealer*), such lake effect snows happen in only four locations worldwide: "The southeast shorelines of the Great Lakes and Hudson Bay, Canada; the eastern side of Great Salt Lake, Utah, and the Japanese island of Hokkaido." These are the only places where winds can sweep across an expanse of unfrozen water, picking up moisture, then move directly onto the colder shore where the moisture will fall as snow.

Even within the borders of Cuyahoga County there are significant geographic and climatic differences; the west side varies from the east, the east from the south, and all differ from the lake shore. These make up microclimates (differences in exposure, moisture, sun, and other factors that alter conditions for plant growth). Some of this region's major climatic variations that most affect gardeners are detailed here:

Lake Effect

Complex conditions that we call the "lake effect" cause this area to have milder weather. Because large bodies of water take a long time to warm up, spring can be cooler very near the lake. "On those warm spring afternoons in April and early May, when baseball first begins, it can be 75° or 80°F at the airport but 55° or 60°F downtown because the lake water is about 55°F. This cooling trend stays near the lake unless there are strong northerly winds," said Alan Ringo, National Weather Service hydrologist.

The Cleveland Botanical Garden (about two and a half miles from the lake) benefits from milder fall weather courtesy of Lake Erie; the water takes longer to cool in fall, and so keeps nearby areas warmer, often delaying the first frost and moderating winter low temperatures. Garden designer Alexander Apanius explained, "The lake keeps cold air from descending near the plants . . . so we can grow plants like umbrella pine (*Sciadopitys verticillata*), Japanese cryptomeria (*Cryptomeria japonica*), Japanese snowball (*Styrax japonicus*), and Franklin tree (*Franklinia alatamaha*) that would not do well in flat open areas away from the lake." At the Rockefeller Park Greenhouse, myrtles, big-leaf magnolias, and albizzias surprisingly survive. The lake also releases moisture into the air that often is taken eastward by prevailing winds. When the moist air hits the higher-altitude areas from Chardon to Bainbridge, the moisture falls as rain or snow. One benefit of this effect: because snow cover insulates plants that are dormant in the ground, marginally hardy plants have a better chance of survival where snowfall is heavier.

The lake effect snows concentrate on the south and east parts of the region. The west side, according to meteorologist Fred Johnson, is spared because the winds tend to run parallel with the shore line there and because it has slightly less elevation.

Rainfall Exceptions

Amount of rainfall can vary significantly between the east and west sides of Cleveland. Like lake effect snows in winter, lake effect rains are caused by moisture rising off the lake, moving east in the prevailing winds, hitting the eastern highlands, rising, cooling, and then dropping as rain. During a 1934 drought, a Cleveland Museum of Natural History researcher calculated that 22.8 inches of rain fell in downtown Cleveland while 39.2 inches fell 15 miles away in the North Chagrin Metropark reservation.

There are occasional variations in this general rainfall pattern, though, because our weather comes from many directions. For instance, in the wet summer of July, 1992, *The Plain Dealer* reported 9.25 inches of rain fell in Parma, the peak area for the month, and close to 7 inches fell across most of Westlake, Olmsted Township, and Strongsville; 8.25 inches fell in Moreland Hills and only 4.25 in Mayfield Heights.

Shelter in the City

Because there is more pavement reflecting heat and more buildings to cut cold winds, city dwellers tend to have milder winters and earlier springs. I have a friend who lives near I-77 in the heart of the city. Every year, he plants his corn in late April or early May—earlier than is normal for this area—but he gets away with it because he gardens in the warmer city zone.

The concentration of buildings in the city also provides more shade than might be accounted for in a general projection for this zone. Local shade patterns can make it difficult to grow sun-loving plants, including common flowers (like roses and geraniums) and vegetables (such as tomatoes and peppers). Similar circumstances occur in the older suburbs, where large old shade trees block the sun. Wherever you garden, count the hours of sun on the site (which will vary during the course of the year): sun-loving plants need six hours or more of sunlight; more shade-tolerant plants usually require four hours. Note that buildings can reflect sun as well as block it; gardens planted near south-facing walls can experience hotter and drier conditions than on other sides of the same building.

The urban landscape affects city gardeners' soil, too, which often stays drier because rainfall is channeled from pavement directly into sewers without moving through the soil.

Slope

Slope is the angle of a land surface (generally measured as a percentage of vertical drop over horizontal distance). Although slope effects may not make dramatic differences in how your plants grow, you will find that plants on slopes facing different directions start growing or blooming at different times. Slopes facing south receive the most sun, so they warm sooner in spring. North-facing slopes have the least sun, so they warm more slowly. Slopes facing east warm slightly sooner than north, because they will receive cool morning sun. Slopes facing west will warm slightly sooner than east, because they receive the warm afternoon sun.

Cool air also collects at the bottom of a slope, sometimes sparing plants higher up on the hill from severe cold or hard frosts. "In one of our outlying collections a true cedar, which is marginally hardy, survives unattended," said Jim Mack, superintendent of the Holden Arboretum grounds. "It's growing on the upper half of a slope, away from where cold air is dumped, and nestled amid other plants that cut the wind."

Climate Statistics

Here are some specific weather data that further describe the Cleveland area climate, and which may help you plan your gardening around the elements:

Frost-free Growing Season

Our average frost-free growing season runs about 160 days, although it can be a month longer near the lakeshore.

Probability of a freeze:

before		after	
Oct 8:	10%	April 30:	50%
Oct 13:	20%	May 13:	20%
Oct 23:	50%	May 20:	10%

"Determining the date for first frost in fall and the last frost in spring is almost a guessing game," said Jack Kerrigan, Cuyahoga County Cooperative Extension agent. "The data the Extension Service provides on the timing of frosts is only an average and mean. You need to look at the extremes, the historical highs and lows for any given day, too. For instance, although we say the first fall frost usually comes around October 15, it has been much later for the past few years."

Temperature

The lowest temperature on record is -19°F (January 1963).

The highest recorded temperature is 104°F (June 1988).

The average annual soil temperature is about 2°F higher than the average annual air temperature.

Precipitation

Total precipitation (rain, snow, hail, etc., measured in water equivalents) averages 35 inches a year, but two years in ten will have less than 30 inches or more than 40 inches.

Usually 60 percent, or 20 inches, of our rainfall comes between April and September. During two years out of any ten, however, it can fall below 16 inches.

Snowfall averages 53 inches a year. About 28 days per winter we have one inch of snow on the ground.

Wind

The prevailing, or most frequent, wind blows from the south and southwest.

Monthly average wind speeds range only slightly from 8.3 m.p.h. in August to 12 m.p.h. in December through March.

Local Climatological Data

Certain climate statistics collected by the National Weather Service are published by the National Oceanic and Atmospheric Administration in a periodical titled Local Climatological Data (LCD). Monthly and annual summaries for Cleveland, Akron, and Youngstown are available by mail from:

National Climatic Data Center
Federal Building
37 Battery Park Avenue
Asheville, NC 28801-2733
(704) 259-0871

Subscriptions to these and other related periodicals are also available.

The local data collection site for the Cleveland area is:
National Weather Service Forecast Office
Cleveland Hopkins Airport
Cleveland, 44135
265-2370

Local all-weather radio is broadcast on 162.55 MHZ and 162.40 MHZ 24 hours a day.

TV8 Weatherline recorded message: 881-0880.

Dealing with Climate: Be Prepared

Your landscape, with the exception of the few lucky plants grown in movable containers, cannot escape these moody outdoor elements. Landscape plants will be exposed to the best and worst of our weather. For these plants to succeed despite such extremes, it's important to plan ahead for difficulties.

Raise planting beds several inches or more above ground level so that excess moisture can drain off. Plan a watering program so you can irrigate when the weather is dry. You can buy inexpensive soaker hoses or high-tech drip irrigation systems. Even save your gray water (the water that is left over from rinsing clothing or vegetables) for use on your plants. Protect tender plants with floating row covers (lightweight fabric draped over plants to keep them several degrees warmer than the surrounding air temperature and also to keep out flying pests). Or make your own light shade with horticultural shade cloth, a lath house, or a sun-blocking trellis to keep cool-season crops alive in unexpectedly hot weather. Look for cultivars that tolerate both hot and cool temperatures, such as newer weather-resistant pansies or multiflora petunias. You can find designs for raised beds, trellises, and similar garden projects in many books available at bookstores and libraries.

Try to remain flexible and be willing to adapt your plans when the unforeseen inevitably comes. A late May frost, an unusually warm winter, or an excessively wet or dry month will affect your garden and landscape. Start a few tomatoes early in movable patio planters if early spring is mild. Bring them indoors, if you must, to escape a late storm.

Working with the weather is what makes gardening so much fun when a project succeeds, and such a challenge when a project progresses contrary to plans. Preparation helps, but flexibility is a necessity. Whether you grow a couple of pepper plants, a backyard of show dahlias, or a high-fashion landscape, northeast Ohio climate will continue to intrigue.

Why the Weird Weather?
by the Ohio State University Section of Communication and Technology in the College of Food, Agriculture, and Environmental Science

What's the reason for the weird weather of the last few years? Is it global warming? The tides of the sun? El Niño? Volcanic activity? Caterpillars?

State climatologist Jeff Rogers just shakes his head when you throw out all the popular theories about weather change. That's not to say that some natural phenomena don't affect the weather. But most popular theories neglect history—one of the best indicators of what the weather will be and why.

Take your pick of these better known theories:

El Niño. Warming of the ocean off the west coast of South America creates shifts in wind patterns when warm and cold water collide. Shifting winds can change weather conditions up into North America. El Niño occurs most often in the winter and spring, so it shouldn't have much effect on summer droughts.

Volcanic activity. The idea is that volcanic ash and dust clog the atmosphere, reflecting sunlight back toward space. This tends to cool the climate, especially in the hemisphere where the eruption occurs. Eruptions that are rich in sulfur may be particularly effective in cooling the atmosphere. A prime example is the cooling that took place over much of North America in 1993 after Mount Pinatubo erupted.

Sun spots. These huge magnetic storms on the sun's surface have been theorized to affect Earth's weather in several ways. The most interesting theory to gardeners is that the cyclical activity of the sun's magnetic behavior correlates to some weather patterns. Winter warmings and some droughts parallel sunspot behavior. However, there's a lot unknown about weather connections to solar activity.

The greenhouse effect. Carbon dioxide absorbs infrared radiation and plays a major role in warming the lower atmosphere. The burning of fossil fuels and tropical deforestation are two major activities blamed for increasing atmospheric carbon dioxide levels. From a weather perspective, this can be both good and bad. The greenhouse effect is blamed for absorbing infrared light from Earth and increasing warming trends. But it also produces clouds that help bounce back sunlight and cause cooling. These contradictions are part of the reason the debate over the greenhouse effect continues.

"Before I'd attribute our climate variations of the last six years to the greenhouse effect or El Niño or whatever, I'd look at the simple fact that history would indicate we're in a period in which we are due for some dry weather," Rogers says. "Weather is so variable and so dependent on the behavior of atmospheric gases that it's most likely a combination of factors—cyclical or not—that creates weather shifts.

Soil

For gardeners, soil means the upper layer of earth that can be dug or plowed and in which plants grow. Soil types vary widely, because their many properties form over time in the complex interaction of minerals, organic matter, and effects of physical relief and climate (such as erosion and decomposition).

Basically, the soils of greater Cleveland were formed in the time since the last glaciers (about 10,000 to 15,000 years ago) and thus are characterized largely by glacial till, a mixture of gravel and clay dropped by the receding ice.

Since that time, a lot has happened to cause local variations. Plants and animals, their type and location determined in part by climate, decomposed with the help of microflora (earthworms, fungi, and bacteria and other microscopic creatures) to release nutrients into the soil. Some of those organic nutrients, along with minerals, washed away with streams and ground water and layered on top of other other soils. Patterns of water runoff and drainage also caused erosion, which lowered some surfaces nearer to bedrock (what was there before the glaciers), exposing them to different minerals. More recently, man has altered the soil by moving it from place to place and by adding fertilizers and other chemicals.

The result of all this is that the Cleveland area provides gardeners with several basic soil types and a wide variety of local variations.

A few generalizations can be made about our soils and their use for gardening:

1. Most soils in this region are naturally acid. Acidity, which will influence the kinds of nutrients available to plants, is measured in pH. An acid soil is rated below neutral 7 on the pH scale, while an alkaline or basic soil, high in limestone, is rated above 7. Most plants grow well from pH 6.5 to 7. If your soil has a lower pH, you can add ground limestone to bring the pH higher. Effects of lime are temporary—based on the type of limestone and acidity of soil. If in a year or so your plants are yellowing or growing slowly, have the pH tested again.

2. Most soils in this region are moderately low in organic matter. Compost, decayed livestock manure, or peat moss will generally benefit the growing of flowers and vegetables.

3. Most Cleveland-area gardeners also struggle with heavy clay soils, which hold water, stay cool and soupy longer in spring, and rot plant roots if you don't provide a route for drainage.

However, a few locations around northeast Ohio have light sandy loams, a welcome relief from clay. West of Euclid and east of downtown, a two- to three-mile-wide, 28-mile-long strip along Lake Erie's shoreline was once occupied by glacial lakes. These lakes left sandy loams, ideal for growing plants. You can see how well these soils grow plants by visiting the Cleveland Botanical Garden or the Rockefeller Park Greenhouse, both of which are blessed with these soils. Similar sandy ridges left by sand dunes or lake beds extend inland west from the Cuyahoga River near Schaaf Road (once a thriving farming area), Detroit Avenue, Triskett, and Hilliard. This soil is also found along Middle Ridge Road in Lake County, an area with many nurseries.

Cleveland's west side, predominately gray clay, is less prone to developing large swampy areas than the east side (although most such swamps are now drained). It tends to be better drained than the east side because it slopes gradually down to the Cuyahoga River Valley.

Beyond these generalizations, it's extremely difficult to discuss the Cleveland-area soil in specific terms, because it can change significantly almost from backyard to backyard. Local soils offer different combinations of minerals and organic matter, consistency, drainage, and aeration to challenge gardeners.

But there is an excellent way for gardeners to find out exactly what's in *their* soil.

Start with the *Soil Survey of Cuyahoga County, Ohio*, a large book of soil maps published by the U.S. Department of Agriculture and the Ohio Department of Natural Resources. The *Soil Survey* gives precise locations of hundreds of soil types found throughout the county. You can pinpoint your own home on aerial photo maps and find out exactly what the name of your soil type is, then call either department to get an explanation of what that soil type means for your garden.

The *Soil Survey* is available free from the County Cooperative Extension Service (Cuyahoga: 631-1890, Geauga: 834-4656, Lake: 357-2582, Lorain: 322-0127, Medina: 725-4911, Summit: 497-1611).

However, in most of the urban areas of Cleveland the *Soil Survey* map's use may be limited, says James Storer, of the U.S. Department of Agriculture's Soil Conservation Service. "In urban areas, often the topsoil has been removed or compacted, or fill dirt has been brought in from other places and layered on top of the existing soil. The soil you have now may not be anything like what was originally there." In the outlying suburbs, such as Bay Village, Westlake, Olmsted Township, Strongsville, Broadview Heights, Solon, and Gates Mills, though, the map remains pretty accurate.

You can run a few simple tests on your soil to verify what the *Soil Survey* reports. To figure out if your soil is clay, squeeze a handful of soil about two days after a rainfall. If the handful of soil stays molded in a ball or if you can squeeze it out into a long ribbon, you have clay. If you have a sandy loam, the handful of soil will break up instead of clinging tightly in a ball or a ribbon.

And you can have nutrient levels in your soil tested by the Cooperative Extension Service for a small fee. Call the county office near you and have them send you a test package.(See phone numbers listed above.)

For more information on soil preparation, look at *The Rodale Book of Composting* (edited by Grace Gershuny and Deborah Martin, 1992, Rodale Press, Emmaus, PA).

Native and Wild Plants

In addition to knowing your local climate and soil, it's helpful to be familiar with the region's naturally occurring vegetation. If there are no woodlands in your neighborhood, use the nearest Metropark reservation or local nature center. Walk around with an identification guide and check out what species are growing in situations similar to your own landscape. One good such guide is: A Field Guide to Trees & Shrubs: Northeast and North Central U.S. and Southeast and South Central Canada, Peterson Guide Series (by George Petrides, 1986, Houghton, Mifflin, Boston, MA).

In more undisturbed rural areas, you can find oaks and hickories growing in drier terrain, including the Brecksville Reservation; beach and maple trees enjoy moister soils on the eastern side of town. Northern species such as yellow birch, Canadian hemlocks, and Canadian yew remain in the cooler ravines of the Metroparks, and white pines grow on the top of 1,300-foot-high Little Mountain in Lake County. Elsewhere, these plants perished as our climate warmed some four thousand years ago and new species—including tulip, poplar, magnolia, hickories, black walnut, red mulberry, sassafras, shadbush, and rhododendron—moved in from the south.

Trees that Grow Naturally in Northeast Ohio
• In drier areas of the west side, you'll find white, red, and black oak, chinquapin oak, and shagbark and butternut hickory.
• In the western lake plain, look for beech, maple, tulip, white ash, tupelo, basswood, and white oak.
• Closer to the Cuyahoga Valley you will find more oaks and tulip trees. In the southern highlands, look for some white pine, hemlock, and yellow birch among the many beech and maple trees.

- The eastern part of greater Cleveland has species such as beech, maple, tulip trees, cucumber magnolia, tupelo, hop hornbeam, shadbush, witch hazel, and spicebush.
- In wetter areas, silver maple, pin oak, sycamore, and tupelo will grow.

Moses Cleaveland Trees

A good way to find a tree that will live for centuries is to find a nearby Moses Cleaveland tree. These trees are thought to be old enough to have been growing when Moses Cleaveland arrived in this area in 1796. Many are labeled with plaques; others are identified by location in the Moses Cleaveland tree records in city hall. As of 1984 (the most recent survey), over two hundred trees were documented in Cuyahoga County. Among them were:

- a White oak on the Baldwin-Wallace College campus in Berea, 44 inches in trunk diameter
- a Black gum at the Cleveland Botanical Garden, 32 inches
- a White oak at Nela Park, Noble Road, East Cleveland, 40 inches
- a White oak at Southwest General Health Care, Middleburg Heights, 58 inches
- a White oak at Sunset Memorial Park, Olmsted Falls, 48 inches
- a White oak at Grantwood Recreation Center, Solon, 47 inches
- a Red oak at Evergreen Cemetery, Westlake, 64 inches

If you know of a tree that might qualify, call the City of Cleveland Tree Commission (664-3104); their foresters will inspect the tree. Once given their okay, the Early Settlers Association gives the tree a seal of approval. Do so before 1996, when these trees will become a prominent part of a meeting of the International Society of Arboriculture that will be held here.

Planting Considerations

Whether using native plants or some of the many plants from other parts of the world that also make excellent low-maintenance garden subjects, plan before planting. When you bring in species from different climates think carefully about how well they will adjust here. Some commonly grown landscape plants relocated here are suffering because our climate is not right for them. Colorado blue spruce and white birch trees, which come from cooler climates, are dying from cankers, borers, and miners. At fault, according to Roger Funk of Davey Tree Service, is not the plants but the climate. It simply has become too warm here for them to grow strongly enough to resist otherwise minor problems.

Another problem arises when Cleveland-area homeowners put species in sites where they cannot grow easily. Our native flowering dogwood, which normally grows beneath the light shade of a taller tree, when put in full sun in the middle of a lawn is more likely to suffer from insects and diseases. It is best set in the rich leaf humus and light shade at the edge of a woodland.

Native Wildflowers

Like trees, wildflowers grow in different habitats (environments made up of different soils, moisture levels, and light in which certain plants usually live). There are two general habitat types in our region: deciduous woodlands and prairies. There are also many variations in the particular site conditions and species found within these two habitats.

In the deciduous woodlands, especially those areas with large mature shade trees, you can find a rich flora of spring-blooming wildflowers. These perennial wildflowers flourish in dark, spongy soil that has been enriched for decades by the decay of autumn leaves. Most of these wildflowers emerge in early spring and bloom before the trees leaf out, peppering the woods with white flowers and occasional pink, blue, and yellow blossoms. Many of these species die back to dormant roots by summer.

If you are willing to build an organically rich soil beneath deeper rooted shade trees (many maples root so thickly near the soil surface that there is little space left for smaller plants), you may be able to start a self-perpetuating spring wildflower garden. You need to look into the specific moisture and light requirements of each species you plant, though—they do vary. Check with the Native Plant Society (see Plant Societies in chapter 7), Holden Arboretum, the Cleveland Museum of Natural History, or the Cleveland Metroparks (see Gardens Open to the Public in chapter 9). Or consult *The Wildflower Gardener's Guide: Northeast, Mid-Atlantic, Great Lakes, Eastern Canada* (by Henry Art, 1987, Storey Communications, Pownal, VT) or *Wildflowers* (by Rick Imes, 1992, Rodale Press, Emmaus, PA).

Some of our more notable spring wildflowers include: wild columbine, jack-in-the-pulpit, Virginia bluebells, Dutchman's-breeches, wild geraniums, violets, foamflower, bloodroot, Solomon's-seal, hepatica, trilliums, and trout lily. You can find some of these species propagated at several nurseries listed in the Specialty Growers section in chapter 6. You can also rescue wildflowers from construction sites, but please don't dig them from the woods (or buy from companies who take them from public woods). If everyone dug up a couple of woodland wildflowers, we would destroy this great natural resource. Unfortunately, our state wildflower, the large flowered trillium (*Trillium grandiflorum*), is quite difficult to propagate and may only be available from sources who collect it in natural areas.

Prairie wildflowers inhabit open fields, and sometimes roadsides, with full sun and drier soil. Prairie plants tend to bloom in summer and fall. Many can spread vigorously when conditions are right, which has led to their use in what many gardeners hope will be low-maintenance meadow gardens. Sometimes the meadow garden works; sometimes it does not. (See Using Wildflower Mixes Conscientiously in chapter 4.)

Some of the native American meadow and prairie species found locally include: purple coneflower, black-eyed Susan, prairie blazing-star, perennial sunflowers, goldenrods, New England asters, butterfly weed, and wild bergamot.

You'll also find plenty of wildflowers from other parts of the world growing locally, including Queen Anne's lace, oxeye daisy, common yarrow, and common chicory.

Iron weed, a prairie wildflower.

CHAPTER 2
Problem Solving

Along with a set of basic natural resources, Cleveland area gardeners share many common concerns. Some general gardening questions are heard again and again all around town: How can I best deal with the clay in my soil? What can I do with a shady lot? What plantings will work best with my landscape? Is it necessary to use garden chemicals or can I manage my yard organically? Should I plant wildflowers to save a bit of our natural heritage? How can I handle temperamental rhododendrens? What should I do about pesky deer?

If you have struggled with any of these issues, you are not alone. It is important to consider these and other major topics of general gardening interest that apply specifically to our Cleveland area gardens.

(For solutions to lawn problems, see chapter 3; for problems with shade, see chapter 4.)

Dealing with Clay

Working in clay is a problem for many Cleveland-area gardeners. In general, where clay is common, be careful to lighten the soil (make it fluffy so excess water can drain out and the roots will have access to air), and eliminate the excess water, or plants will perish. James Storer, district conservationist with the U.S. Department of Agriculture Soil Conservation Service, says, "People think that if you dig a hole and fill it with peat and sand it will be a good place to grow a plant. But that just doesn't work in this clay soil. When it rains, the water will fill up the hole like a bathtub and will only drain out as fast as the surrounding area—which is not fast at all."

An Expert Solution

One gardener who has success in clay soil is Tom Yates, garden superintendent at Holden Arboretum's Lantern Court, a former estate in Kirtland (see Gardens Open to the Public in chapter 9). Yates has found a solution agreeable to hundreds of species and varieties of flowers; rather than attempt to change clay, he exploits its ability to hold moisture and nutrients with a surprisingly simple procedure.

When he began working at Lantern Court in 1972, Yates imagined the estate as an idea garden and showplace. He proposed underplanting specimen trees with perennials and adding drifting beds of flowers, rock gardens, wildflower gardens, and ericaceous (heath-type) thickets. But Yates soon realized that the major problem facing these plans was the heavy yellow clay and wet clay topsoil. He struggled to amend the clay with sand, but it dried into hard brick. He tried to dig the soil especially deep and enrich it with black soil collected near a pond, but the resulting bed stayed swampy and wet.

Then it occurred to Yates to build a new bed over the once-promising black loam. He blanketed the prospective garden with two inches of silica sand and a six-inch layer of wood chips. He could then plant directly in the raised bed without further soil amendment. "The plants grow beautifully there now, and I seldom need to water," he said. The clay acts like a sponge of moisture and a reserve of nutrients that plant roots can reach while the well-drained organic layer on the top stays light and dry so roots and shoots won't rot.

Since that time, Yates has refined his soil blend. Most Lantern Court beds are composed of 40 percent finished compost, 20 percent leaf compost, 20 percent silica sand (which is not alkaline and will not influence the pH), and 20 percent year-old horse manure. This blend supports gardens of daffodils and daylilies, primroses and violets, wildflowers and hosta, barren strawberries, and hardy leadworts—all with equal success.

For acid-loving ericaceous plants (such as azaleas, heathers, bearberry, hudsonia, and cassiope) and for bog plants (such as pitcher plants, cardinal flowers, Japanese iris, and trollius), Yates makes a slightly different blend. He mixes sphagnum peat, oak-leaf compost, sand, and white pine needles and lays the mixture over a six-inch layer of silica sand.

For rare specialities that require an extra-acid soil (trailing arbutus, for example), Yates combines silica sand, pine needles, rotting pine and oak logs, bark, and wood chips. "Although this sounds bizarre, the rotting logs can make the difference between success and failure with trailing arbutus," Yates said.

All of these methods are intended to be easy to imitate in home gardens. "If we claim to need unfamiliar or expensive products, we are not serving the public," Yates said.

Raised beds, (here used at Judson Park) let you build good soil on top of clay.

When Is a Soil Not a Soil?

Eighty percent of Tom Yates's planting mix is not really soil at all but organic matter. "We're greedy for organics," he said. "We chase after utility line crews to get wood chips, collect pine needles from the grove across the street, and use loads and loads of horse manure" (which he lets age for a year before use).

Yates takes all these panhandled materials, as well as seedless weeds, and composts them for about two years in rows that are 20 feet long, three feet high, and three feet wide. Autumn leaves get a slightly different treatment: he puts them in square bins of snow fencing for a year, then moistens the decaying leaf pile and covers them with black plastic for a second year; after that they are ready to recycle into gardens. Both processes take a lot of time and space but require minimal labor and produce a reliable source of organic matter every year.

Clay at Claystone

"There was nothing on our property but a house when we bought it," said Don Vanderbrook, Cleveland-area floral designer and owner of Claystone, his home and four-acre formal garden. "There was a meadow on the hillside behind the house. I began putting in beds of cut flowers there but every time I rototilled, all the clay would slide down. So I terraced the hillside and raised all the beds with railroad ties. Clay soil is very heavy but wonderful when it's broken up. We have lots of horse manure—we keep three horses because they look so great out there, and they supply the fertilizer and compost we've been adding for years. Now the soil is fantastic. You can sink your hands into it and feel the beautiful texture."

Don Vanderbrook created this lovely garden by adding plenty of organic material to his clay soil. (Photo courtesy of Don Vanderbrook.)

Peat Moss Possibilities and Problems

Peat moss! We slather it into the soil around rhododendrons like stadium mustard on hot dogs. We plant all our house plants in it—regular soil just won't do any more. We use it to pack away our precious begonia and canna tubers, pillowing them all winter until we can plant them again in spring.

Just like plastic, juice boxes, and disposable contact lenses, peat moss has become a vital part of modern society.

Well, there's good reason for that. Peat moss is mighty handy. It's concentrated organic matter that helps to fluff up our stiff clay soils—rhododendrons could hardly grow around here without it.

Peat moss maintains a healthy root environment for house plants. Unlike soil, it won't get too soggy or pack down when you water.

And peat moss helps to discourage rotting of roots, tubers, bulbs and other underground plant parts. Like almost finished compost, it supports a thriving population of beneficial organisms that prevent the growth and attack of disease spores. (Compost, however, supports these beneficial organisms longer than peat moss, reports new research from Ohio State University.)

But nothing's perfect—juice boxes are hard to recycle; disposable contact lenses are expensive—and peat moss is no exception!

Peat moss has a highly acidic pH, which is fine around rhododendrons, azaleas, or blueberries. But it may require carefully calculated applications of limestone to counterbalance the acidity when you use it to plant other plants.

Although peat moss makes the soil fluffy, it's greedy for moisture and soaks up much soil water without releasing it to plant roots. And once peat moss dries out—watch out! It's very hard to get wet again. In a pot, it shrinks away from the pot walls so all the water runs down the sides and out, not near the plant roots.

Just like in a dry pot, if you use peat moss on top of the soil in a mulch, it can form a dry mat that repels water. This can be more damaging to plant roots than if you left them unmulched in the first place.

Peat moss also is devoid of nutrients. If you use it to grow pot plants, expect to add fertilizer regularly to make up for this deficiency.

Still, we can work around all of these things with the help of more modern technology. For example, before planting pot plants, you can add soil-moisturizing gels to make moisture easier for roots to access. After planting, you can sprinkle on slow-release fertilizers to provide a regular supply of nutrients.

Still it's hard to overlook one basic underlying problem. Peat moss is mined from natural bogs that are centuries old. That makes some people fear that we are stripping away nonrenewable natural resources.

Why should we degrade these precious natural areas when we can recycle our yard wastes into compost that makes a fine soil amendment? (You also can use compost in potting soil by mixing a gallon of compost, a gallon of sharp sand, and a gallon of good garden loam.)

The Canadian Peat Moss Association says that they are only using a tiny percentage of all the country's peat bogs. And they believe that the bogs do renew themselves fairly quickly after strip-harvesting. I only hope they are right!

Neutralizing Acid Soil

If your soil is overly acidic, as is common around Cleveland, you may need to use lime. Lime is short for limestone, which can sweeten—or raise—a soil's pH value (the measure of soil acidity or alkalinity). You can use lime to change the kinds of nutrients that are available in the

soil, curtail certain fungus diseases, and generally improve the performance of plants that prefer alkaline soils (such as baby's breath). But
lime should never be applied indiscriminately, without knowing if you
need it and how much you need, or the soil's chemistry may be thrown
out of alignment.

Gardeners use lime to counteract acids that are left in soil by decaying leaves, mulches, and other organic matter. Acids also accumulate
from applied fertilizers and from the weathering of minerals within the
soil. If these acids build up to excessive levels and are not counteracted
by soil sweeteners (such as calcium and magnesium), the soil can
become too acidic to grow plants well.

First, Test

To find out if overly acidic soil is causing limited success in your yard,
get your soil's pH value tested. (The pH value is judged on a scale of 1 to
14: 7 is neutral, below 7 is acid, and above 7 is alkaline.) You can buy
inexpensive pH test kits or have soil samples checked by the County
Cooperative Extension Service (Cuyahoga: 631-1890, Geauga: 834-
4656, Lake: 357-2582, Lorain: 322-0127, Medina: 725-4911, Summit:
497-1611).

If your soil's pH value is:

• Near pH 6.5, the optimum pH for most plants, your soil is slightly
acidic, but don't bother to add lime unless you have perennial baby's
breath or plants native to alkaline soils.

• Lower than pH 6, your soil is slightly too acidic for most plants, and
you may need to add some lime. Exceptions are acid-loving ericacious
rhododendrons, azaleas, mountain laurels, Japanese andromeda (*Pieris
japonica*), and leucothoe, which need an acidic soil.

• Neutral pH 7 or even a slightly alkaline pH 7.5, your soil is adequate for many plants except those acid-lovers just mentioned.

• Higher than pH 8, your soil is too alkaline for most plants. This
may mean someone added too much lime in the past. You might need
to counteract the excess lime by adding sulfur.

Adjusting pH

Whenever you manipulate soil pH, follow the recommendations that
come with the soil test results or on the lime-bag label. And choose the
kind of lime you use with care.

Calcitic limestone contains calcium carbonate, which is simply
ground up limestone—inexpensive and effective. Dolomitic limestone
is magnesium carbonate, an alkaline material and source of the nutrient magnesium. Both of these are available in different-sized particles.
Finer grinds will break down in soil more quickly; coarser grinds are

released more slowly. A mixture of fine and coarse grades is good in most cases because it can both correct a pH problem promptly and keep acids neutralized for some time thereafter. Another product you'll see is quicklime, calcium oxide. When you add water to this it becomes hydrated lime, which works fast—fast enough to burn plant roots if you use too much. It also can produce a gas that kills turf if applied at the same time as fertilizer containing ammonia.

Improving Soil with Compost

What Is Compost?

Organic matter (decayed plant and animal debris) lightens heavy soils. It also helps make sandy soils moister, releases a wide variety of nutrients gently, and encourages abundant underground life (earthworms, beneficial bacteria, and fungi) that helps plants grow better.

A fine source of organic matter is compost: properly recycled garden waste and landscape debris. As a soil conditioner, compost can be as good as commercial products sold in garden centers.

Because landscape debris is no longer welcome in most landfills, many communities turn leaves and grass clippings into garden compost, which they then sell or provide free to residents. The independent and nonprofit Greater Cleveland Ecology Program (687-1266) collects landscape and garden waste from several communities and markets Cuyahoga Leaf Humus, which can even be ordered for home delivery. The city of Solon (248-1155) gives finished humus away free to residents who pick it up in their own bags or buckets. Westlake (871-3300) and Bay Village (871-2200) work jointly; they sell and deliver their finished compost within city limits.

Making and Using Your Own Compost

It's not too hard to make your own compost using old vegetation from around your yard. When you have a ready supply, you can:

• Work compost into new beds. Start with a two-inch layer of compost in an eight-inch-deep bed.

• Use compost to mulch existing plantings. The nutrients will trickle down to plant roots with the rain, and the compost will work down to condition the soil when you weed or hoe.

• Put a bucketful into a planting hole and work it into surrounding soil to help a new plant get off to a good start.

When you make your own compost, you can choose from easy but slow-acting compost processes or more time-consuming but quicker-acting methods. The composting process itself is really not much different from gardening. But instead of encouraging plants to grow, you are encouraging them to decay. Create a flora of decomposers (bacteria and fungi) that live in soil and tear apart fallen tissues. They work best when given warmth, moisture, oxygen, and a little nitrogen—all of which you can provide as you build your compost pile.

If you blend the right kinds of plant debris and turn or fluff the pile regularly, decomposers will work most quickly, creating a "hot" compost pile. If you are more casual about the pile, it will still decompose, only slowly and without building up much heat; hence the name "cool" composting.

Hot Composting

The simplest way to start hot composting is by blending a hot pile, which you can leave out in the open or enclose in a frame of wire mesh or snow fencing. Begin by gathering enough plant scraps to build a pile three feet wide and four feet high and deep. To get this much debris takes some planning. Perhaps some Saturday you can renovate a flower or vegetable garden, do a little pruning, rake the leaves, and mow the lawn. On Sunday, assemble the remains of your efforts into a compost pile.

Separate soft greenery, such as lawn clippings and weeds (which provide nitrogen as they decay), from harder dry vegetation, such as straw, twigs, or dried leaves. If you have a lot of really hard material like wood chips, add extra nitrogen fertilizer. Chop clippings and leaves with a lawn mower and soft woody material with a garden shredder if you want them to decompose faster.

Then pile the two components in alternating layers of two inches of green matter and four inches of brown. Sprinkle good organic soil, finished compost, or store-bought inoculant (decay microorganisms in granular form) in between each layer to provide the decomposers.

Keep the pile moist, but not wet. Let plenty of air percolate inside by turning the pile upside down or fluffing it with a garden fork at least once a month. The compost will be finished when it turns into a crumbly brown mound and you can no longer identify the original components.

For those interested in speeding up the process (at a price), there are also several commercial composting systems available. These include spinning barrels or specially ventilated plastic bins that accelerate the heating process and produce compost fast.

Cool Composting

To cool compost, simply add plant debris to a pile as you gather it; then wait for nature to slowly turn it into organic matter. Because decomposition can take a couple years, you should make a new pile every year or else you will simply bury what has decomposed under new debris.

Another easy way to cool compost is to grind up your old plant scraps with a lawn mower or shredder and layer them on top of a garden bed. In a couple of months, they seem to disappear and return to the soil.

What About Animal Manure?

Having both horse and garden makes a lot of sense. But not everyone can, or wants, to keep a four-footed manure machine around. Luckily, there is an excess in this area (including nearby Geauga County, which has a larger horse population than any other county in Ohio). You can get horse manure free at many stables, especially because stable owners are now required by federal and state legislation to meet more exacting manure-handling laws. The changes are coming about because manure, as a recyclable material, is being restricted from landfills. Furthermore, if manure piles up in areas where rainwater can carry nutrients and bacteria into streams and ground water, it is now considered a pollutant.

"It's easy for nutrients to get away if there is any slope to the land at all," said Al Bonnis, agent for the Ohio Soil and Water Conservation District. "Then you are washing nutrients down the drain. We want to see the manure spread on farm fields or pastures where it can do some good, or given to someone who can use it for gardening or compost."

Manure contains a complex blend of nutrients—it's an ideal slow-release fertilizer. The manure produced by one horse in 37 days is enough to produce a bushel of corn. In this area, however, horse manure usually comes mixed with the wood shavings used for bedding, which breaks down very slowly and absorbs nitrogen as it goes. You can avoid the problems associated with wood bedding if you can locate aged manure or a stable that beds their horses in straw. You can also mix thin layers of manure and wood bedding into a compost pile; add a little extra nitrogen (a sprinkling of lawn fertilizer, for example) if there is more wood shavings than manure.

Composting horse manure solves the other problem associated with horse waste: weeds. By letting the manure heat up and decay, you kill many of the weed seeds that horses eat and pass intact. If you use horse manure in a relatively fresh form, be prepared to do plenty of weeding for the next growing season.

Proper Planting

Newly planted trees and shrubs are dying all over greater Cleveland wherever the soils are heavy. Many of these plants are smothering because whoever transplanted them didn't know where the roots were. Fred Robinson, consulting arborist, has been called to the scene of many dying plants and has dug up enough failing trees and shrubs to identify several fatal mistakes transplanters make. Primarily, they over-look the fact that some balled and burlapped plants have deep root collars (the place where the stem emerges from the root system) and thus even deeper roots.

"I have found the root collar to be 6 to 12 inches below the top of the ball in almost all cases of failure," Robinson said. "With the root collar so deep, the root system is limited to the bottom half of the ball."

Where soil is heavy, wet, or compacted, most plantsmen will plant balled and burlapped plants shallowly to keep the roots from drowning. This will hurt plants with deep root crowns. The top half of the ball, which is mostly soil, is left above ground while the bottom half, which contains all the roots, is trapped in a shallow hole. Water fills the hole, driving out oxygen; the plant soon suffocates, or drowns.

How does this occur? Robinson has traced part of the problem back to nurseries that grow material in loose sandy soils. These nurseries tend to plant field material deep for extra stability. The nurseries may also try to protect the roots by covering them more heavily than is ideal. In addition, workers might cultivate between rows, building up even more soil over the roots.

When digging plants, workers may measure the depth of the ball by starting at the top of the soil rather than the root collar. (The size of the ball is predetermined as the size needed to sustain that particular plant.) When they dig the ball of a plant with a deep root collar, they can sever a majority of the roots that would otherwise be in the ball. For instance, if the root collar is six inches deep, the bottom of the ball will not include six inches of essential roots left deeper in the soil. The dug ball does not coincide with the essential root system.

To avoid this problem, before buying any balled and burlapped trees or shrubs check to see where the root collar is. Sway the trunk back and forth slowly and note where the trunk pivots. If it pivots right at the top of the ball, then there are roots all the way to the top. But if you can move the trunk around in the ball, the roots start somewhere lower than the top of the ball. For shrubs and multistemmed trees, you could identify the location of the root collar by probing down the trunk or cutting through the burlap near the stems, working carefully to avoid scarring the plant or weakening the ball.

Once you've located the root collar, measure the root system's depth. Armed with this knowledge, you can dig your holes accordingly.

One Expert's Technique

Richard Kay of Breezewood Gardens recommends the following planting technique, which his landscape crews use quite successfully:

1. Build an elevated planting bed by covering the existing soil with six inches of topsoil and one to two inches of peat moss, leaf humus, compost, or other kinds of organic matter. Mix the soil blend together with a rototiller.

2. Dig a hole deep enough for three-quarters of the root ball. The top one-quarter of the ball should remain above the surface of the soil.

3. Make the hole as wide as possible, at least one foot wider than the diameter of the roots. This will allow roots to grow and spread easily.

4. Amend the soil you will put back into the planting hole. Add thirty to fifty percent organic matter. You can also add a water-holding polymer (a product that looks like crystals in the package but swells to resemble gelatin when moist) that helps plants survive heavy rain by absorbing excess water. The polymer also helps plants tolerate drought by releasing moisture reserves when the surrounding soil has dried out. After amending the backfill, use it to fill the hole in around the root ball.

5. Cover the top one-quarter of the root ball with two to three inches of mulch.

Finally, oxygen is as important for plant roots as moisture. Do not install sod or plant grass seed over the root system of a newly installed tree or shrub.

Filling in the Blanks

Problem 1. You've spent your entire plant budget but still have some vacant areas in your flower garden.

Answer 1. Fill in empty spots with the seed of quick-growing flowers. A packet of seeds costs about $1.

Problem 2. You're tired of having too many tomatoes ripen at the same time in midsummer. This year you are restricting yourself to two tomato plants. What should you do with the rest of the garden?

Answer 2. Plant vegetables that you can only grow from seeds.

Problem 3. The little basil plants you bought last week died. You can't find any more of the right kind. How will you make your famous tomato sauce?

Answer 3. Plant basil seed of the appropriate variety.

Starting plants from seed may be the solution to many landscape problems. But some gardeners hesitate to work with seed. Granted, certain kinds of seed take a long time and a lot of pampering to get going. But you shouldn't be afraid to select foolproof, easy starting seeds and sow them directly outdoors. Here are some good options:

Flowers: Zinnias, nasturtiums, cosmos, sunflowers, annual poppies, marigolds, sweet alyssum, calendula (pot marigold).

Herbs: Basil, cilantro, dill, arugula, chives, catnip, cress.

Vegetables: Beans (snap and bush lima beans), beet, Swiss chard, corn (regular sweet and extended sugar types — super sweet varieties can be hard to germinate), cucumber (both pickling and slicing), lettuce, pumpkins, radishes, squash (both summer and winter).

Tips for Sowing Success:

1. Prepare the seedbed well. Seed arises best in fine-textured, light soil. It may have difficulty emerging through big clumps of clay.

2. Follow depth instructions closely. If you plant too deeply, the seeds may not make it all the way to the soil surface. If you plant too shallowly, they may not get enough moisture to germinate.

3. Keep the soil moist while the seed is germinating and the seedlings are small. But if you have to water, don't blast the hose on the bed full force; you could wash small seeds way. Use trickle irrigation or put an attachment on the hose to break the spray up into a gentle mist.

Pests and Predators

The Problem: while we've been out swimming, picnicking, and riding rollercoasters, the bugs have been at work in our gardens. While we've been eating popcorn (hold the butter, please!) at summer movies, bugs have been nibbling on our plants' leaves, buds, and roots; they've been drinking our plants' sap.

So when you come home from a long day at the beach, take a few moments to inspect your landscape. Are your plants' leaves a healthy shade of green or are they chewed or dotted from insect feeding? Are the new buds or shoots opening normally, or are they curled up or distorted? If you see either problem, look closer for the culprit.

Look under the leaves for any signs of pests clinging there. If you move the leaves and see whiteflies, beetles, or bugs fly away, remember what they look like so you can identify them and learn how to treat them.

If nothing flies away, scan the lower leaf surfaces and stems for sap-sucking insects such as cottony-white mealybugs, smooth waxy scale insects, and soft, pear-shaped aphids.

Here's an overview of some of the most common plant pests in our area and what to do to get rid of them. If you don't see a description that matches the pest you've seen, call the Cleveland Botanical Garden's Horticultural Hotline (721-0400). It's open Tuesday and Thursday, 9 a.m. to 4 p.m., and Saturday 1 to 4 p.m.

Aphids. These are tiny pear-shaped sucking insects with long legs and antennae. They reproduce like mad on new growth, soft stems, or the undersurfaces of leaves on many plants. They excrete a sugary sap that usually is covered with what looks like soot or dirt, but actually is a kind of mold.

Treat aphids early, before they reproduce wildly. Spray them with insecticidal soap or simply blast them off the plant with your hose. Check back in a couple days to see if you need to repeat the treatment.

Black vine weevils. These large, crawling pests are black and beetle-like. They chew ragged holes in the outside of leaves while the grubs feed on plant roots. You'll find them most commonly on rhododendrons, azaleas, yews, hemlocks, and berry bushes.

You can kill black vine weevils with parasitic nematodes (available in organic gardening catalogs). Just mix up a batch in water, pour it over roots of the troubled plant, and keep it moist. The nematodes will attack the weevil larvae. You also can spray the adult weevils with pyrethrin at night when they come out to feed.

Japanese beetles. These handsome, glossy, blue-green and bronze beetles eat almost any plant. They prefer flowers and the soft tissue between leaf veins. The adults can consume entire plants, leaving just a skeleton behind.

You can control Japanese beetles by killing the beetle larvae, which feed on the roots of grasses and other plants. Apply milky disease (available in many garden centers) to the lawn and put parasitic nematodes (available in organic gardening catalogs) on the garden beds. Spray pesky adults with rotenone.

Lacebugs. You can identify these flying pests by their lacy wings and the speckled pattern they leave after feeding on the undersides of leaves—especially on Japanese Pieris foliage.

To treat, spray troubled plants with light horticultural oil.

Scales. There are many different types of scale, but all form tiny firm or soft patches on stems and leaves—the bug is hiding underneath. I've seen a number recently on mugo pines, magnolias, and staghorn ferns, although they will attack many other plants.

Cut off any branches that are severely infested. Wipe the scales off of house plants with alcohol on a cotton ball. Or spray outdoor plants with a light horticultural oil.

Another Answer for Pest Problems

My garden is full of bugs, and I'm glad. Of course, I'm not happy about the occasional plant-eating beetle or sap-sucking scale insect; I'm talking about the beneficial insects. These good guys eat or lay their eggs in garden pests and put the bad guys that are eating my plants out of business.

On one parsley plant that has begun, quite rampantly, to flower I see tiny wasps and hover flies that lay their eggs in aphids, caterpillars, bean beetles, spider mites, scales, and whiteflies. They enjoy flower nectar and pollen when they're not laying eggs.

In the garden, hiding in a cubbyhole beneath the lettuce leaves, I've seen big wolf spiders. They catch all kinds of insects, and do so in large quantities to support their hefty bulk.

I've been looking for lady beetles, which also are great garden allies (they eat scales, whiteflies, aphids, and more), but they're not here in big numbers yet. That's probably because there aren't that many pests in my garden and they need lots of prey to keep from moving on to better pickings elsewhere. But they usually do show up sometime during the summer, just when I need them most!

Getting these beneficial insects to keep a garden fairly free of pests is really quite straightforward. You don't have to buy or apply anything. Here's what to do.

1. Don't be too quick to spray away every pest you see. A few beetles or mealybugs won't do too much damage, and they're necessary to feed your beneficial insects and keep them in your yard. When pests get overpopulated and you have no choice but to use pesticides, apply them only to specific troubled areas, not to the entire garden.

Don't use broad-spectrum insecticides; they'll kill beneficial insects that are trying to eat pests. Try more selective insecticides such as insecticidal soap or Bt, a caterpillar disease, which target only pests and leave the beneficial insects to feed again.

2. Plant a number of different flowers. Most beneficial insects, at some stage in their life cycle, will be attracted to flower nectar or pollen. They tend to prefer plants with lots of small flowers, like parsley, Queen Anne's lace, dill, mints, thyme, sunflowers, and asters.

For your own enjoyment as well as theirs, make sure something fragrant or full of pollen is in flower all the time. (Some of the modern hybrids, such as triploid marigolds, don't have nectar or pollen so they won't help.) The more flowers that are in bloom, the more beneficials you'll attract.

3. In addition to flowers, put in plants of various shapes and sizes. Lettuces, hostas, and ground covers make cool, ground-hugging homes for crawling beneficial insects. More upright plants provide shelter for flying insects.

4. Provide a little water for beneficial insects. It could be a birdbath, water garden in a tub, children's wading pool, or even just a panful.

If you've been an avid advocate of pesticides or have only planted grass until now, be patient. It may take a year or two to convince the beneficials that it's safe to take up residence.

As you start planting more flowers, herbs, and ground covers, keep a close eye on the garden. Beneficial insects work subtly. You'll know that predators like spiders and ladybugs are at work if they're present. You can tell the beneficial parasites are thriving if you see caterpillars, mealybugs, or other pests dotted with funny-looking lumps—egg cases full of parasite babies.

Once all of this happens you can sit back all summer and let your beneficial insects handle the garden bug patrol.

Reducing Chemical Use

I've been an advocate of organic gardening for the past eight years, ever since I had small children toddling around the garden and eating unwashed vegetables. And to my delight, I've seen the organic movement grow in that time.

Organic gardening relies on soil building, adding at least an inch layer of organic material to the soil each year to develop a rich, spongy soil where plants can flourish. This, in turn, develops healthier plants that are less likely to be bothered by pests and diseases. In addition to soil building, organic gardening calls for eliminating synthetic garden chemicals, including fertilizers, pesticides, and herbicides that don't come from plant, animal, or mineral sources. Here's how the two elements work.

1. Soil building. In an organic garden, if you plant generally problem-free plants and have developed fertile, organic-rich soil, you may not have to add anything else to the garden, except some water and mulch.

That's because healthy, organically grown plants are less appealing to pests. I've seen this in my own garden but discovered it's also been documented by the Ohio State University Department of Entomology. In a recent study, corn borers were much less likely to attack corn grown on organically improved soils than on farm fields treated with chemical fertilizers.

The key to increased resistance to insect pests may be that organic soils have a critical balance of seven nutrients, said Dr. Larry Phelan, entomologist. When combined in just the right amounts—a natural occurrence in organic-rich soils—these nutrients turn corn borers off.

Still, many commercial farmers have tended to scoff at organic methods as being too unreliable. But the advantages of organic gardening are beginning to catch up with them.

For example, I visited Fetzer Vineyard and Organic Garden in California recently. In this demonstration garden, they grow wine grapes, fruits and vegetables without a single synthetic chemical. And, they've found that organically grown grapevines produce more and better fruit. So the company, and some other vineyards, too, are gradually converting their grape-growing acreage to organic-only.

2. Controlling chemicals. A National Academy of Sciences report has warned of health risks for children who eat food that contains pesticide residues. (There's also been a possible link between pesticides and breast cancer.) As a result, the current administration is hoping to pass reforms that would reduce pesticide use on 75 percent of American agricultural land in the next six years.

In addition to problems with pesticides used today, pesticides sprayed on some Ohio farmlands 30 years ago are returning to haunt us. Dr. Lynn Willett, from the Ohio Agricultural Research and Development Center, has found that residues of organochlorides (such as DDT) that still linger in the soil will evaporate when the soil is wet. The volatile chemicals condense on plants growing nearby.

If the contaminated land is used for grazing cattle, the organochlorides can pass into their milk and meat. They also can contaminate any vegetable crops grown there, unless the vegetable comes in a husk or shell that you can peel off.

I think that all of these findings are pointing to something you should consider. Isn't it time you tried some organic gardening methods? Improve your garden soil and reduce your use of toxic chemicals. You might be surprised how easy and effective it can be.

Here's some ideas for starters. Add a heap of compost to your garden before planting it instead of relying on fertilizers alone. Plant disease-resistant roses such as Meidiland roses or 'The Fairy' instead of spraying every week or two. Treat soft-bodied insect pests with nontoxic insecticidal soap instead of a toxic synthetic insecticide.

For more information, check out one of the many books on organic gardening in your library or bookstore.

Rhododendron Diseases: Prevention, Diagnosis, and Cure

Greg Payton, Horticultural Technician for the Holden Arboretum Rhodo-dendron Garden
(Reprinted from the *Arboretum Leaves*, Summer 1994)

 Rhododendron lovers have relatively few pests and diseases to contend with—certainly fewer problems than, for example, rose lovers. And happily, many rhododendron problems can be cured or prevented. We deal with five major rhododendron diseases in our region. *Botryosphaeria dothidea* occurs most often and is moderately responsive to treatment. The second most-seen disease, *Phomopsis*, is most responsive to treatment. The third, *Phytophthora*, is least responsive and most serious. Gardeners also contend with petal blight and leaf gall.

General Comments

When pruning diseased branches or plants with a history of disease, sterilize pruning tools after each cut. Pick and destroy all diseased leaves and stems. A 10% solution of bleach and water or of isopropol alcohol works perfectly well for sterilizing tools.

Commercial products are available for controlling a wide variety of pathogens. Keep in mind that it will take some time to see results. People say, "I sprayed, but the leaves still look bad," forgetting that even when the organism is controlled, leaf damage will remain until the leaf drops off.

Botryosphaeria dothidea. *B. dothidea* most commonly causes stem dieback and sometimes also causes leaf blight and leaf spot. Its symptoms:

- most conspicuously, leaves droop and roll downward along midrib;
- an otherwise healthy plant has dying branches, and an entire branch or section of the plant wilts and dies in one to two days;
- diseased leaves turn dull green, then brown;
- dead leaves remain attached;
- xylem turns reddish brown;
- a cross section of discolored stem reveals a brown wedge-shaped discoloration. Tissue can become infected anywhere between the drooping leaves and the crown. If *B. dothidea* kills the main stem, the whole plant dies. It may take time for the plant to die completely. If the plant has layers or multiple stems, these stems can survive. In older plants, large cankers form which can girdle the stem.

Infection occurs through wounds: frost cracks, pruning cuts, or dead rachises (which attach the flower to the stem). The stress of heat and drought increases the incidence of *B. dothidea*, and plants in full sun are more likely to be infected. Counteract the stress of heat and drought by providing water and partial shade during drought. Prune out all infected branches promptly. If a pruning cut reveals a brown discoloration, keep pruning farther down the stem until all infected tissue is removed. Remember to sterilize the pruner after each cut. Spray the plant with fungicide. Remove dying flowers and rachises, and avoid unnecessary wounds.

Phomopsis. This disease occurs in two forms. In evergreen azaleas, symptoms are similar to *Botryosphaeria*:
- stem dieback, most noticeably during drought stress, and

usually just a single branch or flag is affected.

Symptoms in rhododendrons:
• all leaves on the affected branch start to lose color
slightly, just after flowering;
• leaves become brown, die on the edges, and then wilt;
• affected leaves develop gray spots.

Phytophthora. This disease is often fatal. Two common *Phytoph-thora* pathogens are found in this region: *P. cactorum* and *P. cinnomomi.*

Symptoms of *P. cactorum*:
• affected leaves turn dark brown and remain flat;
• mature leaves drop quickly;
• individual shoots are affected, usually dying during growth flush;
• young leaves and stems are particularly vulnerable;
• succulent stems are vulnerable and are quickly affected;
• stems are discolored brown.

Symptoms of *P. cinnomomi*:
• roots rot;
• top growth suddenly wilts and browns, and the plant dies.

Phytophthora is a microorganism that reproduces by creating various types of spores. Some types (chlamydospores and oospores) are resting structures, able to stay in the soil for years, and their sporangia, or sacs, do not survive particularly well.

The most serious types of spores, zoospores, are released from the sporangia in water and swim to the root tips. If water flows over the roots, the zoospores can swim from one area to the next; this situation occurs if the plant is situated in a low area or in poorly drained soil. Improper soils can fail to suppress root rot or can even encourage it. Bark, especially softwood bark, will suppress *Phytophthora*, while peat is actually conducive to its development.

Prevention is the best control. Choose only healthy plants that have dark green leaves, that do not wilt easily, and that have healthy white roots. Plant in well-drained areas, and mix bark into the soil 8 to 12 inches deep. In areas where plants have died from *Phytophthora*, choose particularly resistant varieties. Several commercial products control this disease, but some of them require a special license for application. Home gardeners must therefore rely instead on cultural methods. Use media with 50% or more bark, either hard or softwood, to suppress *Phytophthora*. Soil acidity helps control *Phytophthora* by inhibiting the production of zoospores and sporangia; a pH of 4.0 suppresses zoospore production without being too acid for the plant.

Avoid wetting the foliage in late afternoon. Avoid overfertilizing. Remove all brown, discolored wood in diseased stems, pruning back to a healthy branch, and remember to sterilize the pruner. If the plant dies, remove and destroy the plant and its debris. Place its successor in a new site with the proper soil. If you must put the new plant in the same site, amend the soil and buy a rhododendron resistant to this disease. High soil temperatures increase the growth of *Phytophthora*; cool soil suppresses it.

Petal blight. This disease, *Ovulinia azaleae*, is seen in wet weather conditions during the bloom season and can cause extensive damage. Entire flower heads can rot totally in three days. Petal blight occurs on rhododendrons and azaleas.

Symptoms of petal blight:
• tiny spots on petals, from pale to rust in color;
• spots enlarge rapidly;
• tissue turns soft and water.

To control petal blight, apply 20% Terraclor on the soil under the plants, one to two weeks before flowering on early cultivars. Spray later-blooming varieties as they begin to show color, using Benlate or Benomyl.

If the disease has been severe in past years, spray a second time. As added protection, you can spray open flowers with a fungicide such as Benomyl two to three times weekly. Pick blighted flower heads and destroy them before the petals fall to the ground; the fungus produces hard, black resting structures in the petal tissue that survive on the soil until the next spring.

Educated gardeners can grow great rhododendrons like this one, at Holden Arboretum.

Leaf gall. This disease, *Exobasidium vaccinii*, is very common in early spring on azaleas, particularly native species as opposed to hybrids; it sometimes occurs on rhododendrons.

Symptoms of leaf gall:
• leaves and entire shoots thicken, curl, and turn pale-green to white;
• in later stages, galls are covered with a white powdery substance.

To control leaf gall, pick the diseased leaves and destroy them. The disease is rarely damaging or serious enough to warrant spraying.

Conclusion. The best way to deal with diseases is to prevent them from getting a foothold. The best prevention is to try to duplicate the rhododendron's natural habitat, by planting in rich organic soil.

The best defense is a healthy plant that is situated in the optimum environment.

What to Do About Deer

Jeff Andrey, Dugan's Garden Center

Deer are awfully cute when they're in the wild, but not so nice when they eat your prize rhododendron. White-tailed deer have always been a problem in commercial nurseries; however, their damaging browsing is on the increase and now poses a problem for homeowners as well. The reasons are clear: expanding human population, urban sprawl, and increased deer numbers have made it difficult for deer to survive. With a tasty lunch growing in your back yard (nurtured by you over the years!), it's no wonder their browsing is becoming more common.

While there are no clear solutions to preventing browsing damage, short of installing a very tall and very expensive electric fence, many homemade remedies and commercially made products can reduce the damage to manageable levels.

Soap. Homemade controls vary in their effectiveness depending upon how you apply them. A commonly used method involves hanging bars of soap on or near the plant you expect to protect. Although considered the deterrent, perfumes added to the soaps do not significantly improve the repelling qualities. Rather, the type of soap is the key. Recent tests conducted in New York indicate that tallow-based soaps are most effective. To ensure effectiveness, hang the soap on the perimeters of the protected area.

Human hair is also suggested as a deterrent. Although no research confirms this approach, the reasoning is sound. Deer don't like the smell of humans! Like soap, this method should be implemented by hanging net bags containing hair around the plant or area to be protected.

Hot sauce. An application of hot sauce (mixed with egg whites to make it stick) will help make your prize azalea less palatable to our white-tailed friends. This mix will probably need to be applied frequently for best results.

Commercial products do not differ greatly in their methodology from homemade controls, but they can last longer and be more effective. Products such as Deer-Away or Hinder are applied directly to the foliage and make it unpalatable for the deer. These products seem to "train" the deer, to some extent, to avoid these plants. Bye-Deer is a tallow-based soap flake product available packed in rather nice green sacks ready to hang from your plants.

Fences. Another method of control is erecting fences to control browsing. These need not be permanent—temporary plastic fencing is available—but should be tall to produce effective results. A border of plants along the perimeter of your property may also work, provided these plants are not on the deer's Top 10 list. Suggested varieties include: blue spruce, boxwood, common lilac, forsythia, and most pines (except Eastern white pine). These could be closely planted to provide a natural hedgerow.

The use of all or some of these suggested methods should reduce deer browsing damage by 50 percent or more. However, weather conditions with long cold periods or high snow levels will put increased pressure on the deer population, and more severe browsing damage will occur. Whatever the situation, it is always better to take preventive measures with these animals. They are creatures of habit, and their habit might just become your garden!

CHAPTER 3

Lawn Care

A well-maintained lawn looks good in summer and winter and adds value to your landscape and beauty to your life. It also reduces sun glare and filters air pollutants. For kids, there's nothing better to play on; for garden parties, there's nothing better to stroll on. Few homes are complete without at least a little bit of lawn. And few homeowners have a successful lawn without having some idea of how to care for it.

In the sections that follow, you'll get expert advice on installing turf, adding irrigation, developing a schedule of lawn care, having an organic lawn, and dealing with pests and diseases. Read on and soon you'll find answers to just about any basic questions you might have about maintaining your lawn.

Schedule of Lawn Care

Tom Krupa, Gale's Garden Center

Your lawn is what a lot of people see first as they view your property. A well-maintained lawn adds natural beauty to your home and increases property value. But it takes time and money to keep up. The amount of work and money you put into your lawn will show in the end result. The good news is that almost any homeowner can usually produce a decent looking lawn within the constraints of time and money. How do you go about getting a great looking lawn? The best long-term strategy is to get on a lawn care program, a set schedule of applying the correct products at the correct time. Here is a five-step annual program for your lawn, as a guide.

Step 1

Begin in the early spring with a thorough cleaning and raking of the lawn. This should be done soon after the last snow has melted off the lawn to remove all the debris (leaves, twigs, and branches) left over from the fall and winter. Raking also decompresses the grass blades that have been covered by heavy, wet snow and ice.

After cleaning and raking, it is time for the first cut or mowing of the year. Set the mower at 1.5 inches and use the mower bag to pick up the clippings and other loose debris from the lawn surface. This first cut of the year will also take off the winter-weary, brown grass blade tips. After this first mowing, reset your mower to a cutting height of 2.5 to 3.0 inches and leave it there for the rest of the mowing season, until the last cut.

Next, apply the first control product, pre-emergent crabgrass preventer with lawn food. This product will control annual crabgrass weeds and a few other annual grassy weeds. It works by preventing the seeds from germinating once the soil temperature has warmed to a minimum of 52° to 54°F or higher. This pre-emergent barrier will last from 10 to 16 weeks in the lawn. The lawn food part of this product will provide the necessary nutrients to help green-up the lawn after winter.

Do not sow grass seed at this time, since this product will also prevent grass seed from germinating. If you must seed an area of the lawn at this time, look for a control product containing Siduron. It will let you achieve crabgrass prevention and also plant grass seed. Chemicals that provide pre-emergent crabgrass control in established lawns (grass which has been mowed at least three times) and are available to the homeowner include Balan, Dacthal, Barricade, and Pendimethalin.

Many folks ask for a certain date to apply this first step. Actually, it can change every spring. Weather is the real determining factor for application. If it is an early warm spring, the timetable is moved up. Conversely, a cold, late spring moves our date back a little. Approximate dates for application are the last week in March to the first week of May.

Step 2

The next step is broadleaf weed control. The most common broadleaf weed is the dandelion. When this weed is in flower, you can recognize and identify it in lawns from great distances. Realize, though, that the dandelion is only one of 80-plus common broadleaf weeds that can be found in the home lawn. Other examples of broadleaf weeds include clover, chickweed, ground ivy, oxalis, veronica, spurge, and purslane. Weed identification can be accomplished with the help of a lawn and garden book, or a sample of the weed can be taken to your local garden center. Another source of accurate information is the county extension office.

Once the problem weed is identified, apply a broadleaf weedkiller (herbicide). Most of the broadleaf weed control products available to homeowners are combinations of two or more active ingredients. These products typically contain 2,4-D in combination with MCPP. Dicamba is often added to strengthen the herbicidal performance on some hard-to-control weeds. There are many good, commercially prepared weed and feed products available to the homeowner. The feed part of weed and feed contains fertilizer for nutrient value.

Weedkillers, or weed and feed products, can be applied any time weeds are actively growing, although younger, smaller weeds are easier to kill. Application is best when both day and night temperatures are above 55°F consistently. Do not use any weedkillers above 85° to 90°F, since they may injure grass plants. Always read and follow label instructions.

Step 3

Our time frame now is approximately late June to early July. By now the lawn should be looking pretty good with all your work and proper use of lawn products. This is time for the summer application of fertilizer. We want to use a fertilizer high in nitrogen content. Nitrogen is the most important nutrient for grass plants. It is the first number listed on the fertilizer bag. A typical analysis would be 30–4–4, or 37–5–5. The second number refers to the phosphorus content, and the third number is the potassium content. While potassium and phosphorus are required for any plant growth, including grass, nitrogen is still the most important.

There are two types of nitrogen: slow release and fast release. Slow-release nitrogen (also called water-insoluble nitrogen) is the type recommended. This gives the lawn a slow, steady feeding that promotes a deep green color and controlled, even growth rate. All good quality, more expensive fertilizer products have this type of nitrogen. A feeding should provide about four to six weeks of good color and growth. Remember, all fertilizer is water activated, so water the lawn after application, especially during hot weather. Also, be on the lookout for white grubs. Brown patches may suddenly appear without any apparent cause. Or, the lawn may be dug up by skunks looking for a meal of grubs. More on grubs later.

Step 4

It is now late July, early August. The dog days of summer are here. This is the time to keep a lookout for bugs and disease problems. If brown spots or patches start to appear in the lawn, and you can rule out lack of water as the problem, check for fungus and insects. White grubs can become a major problem in the lawn from mid-August through October. Irregular brown patches and skunks digging in the lawn are the possible warning signals of grub infestation. Make an inspection right next to the browned-out area. This will give you more clues than looking at the dead, brown area. If you cannot determine any apparent cause of the problem, remove a pie-shaped sample of the turf (half brown, half green) for analysis. Take it to your local garden center or county extension office for help.

The lawn should receive about one inch of water per week this time of year. If natural rainfall doesn't fulfill this need, you will have to supplement it with your sprinkler. The general rule here is to water early in the morning (5 a.m. to 9 a.m.) and deeply. It is best to water thoroughly and infrequently. This translates to 0.5 inch of water, twice a week. This practice promotes deep root growth. Also, watering in the evening can encourage fungus development. Another application of fertilizer can be made at this time, but only if you are prepared to keep up with the watering schedule.

Step 5

We now get into a very important time of year for our lawns. Late summer and early fall is a time of shorter days and cooler temperatures that is ideal for improving the quality of your lawn. The period between August 15 and September 15 is an excellent time to establish a new lawn or reseed thin areas. Applications of fertilizer during September to November will do more to improve the color, density, and overall health of the grass than any other time. This is also a good time to kill any broadleaf weeds still growing in the lawn. Try and get the weedkiller applied before temperatures consistently fall to 55°F or below.

Two fall feedings are recommended. The first one should be in September or early October. A high-nitrogen, slow-release fertilizer is recommended for the first feeding; the second feeding should be done between mid-October and late November. This will be the final fertilizing of the season and should be done with a fall- or winter-type fertilizer. The fall fertilizers have a lower nitrogen content and a higher phosphorus and potassium percentage.

This last feeding can be done after you have removed the last of the autumn leaves and made the last cutting of the season. Lower your mower setting to 1.5 inches for this cut, and leave it there for your first mowing next year. Clean, winterize, and get any service work done to the mower at this time. Remember to sharpen the mower blade at least once a year to get a clean cut, versus tearing or shredding the grass.

Oh yeah, one last job, get the snow thrower ready!

A great-looking lawn makes a great landscape, as seen at the Lake County Nursery's Mary Elizabeth Garden.
(Photo courtesy of Lake County Nursery Exchange.)

Diagnosing and Treating Lawn Problems

by Davey Tree Technical Resources Center

Here are some of the most common insect pests and lawn diseases that might take up residence in your lawn. We include information on how to identify and treat these particular problems.

1. White Grubs

White grubs are the soil-dwelling larvae of various species of hard-shelled beetles. These grubs, which commonly feed on turfgrass roots, include the Japanese beetle, the May or June beetle, the European chafer, and the northern/southern masked chafer.

Symptoms: Damage from grub feeding first appears as brown patches of dead grass, usually in sunny or exposed locations. If feeding is heavy, the roots are almost completely severed and the sod can be rolled up like a carpet. Grubs can be found underneath the dead turf and a few inches deeper. They are from 1/2 inch to 1 inch long, often curl into a 'C' shape, are white to off-white in color, have brown heads, a dark area at the posterior end of the body, and three pairs of legs near the head.

Cause: Damage from large overwintering grubs can occur in the spring, but this is unusual because the grass is usually growing vigorously. During early summer, grubs pupate or rest before they emerge from the soil as adult beetles. Adults deposit eggs in the soil from which the grubs hatch. These can cause significant damage from mid-August on, when the grass is growing slowly because of heat and lack of water.

Solution: Controlling white grub populations in turf is often difficult because they are protected from products applied to control them by a layer of sod.

Treatment will depend on the grub species and the degree to which the soil is moisture stressed. For instance, studies have shown that damage does not show on bluegrass that is watered, even with ten Japanese beetle grubs per square foot. But if the turf is not watered, damage can appear with only four grubs per square foot.

The homeowner must water the materials into the soil within 24 hours following application to insure maximum contact with the grubs. Two applications may be required to reduce the grub population to acceptable levels.

2. Chinch Bugs

Chinch bugs are small, black-and-white, thatch-inhabiting insects that can suck the life juices out of turf grasses. Chinch bugs are pests on fine fescues and many other Northern grass species (including corn and wheat crops).

Symptoms: Chinch bugs feed by inserting their beak-like mouthparts into the plant and sucking out the juices. While feeding, the bugs inject toxic saliva into the plant. Because of the toxin, turfgrass plants may continue to wilt and yellow and die, even after the chinch bugs have been controlled.

Damage first appears as yellow to brown patches in hot, moisture-stressed areas of the lawn. Although damage is most apparent in the late summer and early fall, it can appear any time from late June until the first frost.

Chinch bugs prefer hot, dry areas; consequently, damage may be noticed first on slopes and in open sunny areas, such as along sidewalks and driveways. Damaged turf is yellow, then brown with a thin, droughty appearance.

Cause: When the air temperature reaches the 70° F range, overwintering adult cinch bugs emerge from debris in March-April and deposit eggs. Females can produce about 260 eggs over a three to four week period. In many areas of the Midwest there are two generations of insects each year. Adults overwinter in plant debris and around the foundation of homes. The adult cinch bug is about 1/5 inch long, blackish with whitish wings, with a black spot about midpoint on the edge of each wing. The newly hatched, immature nymph is bright red with a white band across the back.

Solutions: To find the chinch bugs, part the turfgrass at the edges of brown spots or in suspected areas. The light irritates the chinch bugs and causes them to move around very quickly. Several different developmental stages may be found because of overlapping generations.

Warm, dry weather early in the season, followed by minimal rainfall, provides favorable conditions for chinch bugs. Wet weather depresses population buildup and favors growth of a fungus disease *Beauveria* sp. which kills many chinch bugs.

Chinch bugs can be effectively managed by the application of appropriate insecticides. Ideally, the turfgrass should be treated when populations exceed 20 insects per square foot around the peak activity period, which would be May-June in the Midwest. Repeated applications may be necessary. Light irrigation after treatment will help move the insecticide to the thatch area and improve results.

Many chinch bug-infested yards are mowed too short (they "hate" shady areas) and the thicker the thatch layer, the greater the number of chinch bugs. Evaluate these concerns to help prevent chinch bug problems.

Predators: Another insect, the big-eyed bug *Geocoris*, is a predator and feeds on the chinch bug. This adult big-eyed bug closely resembles the chinch bug. However, the chinch bug's body is narrow, and it has a small, triangular-shaped head with small eyes, while the big-eyed bug has a wider body and its blunt-shaped head is larger with two large prominent eyes. These fast-moving insects are sometimes misidentified as chinch bugs.

3. Red Thread and Pink Patch

Red thread and pink patch are closely related turfgrass diseases. Both are caused by fungi and are active in spring and early fall.

Symptoms: Infected turfgrass will display a reddish-brown cast. Small patches of infected leaves appear water-soaked at first; they later turn straw-colored and die. On close inspection, red thread disease will have coral-pink fungal "threads" protruding from the tips of leaves at an angle. In early morning, coral-pink masses may be seen over leaves near the soil (in the case of red thread) and on leaves (in the case of pink patch).

Cause: Both fungal diseases can cause severe damage to practically all cool-season turfgrasses, but creeping red fescue is particularly susceptible. The disease is most active when air temperatures are 65° to 75°F. Cultural conditions which favor disease development include: moist soil, low soil fertility, calcium deficiency, and excess thatch.

Solutions: Proper management, such as the careful application of soluble nitrogen fertilizers during the infection period and maintaining a soil pH between 6.5 and 7.0, will aid in offsetting disease damage.
Other cultural management practices include:
1. Removing excess thatch in fall.
2. Improving soil drainage and air circulation to increase turf drying.
3. Watering early in the day to allow drying before evening.

4. Leaf Spot and Melting-Out

Leaf spot and melting-out diseases are among the most prevalent fungal disorders of turfgrasses, and the development of disease-resistant cultivars has been a major factor in breeding programs.

Symptoms: During spring, early summer, and fall, the disease fungi cause indefinite yellowing and thinning of grass in scattered areas. The entire lawn or large sections may have a yellow-to-rust-colored cast. Yellow-brown lesions (spots) with purple-black borders can be found on leaves as a result of both leaf spot and melting-out diseases. Melting-out disease fungus can produce spots on tillers and crown tissue (areas of new growth). In summer, large irregular patterns of turfgrass may die suddenly.

Causes: There are several species of these fungal disorders that attack cool-season turfgrasses, thus providing a wide season of infection. Prolonged periods of cool-to-warm, humid weather are most favorable for turfgrass infections, although the melting-out phase may not become evident until the warm, dry summer months.

Solutions: Fungicidal management practices are effective when applied on a regular basis throughout the developmental period, particularly when a preventive program is followed.
Cultural practices that should be followed to reduce disease severity include:
1. Seed or sod with disease-resistant cultivars.
2. Remove excess thatch.
3. Avoid over-fertilization.
4. Avoid early evening watering.

5. Dollar Spot

Symptoms: Dollar spot is caused by a fungus and produces a characteristic pattern of small spots on the lawn. Infected areas of turf are straw-colored, matted, and the size of silver dollars. Dollar spot can also infect turf along the tracks made by lawn mowers and on lawns mowed higher than two inches. These infected patches are usually larger and more irregular.

Fine, cobwebby fungal threads (mycelium) are evident in the infected area in morning while dew is present. Individual leaf blades have an hourglass-shaped lesion (spot) which is straw-colored with a reddish-brown margin.

Cause: The dollar spot fungus is active from late spring through early fall. Dollar spot is commonly found on leaves with excessive thatch and low soil moisture. Environmental conditions which favor fungal growth include high humidity and air temperatures of 65° to 80 °F.

Solution: During periods of high incidence of dollar spot, a fungicide program may be necessary. Following these cultural practices will reduce the potential for dollar spot to infect your lawn:
1. Remove excess thatch.
2. Do not mow when turf is wet.
3. Maintain adequate fertility.
4. Maintain adequate soil moisture.
5. Seed or sod with disease-resistant cultivars.

6. Fusarium Blight and Summer Patch

Fusarium or summer patch diseases are caused by weak pathogenic fungi that infest turf weakened by adverse environmental or cultural factors.

Symptoms:
• Small, circular, scattered light green patches of turf turn reddish-brown first, and light tan in late spring to early fall.

• "Frog-eye" patterns in turf of healthy green grass are surrounded by border of dead, reddish-brown grass.

• Disease is common in exposed areas subject to heat and drought stress.

• Lesions on grass blades begin as light green blotches, later turning straw-colored with uneven brown borders and streaks of brown.

Causes: These fungal diseases are most often a problem on water-stressed turfgrasses with compacted soils or turfgrasses that are exposed to drought. Sodded lawns of 'Merion' and 'Bensun' cultivars are susceptible, particularly if peat-grown sod is laid over heavy clay without providing a transition between the two different soil types. The peat-clay interface prevents proper penetration of water and chemicals and encourages surface rooting and rapid drying. Seeded lawns rarely have this problem. Aerifying the soil will aid penetration, and the lawn should be watered thoroughly during dry periods.

Conditions that favor disease development include:
• Dry, exposed turfgrass, particularly on southern exposures or near paved areas subjected to heat and drought.
• Excess thatch.
• Compacted soil.
• High temperatures (80° to 95°F) and high humidity.
• Excess soluble nitrogen during summer months.
• Pure stands of susceptible turfgrass, particularly sodded lawns.

Solutions: Fungicide applications alone have little effect on Fusarium blight or summer patch. Ideally, the soil should be wet before applying a systemic fungicide, which should be thoroughly drenched into the root zone following proper watering practices.

Since these fungi attack weakened turf, maintaining turfgrass health and vitality will help prevent the diseases. Cultural practices should include:

1. Keep grass growing vigorously, but avoid rapid succulent growth in summer.
2. Aerify compacted soils.
3. Do not mow when turf is wet.
4. Remove excess thatch.
5. Mow frequently at recommended height or slightly higher.
6. Seed or sod with disease-resistant cultivars.
7. Water thoroughly during dry periods.

Nontoxic Lawn Care Alternatives

Spring has traditionally been the time to douse a lawn with chemicals so that it will grow like green velvet. Recently, however, Cleveland-area communities have been questioning the wisdom of following a regular schedule of pesticide, herbicide, and fertilizer treatments. Many of the synthetic products used on lawns simply are not necessary. They cost a bundle of money, whether you do the application yourself or hire someone else to do it, and the salts and chemicals they leave behind can leach into rivers, lakes, and ground water.

Aerate and Fertilize

Mark Druckenbrod, horticulturist and assistant director at The Cleveland Botanical Garden, says good nontoxic alternatives for improving lawn growth include aeration and organic fertilizers: "Because we have heavy clay that we compact every time we walk across the lawn, aerating the soil in spring will do wonders." Aeration in late summer or fall is recommended by Richard Kay of Breezewood Gardens; he says it encourages root growth, making grasses healthier the following spring.

To aerate, hire a landscaper or rent a heavy-duty lawnmower-type aerator that cuts cores—small cylinders—out of the lawn. The openings they leave behind let air and moisture penetrate down through the thatch and clay to the turf roots. The unearthed plugs break up on top of surface thatch (the matted remains of old grass tillings), speeding its decomposition. Request the kind of aerator that has hollow tubes or cylinders set on a rotating drum. Brands that sport large spikes simply dent the soil and make the compression worse.

"Aerating regularly," according to Druckenbrod, "lets grass plants grow a deeper and better root system. And if you do it every spring for a number of years you'll end up covering about every part of the lawn. Then it is all rejuvenated."

With fertilizers, many lawn experts are finding less can be better. "People need to lower their standards," Druckenbrod said. "There is no need for picture-perfect show-quality lawns. That kind of perfection takes overkill in time, money, and chemicals." When you fertilize three times during spring and summer (an old recommendation), the lawn stays constantly growing and needs a lot of water to stay healthy. This is an extravagant system from an environmental and economic point of view, and also time-wise, because the lawn needs constant mowing.

Lawns that contain bluegrass, as do most of ours, need one fertilization. If you use a standard lawn fertilizer, apply half of a one-time dose in April (or September) and the second half a month or two later. Or use organic or slow-release fertilizers that provide their nutrients over the entire summer. With them, one application is plenty.

If insect or weed problems arise, don't just blanket the yard with a pesticide or herbicide. Take some time to identify the problem and to seek out the least toxic method for dealing with it. Spot-treat, if possible, attacking only the source of the problem and not surrounding areas. If you have a few weeds, pull them out. If you have beetle grubs eating turf roots, treat the lawn with a grubicide in combination with milky spore bacteria, which will help prevent Japanese beetle grubs.

For more information on lawn care, see *Building a Healthy Lawn: A Safe and Natural Approach* (by Stewart Franklin, 1988, Garden Way Publishing, Pownal, VT).

A Victorian Lawn Is an Easy Alternative

There is a special appeal to uniformity in a lawn of grass and nothing but grass, but there is also virtue in a modest amount of diversity. If we all looked alike, life would be boring indeed. The same is true of lawns, although this opinion may represent a minority in these parts. But consider your other options before spraying, treating, mowing, watering, raking, and thatching your way to a model green turf.

Good grass is hard to achieve. It falls victim to too little water, too much water (both common around here), and pests and diseases that easily spread from lawn to lawn. And when you get that wonderful grass growing healthily, what does it mean? Mowing, and lots of it.

Consider instead the Victorian lawn, beloved early in this century when chemicals were not so abundant and when mowing was powered by hand and back. The Victorian lawn in this region had pretty small flowers like forget-me-nots, veronica, violets, creeping phlox, and other desirables that made it interesting. They crept into the grass on their own and grew where they were well adapted. That meant the homeowner didn't have to do anything to ensure their survival and they took much less work.

In today's lawn, homeowners often are upset by white clover that spreads amid the turf. To get rid of it, you can apply herbicides, reseed, water intensively, and hope to encourage new grass growing thickly enough to discourage the colonization of other plants. On the other hand, clover stays green all summer, despite the worst heat and drought. Its flowers are attractive even though they are different from the ordinary green lawn, and because they are legumes they actually can add nitrogen to the soil, fertilizing nearby grasses naturally. Not a bad combination.

This is not to say that you should let dandelions, sedges, and other unattractive weeds spread through the lawn. You will still have to spot-treat those undesirables. But at the same time, you can be a little more tolerant of the handsome wild species while minimizing the amount of chemicals you use.

Irrigating Your Lawn

Bob Hobar, Irrigation Supply

You can install irrigation systems to provide your lawn—and also the rest of your yard—with enough moisture to keep it healthy and green. Here are some considerations when evaluating and setting up a new irrigation system.

Know the location and size of your water line and the water pressure it has. If the pressure is less than 35 pounds per square inch, check with your irrigation supply dealer before proceeding.

Draw to scale a diagram of the area to be watered, being sure to include property lines, house area, sidewalks, driveways, patios, bushes, and trees. You may want to set up separate irrigation systems for areas of shrubs, ground cover, flowers, and vegetables so you can water these more or less than grass areas.

You can water most lawns economically with just two types of sprinkler heads, called fixed-spray and gear-drive sprinklers. Gear-drive sprinklers throw water an adjustable distance, depending on how you set the diffuser pin. Fixed-spray heads have changeable nozzles that will water either a full circle or part circle—such as a half or quarter circle or a strip as narrow as two feet wide. You can adjust the distance the water is thrown by fixed-spray heads by adjusting a screw in the center of each nozzle.

Either type can be installed as pop-up sprinklers in your lawn or they can be placed on elevated pipes in garden areas. For the most economical system, set the sprinklers so each one will cover the most area possible—then you'll need fewer sprinklers.

Now you can sketch the kind of sprinkler heads you'll need on your yard diagram. Use quarter-circle heads in all corners and half-circle heads along walls, foundations, sidewalks, driveways, and other border areas, with the heads spraying into the lawn and away from the walks. In areas not covered by part-circle heads, use full-circle heads.

The amount of area they will cover varies with the number of gallons of water per minute that your water system discharges. For example, a full-circle spray head that discharges 2 gallons per minute can spray up to a 12 foot radius. A gear-drive sprinkler discharging 4 gallons per minute can water up to a 40 foot radius.

You can also design your own piping system, but it is a bit more complicated. A *Do-It-Yourself Home Owners Sprinkler System Design Guide* is available from Irrigation Supply; call 831-0095 for details.

CHAPTER 4
Improving Your Landscape

Landscapes mean different things to different people. For some, the landscape is the entire yard and all the fun and interesting things you can do with it. For others, it is an artistic medium—a canvas upon which to paint with plants. Still others see it as a challenge to make trouble-free, using low-maintenance plants and techniques. In any case, what you do with your landscape says a lot about you and has a vital effect on the appearance of your home.

To make the most of your landscape, here are tips on great ways to plan designs and the best plants to use in any given location. This action-packed chapter is guaranteed to get you excited about the possibilities for your landscape!

Foundation Plantings

Bad landscape design isn't pretty: windows look out into the backs of shrubs, large tree limbs dangle perilously over the roof, and the overall view is awkward, contrived, or overgrown. Such a landscape only gets worse with time. If you're dissatisfied with your landscape, or if you are moving to a new home, it's time to take a fresh look at the plants surrounding your walls.

Some of the most common problems that occur in our landscapes involve poorly designed foundation plantings. Foundation plantings have evolved and expanded over the decades, reflecting changes in home architecture, available plants, and gardening styles. However, some old-fashioned, or even obsolete, concepts still persist in this area; they can stifle a landscape.

Foundation plantings, always in the public eye, can be a way for you to beautify and increase the value of your home and to exercise your creativity. If you invest some time in planning, you can create an attractive design in which maintenance is minimized and plants will flourish for years.

The Purpose of Foundation Planting

The idea of enveloping the face of a house with trees and shrubs originated when basements were shallow and cement walls protruded above the ground to allow space for coal-powered furnaces. To hide the unattractive mechanics of construction, gardeners trooped in shrubbery soldiers and lined them up as a visual barricade.

Modern homes seldom reveal tall expanses of cement foundations, lessening the need for concealment. Still, the home landscape will benefit from carefully designed plantings that soften harsh architectural lines and unite the home with the surrounding property.

Just as homes have changed, plants suitable for foundation plantings are more numerous and better refined. Homeowners are no longer limited to the old landscaping standbys of the historic Western Reserve, such as privet and lilac—both of which mature tall enough to obscure most first-floor windows. Today you can find a wealth of dwarf plants that fit around a foundation without overgrowing (though you may have to seek them out if you buy locally).

Foundation plantings can be simple and understated or elaborate. The simplest option is the traditional line of woody plants in front of a house. More modern alternatives feature beds of arcing lines that may drift out into the foreground of the yard. Either style will be attractive if you pay attention to some fundamental rules of design. How you select and arrange plants should echo interesting house features, soften angles, and draw attention to a focal point—usually the front door.

Start with the House

Begin by thinking about lines. Houses are heavy in vertical lines, which are strongest at the outer corners of the house and the doorway. Neutralize their stiffness with the horizontal branching of rounded shrubs and small trees. The tallest plants, usually located at the corners of the house, should not exceed two-thirds of the height of the roof line. The entryway also can call for tall accent plants, but these should remain lower than eave level. Or you can substitute lower-growing plants instead that draw the eye with color, form, or texture. Fill in between the entryway and house corners with compact shrubs to create a concave or downsloping line that lets the eye pass easily to the doorway.

How high plants should go depends on your house. For a small one-story house, stick with low plants. For a large Victorian house, you can use taller shrubs but avoid blocking doors and windows. A split-level home may call for a small flowering tree at the single-story end and a shrub hedge at the two-story side to balance the shape of the house.

In most cases, the simplest plan is the best. If you limit yourself, for instance, to three different kinds of plants, you can cluster and repeat to give a subtle rhythm to the plan. It's a good idea to mix deciduous with evergreen. The ever-changing deciduous plants progress from flowers to fruits to fall color, while evergreens stand steadfast year-round.

Try to match the plants' ambience to your house. Color is always important, but so is the texture created by leaf size, branching pattern, and bark. For a home of wood siding, a shrub of medium texture will not obtrude. Brick or barn siding is complemented by larger leaves, such as oakleaf hydrangea.

The shape of the planting bed adds to the overall effect. Lines can reflect the shape of the building. Large curves, carefully planned, can further soften architectural angles. However, free-form beds may look contrived and alien. To make them natural, curve and reverse the curve, with large sweeping lines, not little wiggles.

Plant Size

You may decide to let the foundation planting drift out into an entry garden suitable for low shrubs, perennials, or annual flowers. A small specimen tree could be balanced by a cluster of shrubs on the opposite side of the entrance.

Before you run out and buy a single plant, learn the mature height and spread of each shrub and tree you intend to include in your design. Calculate their spacing to let them assume their full size without squeezing their neighbors into odd, one-sided shapes.

A little research into the mature sizes of trees will prevent future problems from limbs that bump into the house or snag utility lines. The height to which some trees can soar may be hard to imagine when you see young nursery stock in a pot: a 5-foot red maple tree can grow to 120 feet in our region; a Christmas-tree-sized white pine can reach 80 feet. Trees of this size should be planted well away from the house. Up close, it is safer to stick with smaller trees, such as the paperbark maple, which reaches 25 to 30 feet, or the fringe tree, which grows 12 to 25 feet tall—both especially good species for this area.

There are giants among shrubs as well. Forsythia, common in landscapes around town, will reach 10 feet—well above most windowsills. Thinning these shrubs annually will keep them in check. So many nice dwarf shrubs are available, however, that it doesn't make sense to bother with an oversized plant. Try viburnums, barberries, false cypress, rhododendrons, spruces, hollies, junipers, and yews; all need little or no care after planting and are available in the Cleveland area (though you may have to order early).

Avoiding Trouble

Once you have identified the right plants for your house, be sure they will receive the sun and rain necessary for good growth. A roof overhang is like an umbrella that keeps the soil below dry and barren. Situate all plants at least one foot away from the roof's outer edge. This safety zone also saves the day when the gutters dam up and drench the soil below with rain, or when heavy wet snow plummets off the roof. Likewise, if you will be planting near a walkway, add from 6 to 12 inches to allow for the mature spread of a plant. This way, branches can droop when wet or snow-laden without invading the walk.

Plants, of course, need sunlight, but houses can be particularly baffling because they will intensify as well as block sunlight. If the foundation planting will be on the north side, shadow may cover much of the bed most of the day. It will stay dark and damp, limiting your plant choices. Light-colored houses will reflect sun, especially on the southern side, and can burn even a hardy sun-lover. Check the number of hours the sun shines in each location, then buy a plant suited to that light exposure. If you try to keep a shade plant in bright sun or vice versa, chances are good that you will be disappointed.

You must reckon with difficulties dealt by pavement and underground utilities as well. Know where underground wires and pipes are located. Avoid disturbing them when landscaping, and keep deep-rooted plants some distance away. Likewise, you may need to give extra space to plantings near driveways and walks; these surfaces radiate heat and limit rooting space and water penetration.

Soil is also a concern. The natural topsoil on your home site may have been removed or compacted during construction. Infertile subsurface soil unearthed when digging the basement may end up on top. This can leave soil heavy and wet, possibly requiring the addition of drainage tiles before plants will grow well.

8 Ways to Create a Better Landscape

Richard Kay, Breezewood Gardens

A new spirit is developing in the field of landscape design, a break with tradition that puts increased emphasis on more dramatic use of perennials, grasses, water features, and rock work.

In response to this freer approach, each plant or plant group seems to leap to life in an unrestrained display. Lush plantings of decorative grasses, bulbs, and perennials are planned for year-round viewing. Perennial flowering plants are woven into luxuriant tapestries; ferns, mosses, and succulents are selected and placed with care to reveal the full beauty of their individual form, color, and texture. Larger trees are massed as dark free-form backdrops, placed to cast layers of delicate shadows over a pathway. Shrubs are chosen for year-round appeal and placed for viewing in the round or strewn about in informal drifts.

Popular, too, is the imaginative use of water—in jets, fountains, cascades, or quiet reflecting ponds—and light, both natural and man-made. The skillful use of evening illumination presents the landscape in a whole new way while extending the hours of enjoyment these new creative design approaches provide.

Have you ever noticed that when you come across a beautiful garden you want to stop, breathe in the fragrance, admire the vivid colors, and just linger awhile? If so, you have come to appreciate a truly successful landscape project.

The following tips will help you transform an unused portion of your property into an area to gather with family and friends. (It has been said that no man hath the pride of the gardener.)

1. Create an "outdoor room" by framing in the designated area with large shrubs, trees, or evergreens. Build in privacy by planting large plants around the perimeter of your outdoor room. Add color on the inside of this perimeter with plantings of smaller blooming shrubs, perennials, annuals, and bulbs. Think of this area as a photograph or painting, with your plant selections forming a visual frame.

2. Plan for use. Think about how you are going to use this outdoor room and plan accordingly. If you want to provide a place for your children to play and your pets to frolic, choose more rugged plants and place the flower beds away from tempting play areas.

3. Ground preparation. Never skimp on the ground work or planting bed preparation. Use top quality topsoil mixed with at least one third part peat moss or composted organic matter for at least the top 12 inches of the planting bed (up to 18 inches is better for many annuals, perennials, and roses). Have the soil tested to determine any deficiencies. In areas of heavy clay soils all plantings should be in raised beds at least 6 inches higher than the surrounding area.

4. Plant choice and placement. Choosing the right plant and placing it in the right place—not only in relation to other plants but also in the right exposure and soil condition—are keys to a landscape that thrives with minimal care. Better garden centers and nurseries have professionals on hand to help you make a good choice.

It's also important to choose high quality plants. Quality plants have the right balance of below ground roots and above ground branches and shoots—essential for future success. Container-grown plants should have well developed roots, but they shouldn't be overgrown in the container or coiled around the inside. Balled and burlapped plants should have root systems that are compact and firm, not loose or cracked.

After inspecting the root system, examine the trunk and leaves, checking for damage or disease. Finally, appraise the plants' overall form and shape. Trees and shrubs have a natural shape and should not be plagued with major bare spots caused by missing or broken branches. Good form, like a healthy root system, is a sign of quality and care.

5. Plant carefully. Place your plants in the garden before you actually plant them. Visualize how they are going to grow together. Then make the proper adjustments after inspecting from all the important angles. When planting, dig a hole only deep enough to accommodate about 80 percent of the root system but twice as wide. Back fill with rich topsoil blended with peat moss, or compost. Create a water dike around the excavation equal to the drip line of the shrub (shade trees should have a slightly slimmer water dike). Mulch to two inches away from the tree and thoroughly water to settle soil and rehydrate the root system.

6. Add water. Add charm while bringing more of nature to your outdoor room by adding a birdbath or water garden. Water gardens are great for rejuvenating the spirit as you listen to the delicate splashing, smell the cool, damp scent, and watch the water slip over the pebbles and rocks.

7. Furnish. Use a deck or patio, a garden bench or gazebo to make your outdoor room a place of easy comfort. Add terra-cotta pots or urns planted with your favorite flowers. Create shade with trees or a trellis covered with vines.

8. Enjoy. Invite a friend over, pull up a chair, sip some lemonade, and relish your friend's praise for a job well done.

Choice Flowering Trees and Shrubs

Alexander Apanius, landscape designer

There are some very attractive and compact trees and shrubs that thrive in the Greater Cleveland area and make excellent landscape plants, even in small yards.

Here are some of my favorites.

Trees

'Bloodgood' Japanese red maple is a small multistemmed tree that has an excellent form and beautiful red foliage.

'Autumn Brilliance' downy serviceberry is a small bushy tree that has white flowers, blue berries in June, red fall color, and attractive gray bark.

'Summer Stars' Chinese kousa dogwood flowers profusely; it bears white, flower-like bracts later and longer than other dogwoods. It is also disease- and pest-resistant.

Japanese flowering crabapple was introduced from Japan years ago and is still the standard against which other flowering crabapples are judged. Pink buds turn into white fragrant flowers and produce yellow and red, 3/8 inch fruit. Better yet, it has a beautiful, slow growing, spreading habit and disease resistance.

'Arnold Promise' witchhazel is a small multistemmed, horizontally branched tree with bright yellow flowers in late winter .

Fringe tree is a shrub or multistemmed tree with medium- to coarse-textured foliage, and lacy, white, pendant flowers in late May or early June. In fall, the foliage turns bright yellow.

Lace bark pine is a slow growing, multistemmed, small tree with an upright oval form, open branching habit, and interesting bark, as the name implies.

Shrubs

English weeping yew is a beautiful, slow growing, spreading yew that does not require shearing. It does well in shade.

'Kallay's Dwarf' pfitzer Chinese juniper is a slow-growing, spreading form with attractive bright-colored foliage. It does not need pruning.

Japanese shore juniper spreads out on the ground, producing a soft natural carpet of medium-textured foliage.

'Blue Princess' and 'Stallion Hybrid' holly have blue-green foliage laced with flowers and red berries. They are slow-growing and very hardy.

'Nordic Dwarf' inkberry holly has shiny round leaves and bushy shape. It tolerates wet soil better than other hollies. Females produce dark blue berries once used as ink by pioneers.

'Prague Hybrid' viburnum is a fine textured, low round shrub that holds its foliage into early winter. It produces white flowers several times a year.

'Burkwood Hybrid' viburnum is a fine-textured, round shrub of medium height that holds its foliage into early winter. Dark green, shiny leaves emerge after fragrant, early spring pink flowers fade.

'Blackburn' cranberry cotoneaster has large red fruits that fill this low-spreading shrub in late summer and fall, and become especially attractive after the red fall-colored foliage drops off.

Compact burning bush has attractive fall color every year.

Making the Most of Shade

Mike Wells, Gali's Garden Center

 There are three main types of shade you may have to contend with. The first is partial or half-day shade, which is also known as partial sun. Found on either the east or west side of a house or tree, it's an area that is sunny for part of the day and shaded for the remainder. Most common garden plants, even those that require full sun, will grow there.

The second type of shade is dappled or light shade, found under high tree branches where the shadows cast by the leaves shift with the sun. This type of shade is found most often at the edges of large trees or woodland groves.

The final type of shade is permanent shade—areas north of a house, fence, or wall that casts a permanent shadow over the growing bed. This is the most difficult type of shade to plant in, and always seems barren and in need of something to fill it out.

The plants listed in this article will grow in all these areas.

To identify which kind of shade you have, survey the site carefully: is there a little sun in the morning, the afternoon, or both? Can you remove some of the lower tree branches to allow more light into the area without spoiling the tree's appearance?

Think about the amount of moisture available to the plant, too. Because trees are vast consumers of water, little extra may be available under the tree for a rhododendron or an azalea. In dry sites, you may have to water under the tree once, even twice per day, to insure the survival of your planting. Now look at the condition of the soil under the tree. If the soil is poor or full of tree roots, build a raised bed for planting. A simple mound of soil topped with a heavy mulch is the easiest method. You may get more elaborate by building a doughnut-shaped ring under the tree, keeping the center at least two feet from the trunk and extending it out as far as you would like beyond the tree. You also could dig out the roots and install a barrier to contain them and prevent re-entry to the planting site.

Now, choose your plants carefully. The hardier and less demanding they are, the better they will grow.

Plants Suitable for Shade

1. Shrubs and Small Trees

Taxus or yews. These are evergreens of various shapes that mature from 3 to 60 feet tall. They prefer a peat-rich, acid soil, but will tolerate poorer soils. You can prune them heavily.

Oriental arbor vitaes. These evergreens vary in height from 4 to over 60 feet at maturity and are grown for the rich emerald-green color that remains constant through the year. If these thin out in heavy shade, prune to keep them attractive.

Junipers. These stately trees or low ground-cover-like shrubs range from deep green to blue in hue. All junipers, particularly the "blue" junipers, need a spot with less dense shade. The darker green varieties fare better in deeper shade.

Barberries. These colorful spreading shrubs range in height from 2 to 10 feet at maturity. They lend a different accent to a shaded area.

Dogwoods. There are two notable varieties suited for growing in the shade. The first is the variegated red-twigged dogwood (*Cornus alba*). It's a lower-growing shrub reaching about 6 to 7 feet high with a wide spread. Its bright red twigs bring winter color to the area, and it is tolerant of wet locations.

The second is the common white-flowered eastern dogwood (*C. florida*). Growing to about 7 to 10 feet in cultivation, it blooms in spring. Later in the season, it has shiny red berries and dark red autumn foliage. Both of these dogwoods prefer moist neutral soil but will tolerate drier conditions.

Hydrangeas. The familiar snowballs of your grandparents' yard are large bushes to small trees with pink-to-white or blue flowers in mid-summer. They are truly a showstopper in a shaded area.

Cotoneasters. From less than 2 to more than 12 feet, these spreading shrubs are good underplantings in tough spots. Tolerant of both heat and drought, the semi-evergreen foliage on purplish-brown stems and brilliant red berries provide good fall and winter color.

Euonymus. This group includes the showy burning bush. In bright shade situations, this plant has dense, dark green foliage that turns flaming red in autumn. Others of the group have evergreen foliage which is green and white, or yellow and green on the lower-growing varieties of these shrubby plants.

Magnolia. In shade areas, the star magnolia cannot be rivaled. Lightly fragrant, loose, showy white blossoms appear in early spring and cover the tree before the leaves. Others of the group are equally tolerant of shade.

Pyracantha. The common firethorn is a rampant grower in shady conditions, though it tends to be straggly. Semi-evergreen, this shrub produces umbels of greenish-white, honey-scented blossoms followed in fall by bright orange berries that are attractive to birds.

Viburnum. These deciduous shrubs range in height from 3-foot bushes to 12-foot thickets. They make excellent early summer blooming plantings for a woodland setting. Black-purple fruits follow white flower clusters held erect on the grayish-brown twigs. The oak-leaved viburnum flower heads rival those of the hydrangeas for showy color.

Azaleas and rhododendrons. Nothing can rival these shrubs for spring color in shaded areas. Ranging in height from 2 to 10 feet, they need a moist, acid soil rich in peat. Some winter protection is necessary if the area is exposed to harsh winds and late afternoon sun.

Privets. Able to hold their own against all odds, privets make excellent choices as underplantings in any well drained spot. 'Golden Vicary' is a good choice for alternative color.

Mock orange. An old-fashioned flowering shrub, mock orange justly deserves a place in the shade garden. Blooming in June, the sweetly scented blossoms are reminiscent of orange trees. Prune heavily after flowering to prevent legginess.

2. Vines

The following plants are well suited to shade locations. Most are tolerant of poor soil and dry locations but require late-winter pruning to keep them in check. Exceptions are noted.

Porcelain berry (*Ampelopis brevipedunculata*). This grapelike vine reaches to 25 feet and bears variegated leaves. The tiny clusters of insignificant flowers produce porcelain-blue berries for fall display. Provide support.

Japanese clematis (*Akebia quinata*). The five-lobed, semi-evergreen leaves add texture and contrast to the shaded area. Flowers (which appear in late spring and early summer) are small and very unusual. They are followed by edible berries in late summer or early fall. Provide support.

Climbing hydrangea (*Hydrangea anomala petiolaris*). This is an excellent vine for the shaded garden. It has slow growth, deep shiny green leaves and, in early summer, many large panicles of creamy white flowers that have a greenish tinge. It will support itself by means of holdfasts, but requires a richer soil than most vines. Prune after flowering.

Honeysuckles. 'Goldflame' honeysuckle, which reaches 12 feet high, is the showiest of the group. Red flowers with a golden-white interior appear in summer at each growing tip. Provide support or grow as a ground or bank cover.

Bittersweet (*Celastrus* spp.). Simple, heart-shaped leaves and tiny greenish flowers are followed in fall by a glorious show of yellow foliage and a multitude of burnt orange and red berries on twisted, rich brown wood stems. Growing to 20 feet, this vine will support itself.

English ivy. This ubiquitous, evergreen vine is used extensively for a ground cover. It requires moisture for best growth.

Myrtle. This delightful evergreen plant is very low growing and adapts well to any situation. In the right location, it produces periwinkle blue blossoms twice a year. Mow it back in late spring after flowering for better growth and second bloom later in the season. Myrtle prefers an acid soil.

Silver lace vine (*Polygonum aubertii*). This vine has deep green, triangular-shaped leaves, topped out at the growing point by airy, white, fragrant blossom clusters. It tolerates dry locations because of its deep root system, but it needs support.

The vine-covered pergola at the Cleveland Botanical Garden makes a home for unusual shade plants.
(Photo courtesy of the Cleveland Botanical Garden.)

Great Long-Lasting Flower Bulbs

Peter Brumbaugh, Wood and Company

 If you want to grow bulbs that you can enjoy for a long time, check out these favorites. The following bulbs are great for naturalizing or are as long lasting as a bulb can be. They are organized by order of bloom, starting with early spring and progressing into fall.

Snowdrops. *Galanthus nivalis* is a lovely early snowdrop that spreads nicely. But buy only this species, not Asiatic types which don't do as well here.

Squill. *Scilla tubergeniana* bears light blue flowers for an especially long time.

Chionodoxa luciliae. These flowers are bright blue with a white heart and can self-seed and spread well.

Puschkinia libanotica alba. For pure white flowers, look for this long-blooming bulb.

Tulipa dasystemon. This is a species tulip that looks a little like a crocus—it's only about 7 inches high and has yellow flowers that are violet on the outside. It is very long lived.

Tulipa kaufmanniana. This species tulip and its hybrids will bloom for years. The flowers, which open when the sun shines, are small and available in many different colors.

Tulip, Early Single. The longest lasting cultivar in this class of tulips is 'Keizerskroon', an old-fashioned bulb that dates back to 1750 and has red and yellow flowers. It lives a long time in our climate and might even multiply if given a little care.

Cottage tulip. Late blooming 'Halcro', a reddish pink, and 'Mrs. Scheepers', a yellow tulip, will live a long time in our climate.

Short and early daffodils. 'Tête-à-Tête' is a charming, small, yellow-flowered daffodil that's long lasting. 'Fortune's Bowl', which has a flat golden cup with a yellow perianth, blooms a long time and tolerates poor weather. Better yet, it doesn't need to be lifted and divided every three years like 'King Alfred'.

Fragrant daffodils for cutting. For great late-blooming cultivars , try white-flowered 'Cheerfulness' and yellow-flowered 'Yellow Cheerfulness'.

Poet's daffodils. 'Actaea' is large for a poet's daffodil and has a white perianth, and yellow eye with a red rim. It blooms late for a daffodil and grows vigorously, even in slightly wet, naturalized locations.

Recurvus is a smaller-flowered poet's daffodil that blooms very late.

Bluebells. English bluebells (*Endymion non-scriptus*) are shorter and earlier than Spanish bluebells—better yet, they're also fragrant. Spanish bluebells (*E. hispanicus*) can multiply well—almost too well—if naturalized.

Flowering onions. Giant flowering onion (*Allium giganteum*) produces a spectacular large, lavender, globe-shaped bloom if given plenty of sun and well drained soil. *Allium caeruleum* produces smaller, knee-high, clear blue flowers.

Hardy amaryllis. *Lycoris squamigera* produces pink flowers on leafless stems in midsummer. It can return year after year if planted in a well-drained location and protected from damage when the flower suddenly appears.

Oriental lily. 'Imperial Crimson' is a very fragrant, large, and fairly flat flower that blooms in August. It needs rich but well-drained soil, afternoon shade, and good care, but is well worthwhile.

Colchicum. 'The Giant' produces large, lavender, crocus-like flowers in fall. They are not knocked down by rain, like some colchicums, and rebloom year after year. The leaves appear in spring but die back in summer.

Autumn flowering crocus. *Crocus speciosus* has charming clear blue flowers, a color not available in the spring-blooming crocus. It will bloom reliably and even multiply in full sun.

Puschkinia Libanotica alba is a long-blooming bulb.
(Photo courtesy of Netherlands Flower Bulb Information Center.)

14 Low-Maintenance Perennials

Robin Armstrong Siktberg, Cleveland Botanical Garden

 I have a fairly large perennial garden at home, but my busy lifestyle does not allow me much time to take care of it. I have to be careful to choose low-maintenance plants that do not need to be fussed over. The plants on the following list are some favorites that have been successful. I must stress that proper soil preparation, in addition to the right choice of plants, is the key to a low-maintenance garden.

Plants for Sun

Gayfeather (*Liatris spicata*) 'Kobold'; 18 to 30 inches; bright lavender flowers in mid-late summer.

No staking is necessary for this striking plant, which is shorter than others in its genus. Gayfeathers are natives of the prairie and are used to long periods of drought. The flower spikes and upright stems give a nice vertical effect to the garden, and it's a butterfly favorite!

Montbretia (*Crocosmia* x *crocosmiiflora* 'Lucifer'); 3 to 4 feet; orange-scarlet flowers in late summer.

Aside from the really stunning display of flowers, 'Lucifer' attracts hummingbirds. Other Crocosmias need to be lifted for the winter, but 'Lucifer' is hardy. No staking is required, despite the plant's height.

Purple coneflower (*Echinacea purpurea* 'Magnus'); 3 feet; lavender flowers in mid-late summer.

'Magnus' is superior to the other *Echinacea* cultivars because its petals do not droop. All the varieties share the same tolerance of drought and heat, however, and if the dead flowers are removed the plant will bloom for several months. Butterflies are attracted to *Echinacea*, another plus.

Russian sage (*Perovskia atriplicifolia*); 3 to 4 feet; large clusters of tiny lavender-blue flowers in mid-late summer.

This plant is an attention-getter in the border with its combination of grayish-white leaves and lavender-blue flowers. Like other members of the mint family, the leaves are fragrant, too. Perovskia needs a well-drained, but not necessarily fertile, soil in full sun. There's no extra watering or staking required.

Stonecrop (*Sedum* 'Autumn Joy'); 18 to 24 inches; green-to-pink-to-mauve flowers in late summer-fall.

This plant has become quite common, and for good reason. It probably requires the least maintenance of any perennial plant—no staking, no dividing, no watering, no deadheading. Butterflies like the flowers and the succulent bluish-green leaves are attractive in their own right. What more could I ask?

Tickseed (*Coreopsis verticillata* 'Golden Showers'); 2 to 3 feet; yellow flowers in mid-late summer.

All of the *C. verticillata* cultivars are nice, but the large yellow flowers of this one make a bigger, bolder statement. 'Golden Showers' thrives in dry, sunny places and its lovely delicately textured leaves make a nice backdrop for shorter plants. Cut it back after flowering for a second bloom.

Plants for Shade

Barrenwort (*Epimedium* cultivars) 8 to 12 inches; yellow, pink, white, or violet flowers in early spring.

Epimedium is a wonderful alternative to other overused and less suitable shade groundcovers. It requires moist, well-drained soils, but has no serious pest problems. Once established, it spreads fairly quickly. It does well under trees, and the overlapping heart-shaped leaves create a nice look.

Goldenstar (*Chrysogonum virginianum*) 6 to 8 inches; yellow flower in spring and fall.

Goldenstar spreads quickly in good soil and is a great filler between more dominant plants. The yellow flowers are bright and last for many weeks. This plant provides the yellow color that is so difficult to find in shade plantings.

Japanese anemone (*Anemone* x *hybrida*); 2 to 4 feet; white or pink flowers in late summer-fall.

If given good soil with ample moisture, Japanese anemones require no other care except for possible staking when in bloom. There is no better plant for a shady, late-season garden.

Kamchatka bugbane (*Cimicifuga simplex* 'White Pearl'); 3 to 5 feet; white flowers in late summer-fall.

The airy white spires of 'White Pearl' are self-supporting. Like most shade-loving plants, cimicifugas need moist, well-drained soil but no special attention. I forget mine is there until the flowers are waving gracefully in the back of the border.

Old-fashioned bleeding-heart (*Dicentra spectabilis*) 2 to 3 feet; pink flowers in May-June.

This plant has long been a favorite of mine. Fortunately, it requires almost no effort on my part to grow it. Given partial shade and moist, well-drained soil, bleeding heart will appear each spring, bloom profusely, and disappear by July. I am always fascinated by the complexity of the heart-shaped flowers.

Plantain lily (*Hosta* cultivars)

Hostas come in all colors and sizes and are grown primarily for their attractive foliage. They are the most useful plant for the shady border and are carefree except for the fact that slugs enjoy them. This is not a reason to avoid planting them, though—the slug problem can be controlled with a minimum of effort. Many of the blue-leaved cultivars, including two of my favorites, *Hosta* 'Krossa Regal' and *Hosta sieboldiana* 'Elegans', seem to be less attractive to slugs.

Toad lily (*Tricyrtis hirta*) 24 to 30 inches; lilac flowers in late summer.

You have to get up close to see the flowers of the toad lily, but once there you will marvel at their unique shape and markings. The arching stems with their leaves are always attractive and you won't have to do a thing except provide moist, well-drained soil.

Variegated Solomon's seal (*Polygonatum odoratum* 'Variegatum'); 2 to 3 feet; creamy-white flowers in spring.

This graceful plant is one of the best and most reliable for a shady garden, but is still unusual enough to satisfy experienced gardeners. The arching stems are reddish, bearing green leaves streaked and edged with white. The clump will increase at a steady pace, producing three to five additional shoots each year. No special attention is needed, unless you want to divide it and give some to friends.

More Plant Ideas for Local Landscapes

Lake County Nursery Exchange

Plants for Hedges and Windbreaks

Hedge maple	(*Acer campestre*)
Amur maple	(*Acer ginnala and cvs.*)
Japanese barberry	(*Berberis thunbergii and cvs.*)
Barberry	(*Berberis – Bonanza Gold*™)
European hornbeam	(*Carpinus betulus 'Fastigiata'*)
False cypress	(*Chamaecyparis obtusa 'Gracilis'*)
Tartarian dogwood	(*Cornus alba 'Siberica'*)
Paricled dogwood	(*Cornus racemosa*)
Smoke tree	(*Cotinus coggygria and cvs.*)
Hawthorn	(*Crataegus crus-galli and cvs.*)
Hawthorn	(*Crataegus phaenopyrum*)
Hawthorn	(*Crataegus x 'Vaughn'*)
Russian olive	(*Elaegnus angustifolia*)
Russian olive	(*Elaegnus – Titan*®)
Burning bush	(*Euonymus alatus 'Compacta'*)
Beech	(*Fagus spp. and cvs.*)
Witchhazel	(*Hamamelis spp. and cvs.*)
Holly	(*Ilex, China Series*)
Holly	(*Ilex x meserveae Blue Series*)
Juniper	(*Juniperus scopulorum 'Moonglow'*)
Mountain laurel	(*Kalmia latifolia*)
Privet	(*Lingustrum, most*)
Spice bush	(*Lindera benzoin*)
Honeysuckle	(*Lonicera maackii and cvs.*)
Honeysuckle	(*Lonicera tatarica 'Arnold's Red'*)
Magnolia	(*Magnolia, most*)
Apple	(*Malus, most*)
Bayberry	(*Myrica pennsylvanica*)
Mock orange	(*Philadelphus 'Minnesota Snowflake'*)
Spruce	(*Picea spp. and cvs.*)
Austrian pine	(*Pinus nigra*)
White pine	(*Pinus strobus*)
Scotch pine	(*Pinus sylvestris*)
Firethorn	(*Pyracantha – Gnome*®)
Firethorn	(*Pyracantha x 'Mohave'*)
Buckthorn	(*Rhamnus frangula and cvs.*)
Rhododendron	(*Rhododendron, most*)
Willow	(*Salix discolor*)

Willow	(*Salix x 'Golden Curls'*)
Willow	(*Salix Scarlet Curls™*)
Willow	(*Salix purpurea 'Streamco'*)
Lilac	(*Syringa, all*)
Yew	(*Taxus, all*)
Arborvitae	(*Thuja, all*)
Canadian hemlock	(*Tsuga canadensis*)
Viburnum	(*Viburnum, all*)
Weigela	(*Weigela flnorida and cvs.*)

Plants that Tolerate Heavy Clay Soils

Trees

Hedge maple	(*Acer campestre*)
Red maple	(*Acer rubrum and cvs.*)
Sugar maple	(*Acer saccharinum*)
River birch	(*Betula nigra*)
Hawthorn	(*Crataegus ssp. and cvs.*)
Russian olive	(*Elaegnus angustifolia*)
Red ash	(*Fraxinus pennsylvanica and cvs.*)
Honey locust	(*Gleditsia triacanthos inermis and cvs.*)
Golden-rain tree	(*Koelreuteria paniculata*)
Sweet gum	(*Liquidambar styraciflua and cvs.*)
Apples	(*Malus, most*)
Spruce	(*Picea spp. and cvs.*)
London plane tree	(*Platanus x acerifolia 'Bloodgood'*)
Pear	(*Pyrus, most*)
Willow	(*Salix, most*)
Bald cypress	(*Taxodium distichum*)
Elms	(*Ulmus spp. and cvs.*)

Ground Covers

Bugleweed	(*Ajuga spp.*)
Euonymous	(*Euonymus fortunei 'Colorata'*)
Grasses, ornamental	(*Grasses, ornamental*)
Daylilies	(*Hemerocallis, all*)
Hosta	(*Hosta, all*)
Juniper	(*Juniperus, low types*)
Honeysuckle	(*Lonicera japonica 'Halliana'*)
Honeysuckle	(*Lonicera xylosteum 'Emerald Mound'*)
Pachysandra	(*Pachysandra terminalis and cvs.*)
Virginia creeper	(*Parthenocissus spp.*)
Fragrant sumac	(*Rhus aromatica and cvs.*)

Shrubs

Barberries	(*Berberis, most*)
Flowering quince	(*Chaenomeles, most*)

Dogwood	(*Counus, shrub types*)
Deutzia	(*Deutzia, most*)
Russian olive	(*Elaegnus, most*)
Euonymous	(*Euonymus, most*)
Forsythia	(*Forsythia most*)
Witchhazel	(*Hamamelis spp.*)
Juniper	(*Juniperus, most*)
Privet	(*Ligustrum, most*)
Honeysuckle	(*Lonicera, shrubby types*)
Bayberry	(*Myrica pennsylvanica*)
Firethorn	(*Pyracantha, most*)
Sumac	(*Rhus, most*)
Alpine currant	(*Ribes alpinum and cvs.*)
Rugosa rose	(*Rosa rugosa*)
Willow	(*Salix, most*)
Spirea	(*Spiraea, most*)
Yew	(*Taxus, most*)
Arborvitae	(*Thuja occidentalis and cvs.*)
Viburnum	(*Viburnum dentatum*)
Viburnum	(*Viburnum lentago*)
Viburnum	(*Viburnum opulus and cvs.*)
Viburnum	(*Viburnum prunifolium and cvs.*)
Viburnum	(*Viburnum sargentii and cvs.*)

Plants that Tolerate Poor, Dry Soils

Trees

Hedge maple	(*Acer campestre*)
Amur maple	(*Acer ginnala*)
Sugar maple	(*Acer saccharinum*)
Birch	(*Betula spp. and cvs.*)
Turkish filbert	(*Corylus corlurna*)
Hawthorn	(*Crataegus spp. & cvs.*)
Russian olive	(*Elaegnus spp.*)
Red ash	(*Fraxinus pennsylvanica and cvs.*)
Honey locust	(*Gleditsia trlacanthos inermis and cvs.*)
Kentucky coffee tree	(*Gymnocladus dioica*)
Golden-rain tree	(*Koelreuteria paniculata*)
White pine	(*Pinus strobus*)
Chinese elm	(*Ulmus parvifolia*)

Ground Covers

Hosta	(*Hosta spp. and cvs.*)
Virginia creeper	(*Parthenocissus spp.*)
Sedum	(*Sedum spp and cvs.*)

Shrubs

Barberry	(*Berberis x mentorensis and cvs.*)
Barberry	(*Berberis thunbergii and cvs.*)
Flowering quince	(*Chaenomeles spp. and cvs.*)
Gray dogwood	(*Cornus racernosa*)
Smoke tree	(*Cotinus coggygria and cvs.*)
Broom	(*Cytisus spp. and cvs.*)
Russian olive	(*Elaegnus angustifolia*)
Russian olive	(*Elaegnus Titan®*)
Heath	(*Erica x darleyensis and cvs.*)
Witchhazel	(*Hamamelis spp. and cvs.*)
Juniper	(*Juniperus spp.*)
Beautybush	(*Kolkwitzia amabilis*)
Privet	(*Ligustrum spp. and cvs.*)
Bayberry	(*Myrica pennsylvanica*)
Potentilla	(*Potentilla spp. and cvs.*)
Buckthorn	(*Rhamnus spp. and cvs.*)
Sumac	(*Rhus, all*)
Alpine currant	(*Ribes alpinum and cvs.*)
Rugosa rose	(*Rosa rugosa and cvs.*)
Viburnum	(*Viburnum lentago and cvs.*)
Viburnum	(*Viburnum prunifolium*)
Yucca	(*Yucca filamentosa and cvs.*)

Using Wildflowers Conscientiously

Wildflowers, common along Ohio roadways and in unused fields and vacant Cleveland lots, are on the move, aided by natural and unnatural forces. Birds carry fleshy berries. Water tosses buoyant seed downstream. Winds lift lightweights with vegetable wings or plumes. In addition, people, trucks, and airplanes are moving more than their share. Thanks to modern communication and transportation systems, you can bring wildflowers from anywhere in the world to your doorstep. And Cleveland-area gardeners are doing so in ever-increasing numbers.

We no longer need to go out and cull seed or cuttings by hand. Instead, many gardeners will call one of the catalogs featuring color photos of thousands of Texas bluebonnets and California poppies all in riotous bloom. The UPS truck will deliver their blue mix or northern mix or can-of-color mix, which, it is hoped, will turn out like the catalog picture.

This scenario poses many exciting possibilities. But if you import wildflowers from far away, your wildflower garden is likely to prove disappointing. You may wish you had stuck with older methods and hand selected the best of the local wildflowers that are naturally fine-tuned to our climate and soil.

Among those who have been disappointed is the state of Ohio. When our state government decided to plant wildflowers along the highways in 1984, the job fell to the Ohio Department of Transportation (ODOT). Their staff soon discovered that there was no bulk source of Ohio seed for sale. So the Department of Transportation opted to buy seed mixes from a nursery in Colorado. They ended up with about thirty species of annuals, perennials, and biennials, many of which would never occur naturally in Ohio. One of the mixes included cultivars of baby's breath, purple and yellow coneflower, and bachelor's buttons; these were garden varieties and not wildflowers at all. Most of the mixes included European dame's rocket. With the exception of dame's rocket, none of these became self-proliferating.

"These plants grew fast and were showy. The gardens were so successful that people were pulling off the road to pick flowers or take photographs. However, soon they were overwhelmed by our natives and weeds. We found we had to replant annually," said Guy Denne, assistant chief of the Ohio Division of Natural Areas and Preserves. "We also found if we used dame's rocket by a waterway, it could escape into the surrounding countryside." It now blooms in abandon each May along Cleveland-area flood plains.

Select Carefully

These two problems—mixes of species doomed to failure or of those so aggressive they spread like a curse—occur again and again in mass plantings and intimate home wildflower meadows. But both can be avoided with careful species selection. One must assume the ODOT evaluated the mixes before they began the project, although their decision to plant non-natives has received criticism since then. Yet many home gardeners, including some of my own friends, admit to buying wildflower seed mixes blindly. They never stop to question what they are doing. They see the picture of the finished garden, read the promises, and are sold on the idea. If only people would approach purchasing wildflowers like grocery shopping. Would you buy a can of synthetic meat product if you didn't know what it was made of? Probably not. Likewise, how can you plant species if you don't know what they are?

Instead of jumping into wildflower gardening with your eyes closed, look closely at the fine print of the catalog or label before you buy a meadow mix. In many cases, you have to dig beneath the graphics and punchy language. Are the species identified somewhere? Is the product sanctioned by a reputable conservation association or native plant society? This is something the Eastern Native Plant Alliance hopes to begin soon. What percentage of the mix is short-lived annual seed, and what is longer lived perennial seed? Where does the seed come from? You probably won't find all the answers, but they are good questions to ask before you buy.

If there is no significant information on the package label, which does happen despite U.S. Department of Agriculture and state seed-labeling laws, look for a customer service phone number to get your answers. In most cases, you will find the wildflower mix you had your eye on is not local. Seed in it may come from out of state, region, or even country. With a little research, you might determine there are no species even remotely similar to those that grow in our neighborhoods.

Importing Trouble

Importing non-local wildflowers tends to disturb conservationists rather than to please them. "I have been among the people that complained to the Ohio Department of Transportation," said Allison Cusick, chief botanist for the Ohio Department of Natural Resources. "They shouldn't be using any European species, but the European stuff is cheaper than American natives."

Most naturalists and botanists agree that what you do in the privacy of your cultivated gardens is your own business. But what you do near wild areas affects everyone. European species such as dame's rocket can escape and spread into wild areas. This lanky white-to-purple flowering early summer bloomer is "a real weed," according to Jim Bissell, curator of botany for the Cleveland Museum of Natural History. "It seems we still have the same diversity of native species in those areas but the numbers of each species is way down," said Bissell.

Other aggressive alien species are worse than dame's rocket. You might compare the effect of these runaway aliens to foreign insect pests, such as gypsy moth, elm bark beetles, and Japanese beetles.

Perhaps the worst introduction in this area is purple loosestrife (*Lythrum salicaria* and *L. virgatum*), which have been sold as cultivated garden plants and wildflowers. These showy lavender-spiked wildflowers seed so prolifically that they have taken over thousands of acres of Ohio wetlands from native species. Even self-sterile garden cultivars of purple loosestrife can hybridize with the native species, *L. alatum*, and reproduce prolifically once again. Purple loosestrife has been a big problem in the wetlands along Lake Erie, but now the weed has spread along highway drainage ditches and the Ohio River. "I consider it one of the ten worst weeds in the state," said Cusick.

Dr. John Averett, botanist and director of research for the National Wildflower Research Center, explained the consequences of this kind of escaped alien. "Species like purple loosestrife take over and take up space that would have housed native plants. You alter the ecosystem by replacing a unique local plant with a species already present in another part of the world. The species tally comes up short in the end: the list of extinctions grows. And, since plants are at the bottom of the food chain, the effect reverberates up the ladder. Scientists estimate fourteen species of animals depend on each plant species. For each plant species lost to extinction, some wildlife will perish also," said Averett.

In Ohio, according to Cusick, purple loosestrife is threatening many of the common wetland plants, including broad-leaved cattail and pickerel weed, and pushing endangered species such as white flowered wapato (*Sagittaria cuneata*) closer to extinction.

Loosestrife and dame's rocket are only two of the newest runaway aliens. Many of America's most common roadside wildflowers are actually European weeds or garden plants that have escaped and spread nearly nationwide. These include Queen Anne's lace, yarrow, chicory, and oxeye daisy. These four coexist with, or replace, other opportunistic native species in disturbed soils and along roadways. They are not the threat that purple loosestrife and, to a lesser extent, dame's rocket are because they seldom mass in more pristine sites where you would find rare and endangered plants.

Queen Anne's lace and its like are called naturalized exotics or aliens because they clearly came to America with the European colonization of the last five hundred years and thus are not native. But they have been on the continent over two hundred years, long enough for the more liberal nurserymen and gardeners to give them native status. You can find naturalized aliens included in many wildflower meadow seed mixes. Since they are likely to sneak into the planting anyway, though, they add little value to such a package.

A 1990 survey of the New England Wild Flower Society showed that 7 out of 15 major wildflower meadow seed suppliers supplemented native species with exotics and naturalized aliens in their mixes. Knowing that exotics and naturalized aliens can be over, or under, aggressive, you might be more satisfied in the long run if you plant native species rather than imported European weeds. The Ohio Department of Transportation is trying to do just that.

The problem is finding a commercial source of natives that are indigenous and well adapted to the idiosyncrasies of your area. Obviously, large wildflower seedsmen cannot produce native plants from every state in the country. California-based Clyde Robin Seeds, one of the first large meadow mix suppliers, collects seed from around the United States. But they can only harvest seed from those species that thrive in the company's far-western production ranches. The company does its best—albeit imperfectly—to address requests for locally adapted seed. They sell generic, generalized regional mixes for North and South, East and West. For larger orders, they will run a computer simulation of a particular geographic area and custom-blend to match its flora. However, the seed stock may still not be local.

Despite the difficulties involved, there is room for some big gains if more gardeners would explore the virtues of local wildflowers. You can grow a wildflower meadow that is long-lived and conservationally appropriate. And, if you are willing to experiment with species growing in tough sites or not commonly used in commercial mixes, you may just discover unknown garden uses. Although you will not find Ohio wildflowers in a fancy catalog, you can find some species cultivated at Ohio botanical gardens and arboreta, including the Holden Arboretum in Kirtland and Cox Arboretum in Dayton (6733 Springboro Pike, Dayton, 45449; 513-434-9005). You also can dig up and rescue plants from natural sites that are going to be cleared for construction (though caution should be used not to disturb protected varieties). Or collect seed and grow your own, as people used to do just a few decades ago.

10 Favorite Cut Flowers

Don Vanderbrook, D. K. Vanderbrook Florist, Inc.

Here is a sampling of Don Vanderbrook's favorite cut flowers—flowers that look great in arrangements and are easy to grow in northeast Ohio.

Lady's mantle (*Alchemilla mollis*): This perennial, which blooms in late spring, often reblooms if deadheaded. It is a low, clump-forming plant usually smothered with greenish-yellow flowers for cutting; they last about two weeks. Use them as a filler flower; the color complements pinks and white very well. The larger, more mature leaves with their wondrous slivery, serrated edges are arranging materials as well. Lady's mantle can be multiplied by seed or divisions.

Coral Bells (*Heuchera* x *brizoides*): The flowers on this perennial have a delicate bell-shape on 18 inch stems. They come in many shades, including pale lime green, white, pinks, corals, and bright reds. This flower adds a soft dimension to an arrangement that few other flowers accomplish. We often use it clumped together in six-to-eight stems so it doesn't get lost in a mixed flower arrangement. Coral bells bloom in late spring and will sporadically bloom all summer long. Be on the lookout for a new variety that is beginning to show up in catalogs, called 'raspberry regal.' It is the most spectacular *Heuchera*.

Tree mallow (*Lavatera trimestris*): This annual plant grows to 24 inches high, bearing hibiscus-shaped flowers in intense raspberry pink through shades of lighter pink to white. The flowers of this plant hold well as a cut flower. Their form and display of color allows them to be used as focal flowers in an arrangement. The buds are interesting to watch develop because the petals open in an intriguing swirl pattern.

Peonies (*Paeonia* spp.): If I had a choice of which flowers I would like to extend the season for, or have all year, peonies (a perennial that blooms in late spring) would be at the top of the list. There is nothing that makes as bold an expression or pulls the arrangement together as do peonies. Peonies come in many shades of white, cream, and pale pink through raspberry to a deep rich red. Be selective in the number of flowers and stem lengths you cut from any one bush, because the plant does need a large number of leaves to produce flowers for the next year. The tight buds can be stored up to a month wrapped dry in newspaper, standing upright in a 35° to 40°F refrigerator.

Flowering Onions (*Allium* spp.): Alliums, perennial bulbs that bloom at different times of the growing season, come in many colors, but generally all are globe-shaped umbels. The onions, garlic, and leeks are *allium*. Therefore, some of the relatives have bad breath that becomes a serious problem in an enclosed house; but generally it is the cut stems that smell bad, not the flowers. The form is good in arrangements because there are not many flowers available in this golf-ball shape. The small buds on *allium* will open up after they are cut, extending their life as a cut flower.

Tulips (*Tulipa* spp.): Tulips, perennial spring-blooming bulbs most often treated as annuals, are celebrating their 400th year in commercial existence and are still one of the favorite cut flowers. These flowers require some forethought, because they are planted about six months ahead of harvest. Tulips are probably one of my most difficult flowers to cut out of the garden because they have defied the cold, adverse weather and stand proud and tall to let us know that the good weather is coming. We usually pull the flowers from the bulbs because we get longer stems and cannot wait for the bulbs to mature correctly for next year's bloom. We need the land for a summer crop.

Dahlias (*Dahlia* spp.): The most critical point about dahlias (which bloom late summer and fall) is that they are not hardy and the tubers need to be dug up and stored in a frost-free place until next spring planting. Dahlias seem to defy the rainy weather we often get in late summer that knocks out the zinnias, marigolds, petunias, and asters. Their blooming is not slowed down by short days as many flowering plants are.

I have had extremely good luck with starting my crop of dahlias from seeds, especially when we lost our whole crop of dahlias one winter because of the extreme cold storage. My plants from seeds produce more flowers and are taller than the plants from purchased tubers. I also get a greater variety of colors and forms to save and propagate for next year. Remember that the large dinner-plate flowers are great for show prizes but are difficult to use in arrangements. Select varieties that have long stems for cutting and that are medium- to small-sized. The color variation is unlimited except for blue. Dahlias last a good length of time in the cut flower cycle.

Hydrangea (*Hydrangea paniculata* 'Grandiflora'): There are many forms of hydrangea available for cutting; this one blooms in mid- to late-summer. I believe that my soil is a bit too heavy for over-wintering the typical blue, pink, white snowball-shaped hydrangeas. The tall cone-shaped hydrangea is our best bet. First of all, it needs to be pruned severely in the fall to produce nice strong, sturdy stems for next year; it responds to cutting.

This chameleon of the plant world goes through many color changes throughout its life, from frail delicate white to soft pinks, then greenish-pinks to green, to its final resting of tawny brown. It can be used fresh or allowed to dry in any of its color stages except white. The flowers need to be firm before they are cut or they will shrivel and lose their shape. If you want to keep the flowers more compact, hang them upside down. If your wish is for a more open look, strip the leaves off and place them in a cylinder container with a small amount of water in the bottom so the flowers will dry a slow and natural way. Keep an eye on the blooms still on the bush because they can change color in a day or two, especially with cold nights.

Montbretia (*Crocosmia* x *crocosmiiflora*): This bulb can be perennial with some winter protection. *Crocosmia* has increased in popularity over the past few years and it is becoming a more visible asset in the garden. The variety 'Lucifer' is especially spectacular in the summer garden. Everyone who sees it asks, "What is that?" It is probably the color as well as the unusual shape that attracts attention.

The plant belongs to the iris family and is not unlike a freesia flower blossom, which belongs to the same family. The flower stem emerges from strong, strap-shaped leaves, also useful in arrangements, to a height of three feet. The stem crooks over at a right angle and creates a straight crown of brilliant red-flared tubular flowers.

As with freesia, the buds open up along the stem and you remove the spent flowers to have a longer blooming cut flower. *Crocosmia* always adds punch and excitement to the arrangement. As the seedpods form, they lengthen the season of interesting cut materials. That is, if you have any left after cutting the flowers.

Roses (*Rosa* spp.): These plants bloom from spring to fall and are probably the most popular of all flowers—yet they are among the most difficult to produce. I remember once destroying a rose garden of 300 bushes because I had had enough of the "Tender Loving Care," but now I'm back at it. I have a garden of over 1,000 rose bushes because my business partner, Tony Badalamenti, takes care of them. Garden roses are worth the effort when you bring them in the house. Unless we are talking about arranging spray roses or species roses, I prefer that hybrid tea roses be multicolored, placed, not arranged, in bowls around the house with only their own foliage and no accessories.

Tulips are one of Don Vanderbrook's favorite cut flowers
(Photo courtesy of Netherlands Flower Bulb Information Center.)

What Makes a Great Daylily?

Ron Zayac, Warren Road Garden Center

I first became interested in newer daylily cultivars because, unlike many other modern plant-breeding efforts, premier daylily breeders have kept their focus on continuing the vigorous, maintenance-free characteristics of the daylily. They also have made incredible advancements in flower form, plant characteristics, and colors.

The modern daylily reblooms, or produces more than one set of flower stalks, approximately two to four weeks apart. It has a higher bud count (40 to 60 flowers per stalk is not uncommon), larger and lovelier flowers (up to 8 inches across), and clear vibrant shades of every color but blue. We are not seeing a generation of plants that bloom for months with hundreds of large, ruffled flowers on strong, well-branched flowering stems.

Here are some of my favorite daylily cultivars that are being sold for moderate prices (with the year of introduction and a brief description):

'Mariska' (1986) has clear pink flowers 30 to 35 flowers per stalk, and blooms for six weeks or longer.

'Celestial City' (1991), has ruffled, pale pink flowers with pink and yellow veining and a well-spaced rebloom (it blooms a week or two longer than 'Mariska').

'River Nile' (1992) has lavender-violet flowers that come as close to blue as any daylily to date. It has over 30 flowers per stalk and reblooms two to three times for two months of color.

An assortment of daylilies are on display at Holden Arboretum.
(Photo by Lydia Bailey, courtesy of the Holden Arboretum.)

'Chanteuse' (1992) has flowers with a beautiful pastel blend of salmon, rose, and pink. There are over 35 flowers per stalk and dependable reblooming.

'South Seas' (1993) has pinkish coral-tangerine flowers with a deeper red-coral band. There are over 35 flowers per stalk and reblooming qualities.

'Hacienda' (1988) has flowers of hot jalapeño-orange edged golden amber and reblooming qualities.

'Strutter's Ball' (1986) has deep blue-purple flowers with over 50 buds per stalk. It won't rebloom but will flower for six weeks because of its high bud count.

'Avante Guarde' (1990) has bold red flowers with a watermarked eyezone that explodes out to within 1/4 inch of the ruffled tan-edged petals. There are more than 35 flowers per stalk and reblooming.

'Pygmy Pirate' (1991) has small (4 inches wide), dark crimson flowers on dwarf (20 inches high) plants, over 30 buds per stalk, and reblooming.

'Vera Biaglow' (1986) has flowers with a vivid shade of pink-rose; it blooms dependably for six weeks.

10 Tips for Combining Perennials

Bobbie Schwartz, Bobbie's Green Thumb

 The creation of a perennial garden is an evolution in which one considers several aspects of a plant (height; time of bloom; color of bloom; type, size and color of foliage; fragrance; and winter interest) and uses these factors to achieve a satisfying marriage of plants. Ten tips should help you achieve the vision in your head.

1. Use the foliage of a nearby plant to echo the blossom color of a neighbor, e.g., maiden grass (*Miscanthus sinensis* 'Strictus') with green and yellow striped foliage near or next to tickseed (*Coreopsis verticillata* 'Moonbeam') with lemon yellow blossoms.

2. Use varying foliage textures to give interest to a grouping of plants, e.g., hosta 'Frances Williams' (large and quilted), lady's mantle (*Alchemilla mollis*) with medium, pleated, and scalloped leaves, and *Corydalis lutea* with small and slightly scalloped leaves.

3. Vary the colors of foliage: shades of green from light to dark, types of green from matte to shiny, blue-green, yellow-green, yellow, purple, and variegated.

4. Always keep in mind what the foliage of each perennial looks like when it is not in bloom (which is usually most of the time). Try to vary the foliage textures and sizes (as in 2) and colors (as in 3).

5. Use varying heights, but do not be rigid in their placement, i.e. ,short in front, medium in the middle, tall in the back. Vary their placement and do not be afraid to use tall plants in the front of the bed, particularly if they are wispy or give a veiled effect, e.g., colewort (*Crambe cordifolia*), a tall, airy, white perennial which has short but large foliage or vervain (*Verbena bonariensis*), which is a tall, narrow, purple reseeding annual.

6. If the colors you like seem to clash or to be too strong, use silver-foliaged perennials as mediators, not white-flowering plants as you might have thought. White is the strongest color of all and will compete, not mediate.

7. If your garden will be viewed primarily in the evening or is in shade, combine perennials that have white or pale blossoms with others whose foliage is silver or has a lot of white variegation, e.g., peach-leaf bellflower (*Campanula persicifolia alba*), hosta, and lilyturf (*Liriope spicata* 'Silver Dragon').

8. Don't be afraid to use the element of mystery. Plant something tall and dense, e.g., New England aster (*Aster novae-angliae* 'Hella Lacy') or one of the maiden grasses *(Miscanthus)*, in the middle of a curve so as to block sight of the rest of the bed or landscape, thus beckoning the viewer onward.

9. Remember that there are four main types of blossoms (daisy, rose, flat, and spike) and try to use as many as possible, e.g., coneflower (*Rudbeckia fulgida* 'Goldsturm'), globeflower (*Trollius* 'Lemon Queen'), yarrow (*Achillea* x 'Paprika'), and speedwell (*Veronica* x 'Icicle'). A garden of only one type will be boring.

10. Try to use some plants that will provide winter interest, e.g., Siberian iris (*Iris siberica*), which has orangy-bronze foliage and stiff-stemmed seedpods (assuming that you didn't cut them down when the blooms were finished); *Allium tuberosum*, which has grayish-bronze seed heads; *Sedum* 'Autumn Joy,' which has flat bronze heads, and *Pennisetum alopecuroides*, a grass that turns beige in fall and maintains that color throughout the winter.

Bloom Sequence for Perennial Flowers

One of the delights and challenges of growing perennial flowers is that they do not bloom all season. This allows perennial gardens to be constantly changing but requires garden planners to include a variety of flowers that bloom in sequence. Here's a list to help you plan for a great garden, all season long.

Note: Some flowers are listed in two or more months because their bloom overlaps or they could bloom in either month, depending on the weather. Some may bloom even longer if you remove the faded flowers promptly. Perennials are listed here by botanical name so you can order them easily from nursery catalogs.

April

Pasqueflower	(*Anemone pulsatilla*)
Virginia bluebells	(*Mertensia virginica*)
Lungwort	(*Pulmonaria spp.*)
Sweet violet	(*Viola odorata*)

May

Bugleweed	(*Ajuga reptans*)
Windflower	(*Anemone vitifolia*)
Columbine	(*Aquilegia spp.*)
Seathrift	(*Armeria spp.*)
Sweet woodruff	(*Asperula odorata*)
Lily-of-the-valley	(*Convalaria majalis*)
Tickseed	(*Coreopsis spp.*)
Pinks	(*Dianthus spp.*)
Bleeding heart	(*Dicentra spectabilis*)
Coral bells	(*Heuchera sanguinea*)
Candytuft	(*Iberis sempervirens*)
Woodland phlox	(*Phlox divericata*)
Jacob's ladder	(*Polemonium caeruleum*)
Solomon's seal	(*Polygonatum spp.*)
Llungwort	(*Pulmonaria spp.*)
Ffoamflower	(*Tiarella cordifolia*)
Sweet violet	(*Viola odorata*)

June

Yarrow	(*Achillea filipendulina*)
Monkshood	(*Aconitum napellus*)
Bugleweed	(*Ajuga reptans*)
Windflower	(*Anemone sylvestris*)
Goatsbeard	(*Aruncus sylvester*)
Astilbe	(*Astilbe x arendsii*)
False indigo	(*Baptisia australis*)
Tufted bellflower	(*Campanula carpatica*)
Clustered bellflower	(*Campanula glomerata*)
Shasta daisy	(*Chrysanthemum maximum*)
Tickseed	(*Coreopsis spp.*)
Delphinium	(*Delphinium spp.*)
Pinks	(*Dianthus spp.*)
Bleeding heart	(*Dicentra spectabilis*)
Foxglove	(*Digitalis spp.*)
Blanket flower	(*Gaillardia x grandiflora*)
Hardy geranium	(*Geranium sanguineum*)
Hardy geranium	(*Geranium endressii* 'Wargrave Pink')
Coral bells	(*Heuchera sanguinea*)
Siberian iris	(*Iris siberica*)
Lavender	(*Lavandula angustifolia*)

Peony   (*Paeonia officinalis*)
Garden phlox   (*Phlox paniculata*)
Jacob's ladder   (*Polemonium caeruleum*)
Salvia   (*Salvia superba*)

July

Yarrow   (*Achillea filipendulina*)
Monkshood   (*Aconitum napellus*)
Lady's mantle   (*Alchemilla mollis*)
Tufted bellflower   (*Campanula carpatica*)
Clustered bellflower   (*Campanula glomerata*)
Shasta daisy   (*Chrysanthemum maximum*)
Tickseed   (*Coreopsis spp.*)
Foxglove   (*Digitalis spp.*)
Purple coneflower   (*Echinacea purpurea*)
Blanket flower   (*Gaillardia x grandiflora*)
Hardy geranium   (*Geranium sanguineum*)
Hardy geranium   (*Geranium endressii 'Wargrave Pink'*)
False sunflower   (*Heliopsis helianthoides*)
Beebalm   (*Monarda didyma*)
Garden phlox   (*Phlox paniculata*)
Balloon flower   (*Platycodon grandiflorum*)
Coneflower   (*Rudbeckia spp.*)
Salvia   (*Salvia superba*)
Stoke's aster   (*Stokesia laevis*)

August

Yarrow   (*Achillea filipendulina*)
Windflower   (*Anemone vitifolia*)
Butterfly milkweed   (*Asclepias tuberosa*)
Aster   (*Aster x frikartii*)
Tufted bellflower   (*Campanula carpatica*)
Leadwort   (*Ceratostigma plumbaginoides*)
Tickseed   (*Coreopsis spp.*)
Purple coneflower   (*Echinacea purpurea*)
Blanket flower   (*Gaillardia x grandiflora*)
Hardy geranium   (*Geranium endressii 'Wargrave Pink'*)
False sunflower   (*Heliopsis helianthoides*)
Beebalm   (*Monarda didyma*)
Russian sage   (*Perovskia atriplicifolia*)
Balloon flower   (*Platycodon grandiflorum*)
Coneflower   (*Rudbeckia spp.*)
Salvia   (*Salvia superba*)
Stoke's aster   (*Stokesia laevis*)
Toad lily   (*Tricyrtis hirta*)

September

Japanese anemone	(*Anemone hupahensis*)
Butterfly milkweed	(*Asclepias tuberosa*)
Aster	(*Aster x frikartii*)
Tufted bellflower	(*Campanula carpatica*)
Leadwort	(*Ceratostigma plumbaginoides*)
Chrysanthemums	(*Chrysanthemum spp.*)
Tickseed	(*Coreopsis spp.*)
Russian sage	(*Perovskia atriplicifolia*)
Coneflower	(*Rudbeckia spp.*)
Stonecrop	(*Sedum spectabile*)
Toad lily	(*Tricyrtis hirta*)

October

Japanese anemone	(*Anemone hupahensis*)
Windflower	(*Anemone vitifolia*)
Aster	(*Aster x frikartii*)
Chrysanthemums	(*Chrysanthemum spp.*)
Coneflower	(*Rudbeckia spp.*)
Stonecrop	(*Sedum spectabile*)

Ideas from Residential Gardens: Some of the Best of East and West

Suzanne Hively, garden editor for *The Plain Dealer*

Clevelanders love their gardens. It would be difficult to walk more than a block without finding an intriguing garden. Here are just a few that I viewed recently.

Meticulous about color. After five or so years of planting annuals, Thomas Sheehan, who lives along Cleveland's Gold Coast, discovered perennials and landscape design. Since then ideas have been flowering faster than Sheehan can implement them.

Sheehan, an attorney, rented a small bulldozer and excavated a pond in the back yard. He built an arched bridge over it and an elevated deck behind it. The observation deck is surrounded by evergreens. Other "garden bones" constructed by Sheehan include a rustic teahouse.

Although Sheehan is meticulous about harmonious color schemes, he sometimes buys plants or trees just because he likes them; then he creates a place for them. He has selected a palette of blue, purple, lavender, and pink flowers. Varying textures and colors are repeated throughout the garden.

Sheehan believes that the most important element in gardening, next to watering, is good soil. He composts his own humus. Five wire mesh composters, which he made for less than $30, generate six to seven yards of humus a season.

Learn as you go. Robert Brigden of Shaker Heights believes that if you want a beautiful garden, you should start with a plan or sketch. Then take a shovel and start digging. Learn as you go. Because Brigden and his wife, Nancy, both work at home, having a lovely garden as an extension of the house is especially important to them.

The old back yard was typical, a small expanse of lawn approximately 40 by 40 feet surrounded by a border of trees and shrubs. The new garden has multiple levels, many seating areas, places for serving food, and a hot tub. Some areas are shady; others are sunny; others are protected from the elements by lattice arbors. This permits a great diversity of plants.

Brigden wanted a curving brick walk, but he didn't want to lay it in good topsoil so he scraped six or so inches away down to the clay. The good topsoil was piled to one side as a raised rose bed. Brigden constructed a pond and piled the excavated earth as a backdrop behind it. He also built a deck and salvaged some old sidewalks to be used as a "stone" patio.

Something is always in bloom. Spring-flowering bulbs are replaced by magnolia blossoms and dogwood. Brigden rejuvenated an old lilac by gradually removing the oldest branches. As this ends its bloom, the peonies and irises are starting to flower. Later, roses and a wide variety of perennials will add their color. The garden is especially pretty in the evening when soft lighting points up at featured plants.

Natural and cozy. Ruth Love, who lives near I-480 on Cleveland's west side, has a row of evergreens, deciduous trees, and shrubs to provide privacy from the traffic. An intriguing cottage garden is for Love's eyes only. She takes a casual approach to gardening. "If nature plants it, I leave it," she said. Yet her garden is charming and cozy.

It is the type of garden that invites visitors to explore. Love refers to her raised bed perennial garden as "my stained glass window." During the summer it is a kaleidoscope of color.

After attending a bonsai demonstration, Love came home and whacked a rather large Scotch pine into a graceful Oriental silhouette. A rustic bridge leads past the "stained glass" garden to a charming tea house that Love built with scrap lumber and materials found along roadsides. Few of the angles in the structure are 90 degrees, but that is part of its character.

Love has a great diversity of plants throughout the property, but her pride and joy is a large old magnolia tree at the corner of the house.

A Japanese garden. No one would ever guess that Kay Coss's glorious Cleveland Heights garden was just a typical suburban landscape a decade ago. When she tired of cutting grass, she hired a landscape architect to redesign her yard into a Japanese garden. The garden developed into a three-year project and a lifetime interest. Coss, a librarian, reads every book that she can find about Japanese gardening.

She kept redesigning her garden until about one-third of the landscape architect's work remains. She even had the boulders that serve as a backdrop for the pond repositioned. A variety of Japanese deciduous trees and evergreens are placed in the best viewing points. The evolving design reflects Coss's widening horticultural interests as her penchant for gardening grows. For instance, she has added a number of flowers to attract birds and butterflies.

"A Japanese garden needs little echoes of not quite the same thing, but something similar near it," she said. Color of different varieties of flowers is repeated on both sides of a walkway.

Outdoor rooms. Ray Kowalski's garden in Cleveland Heights functions as a series of outdoor rooms. Each "room" introduces a view of the next, making one want to explore every path and plant.

A well-known artist, Kowalski uses his painterly skills to play with perspective and optically achieve effects such as increasing the size of the yard, altering the length of a stone patio, or even making some things disappear.

He constructed a small pond with a gentle waterfall. The stones surrounding the pond are an example of the relationship of color and shape at its finest. Flat black, rectangular-shaped stones form the pond's edge. Rose-colored spherical shaped stones are used as accents in strategic areas. The black is repeated in smaller river-washed stones.

Water and serenity. In three years, Ann Weiss has achieved a comfortable "lived-in" garden in Moreland Hills that speaks of serenity and beauty.

A large raised flower bed filled with blue, lavender, pink, and white perennial and annual blooms reaches across the front of the property and suggests an impressionist painting. It serves as an introduction for a small but magnificent lake that stretches nearly to the house.

Irises grow at the water's edge and a lone waterlily sends a profusion of pink blooms to the surface. A graceful old willow leans over the water as if to catch its reflection.

Weiss brought many of the plants from her former home in Newbury. The plants were virtually all that was left after a gas explosion destroyed the house and killed her husband.

Weiss said that she finds gardening to be soothing. She mixes annuals with perennials to provide a continuous blaze of color as the various perennials end their bloom. "I feel sadness when they leave, but I know they will be back and I look forward to that," she said.

Pets allowed. Leslie Scott, a landscape designer who lives in Cleveland Heights, found that it is possible to have both pets and and a beautiful garden. She literally designed a garden around her two Gordon setters by observing the routes that the dogs took when she let them loose in the fenced back yard.

The yard is designed as two spacious outdoor rooms. The first has a large raised flower bed occupying the center of the space. The bed is defined by a retaining wall of recycled stone and surrounded by brick paths that lead to other flower beds.

Little plants are tucked here and there to be discovered by walking along the many brick and stone paths. Each turn or curve along the path brings a new delight.

The second room has a square of lush green lawn surrounded by a brick path, like an area rug with a border. A vine-covered arbor harbors a hammock that encourages one to take an occasional break from gardening chores.

Landscape designer Jane Scott planned her garden to have space for frisky dogs. (Photo by Leslie Scott.)

A large country home. Surrounded by gardens, it is not visible from the quiet country roadside in Kirtland Hills. The winding drive leading to the house is blanketed with crabapple and ornamental pear trees, shrubs, and masses of perennials.

Before reaching the house, visitors see a large pond with a waterfall off to one side. Dwarf conifers provide winter interest around the pond after the perennials have gone to sleep. Variegated grasses and masses of violas are summer attractions. Pink waterlilies bloom in the pool.

A smaller pond, off to the other side of the drive, is blanketed by grasses and masses of perennials. A pair of elegant sculpted herons are a focal point.

Scene from a quiet country home.

The flagstone walk leading to the house was strategically placed to lead past small plantings of rhododendrons and to offer a panoramic view of the spacious grounds. A split rail fence serves as a backdrop for a border of perennials. A magnolia tree frames the entrance to the rear of the house. Front doors are seldom used in the country.

A third pool is located near a backdrop of hillside woods. A pump recirculates water from a small waterfall and another jets a small stream into the air. Masses of red cardinal flowers, blue lobelia, red salvia, and a huge collection of daylilies and other perennials color the area.

An urban oasis. The garden at Radisson Plaza at 1701 E. 12th Street is one of Cleveland's best kept surprises. From the street the 11,000-square-foot garden atop the hotel and Reserve Square apartment's five-story garage is not visible. A bird's-eye view of the garden from the upper levels of the apartments and hotel is a visual oasis in a desert of concrete.

Stone paths and benches throughout the garden invite restaurant diners to explore or to sit for a while. The garden is also accessible to apartment dwellers.

Flowers and vegetables are intermixed. Giant tomato plants almost hide some of the smaller evergreens. Squash are planted among the roses. Spring and fall-flowering clematis are planted on the same standard so that when one stops blooming, the other starts. Sometimes the flowers are picked for the restaurant's tables and for receptions. When the Radisson's chef needs fresh herbs, all he has to do is step outside the kitchen and into the garden.

John Popa, the gardener, digs some 6,000 tulip and daffodil bulbs after they have finished flowering and replants them in fall. The garden has an underground irrigation system with above-ground sprinkler heads on automatic timers to keep the garden watered. In most places the soil, which was trucked in via the freight elevators, is less than a foot deep. Popa has mounded it in other areas where more depth is needed.

Fragrant Favorites

Kathleen Gips, Village Herb Shop

Scented plants are fun to grow and great to use in many ways. Here are some of my favorites.

Lemon Verbena

The fresh scent of a lemon drop makes lemon verbena a favorite to everyone who pinches its leaves. Although it is destroyed by frost and a horrible house guest because of its persistent white fly affinity, lemon verbena is a must for every herb garden. The simple delight of pinching the leaves as it grows in a container is reason enough to keep this scented plant.

Lemon verbena's main enemy when grown both indoors and out is whitefly. Hose the plant off with a strong water spray every day to eliminate this pest without chemicals.

Using lemon verbena in cooking is a sensual pleasure. Try a few leaves in iced water or in a finger bowl at a barbecue. In pound cake, tea, and cookies it lends its lovely lemon flavor. Lemon verbena is my most popular herb jelly flavor. It makes a fragrant addition to potpourri and an ingredient in herbs used for bathing.

Lemon Verbena Herb Tea

1/2 cup lemon balm, dried and crushed
1/2 cup lemon verbena, dried and minced (use scissors or mincer)
1/4 cup lemon-scented leaf geranium
1/4 cup lemon peel, dried (use only the zest and chop finely)
1 T. allspice, slightly crushed
1 cup black tea leaves, optional

Mix all ingredients and store in an airtight container out of direct light. Use one teaspoon per 6 ounces of boiling water. Steep for 3 to 5 minutes. Sweeten to taste.

Rose-scented Geranium

The rose-scented geranium is a must in the kitchen year-round. If you plant it in the ground in May, the popular 'Attar of Rose' scented geranium will grow to three or four feet in height, providing rose-scented leaves to be used throughout the summer until you harvest the entire plant before frost (usually mid-October). The lush growth will be most prolific and fragrant in full sun, but it is equally at home in a container on the patio in filtered light and in a sunny, cool windowsill through the winter months.

The delightful fresh rosy scent makes pound cake a hit at every event. Placing a few fresh leaves in a sugar bowl gives the sugar a rosy flavor for use in tea, cakes, and cookies. A popular potpourri is rose pine, or friendship potpourri. It combines herbs and the language of flowers: rose geranium for preference, balsam for warm friendship, pinks for bonds of affection, and roses for love. Rose geranium leaves retain all of their fragrance when dried.

To prevent the leaves from yellowing while they dry, remove them from the stem and dry them quickly in a single layer on top of the refrigerator, which is warmed by the motor. They can also be dried in a low oven until crisp. Use dried leaves for tea, cooking, and potpourri.

Rose Geranium Pound Cake with Rose Water Icing

Heat from the baking process allows the fragrance and taste of the rose geranium to permeate the pound cake.

Betty Crocker Pound Cake Mix (makes 2 small loaves)
1/2 cup rose water (available at Village Herb shop and specialty markets)
6 large fresh rose-scented geranium leaves

Prepare 2 small loaf pans by greasing and dusting with flour. Place fresh rose-scented geranium leaves on the bottom of each pan. Prepare pound cake mix according to box directions, substituting rose water for water required in recipe. Bake as directed.

Cool cakes on wire rack and remove from pans. Rose-scented geranium leaves will be on the bottom. Frost when cool with rose water icing. Decorate with edible flowers such as heartsease and violas, or sprinkle with minced fresh rose geranium leaves.

Rose Water Icing
Mix 1/2 cup confectioner's sugar with 1 teaspoon rose water and 1 drop of red vegetable-based food coloring. Mix well and drizzle on cake.

Lemon Thyme

Lemon thyme is an irresistible herb in the kitchen. Lemon thyme tea bread with a fresh lemon juice and confectioner's sugar frosting is delicious at teatime, breakfast time, or anytime! Decorate the loaf with edible flowers such as tiny purple heartsease, with bunches of variegated lemon thyme at the base. I have found this delicious bread will convert many suspicious onlookers into herb lovers.

Lemon thyme is as welcome in a cup of tea as it is infused in water for a bath. Thyme contains an essential oil, thymol, which is antibacterial. Lemon thyme, decorative as well as fragrant, is used in wreaths and tussie mussies. (Tussie mussies are special gift posies composed of herbs and flowers that have meanings in the floral language.) It stands for happiness in the language of herbs and flowers. Thyme is the favorite plant of the fairies, so it cascades from my miniature fairy garden, providing cover and protection for the tiny nymphs.

This thyme variety is low-growing, compact, and seldom gets center fungus—a frequent problem for thyme varieties. This crisp, citrus-scented plant is often used to border walks and fill in between stepping stones. When the leaves are stepped on, the delightful fragrance is released. Thyme thrives next to gravel or stones. The added heat absorbed from the sun produces lush growth with a high concentration of essential oils in its cells.

Lemon Thyme Tea Bread
Makes one large loaf or two small loaves.

```
6 T. margarine
1 cup sugar
2 eggs
1/4 cup lemon thyme, finely chopped
1 T. grated lemon rind (zest)
2 cups flour
1 1/2 T. baking powder
3/4 cup milk
```

Cream butter, sugar, and eggs until light and fluffy. Beat in lemon zest and lemon thyme. Mix together dry ingredients and add alternately with milk. Mix just until blended. Turn batter into a greased and floured loaf pan. Bake about 45 minutes at 325°F or until a toothpick inserted in center comes out clean. Cool on a wire rack and remove from pan when cool. Frost with lemon icing. Unfrosted bread freezes well.

Lemon Icing

Mix confectioner's sugar with fresh lemon juice and one drop of veg-etable-based yellow food coloring until of spreading consistency.

Rosemary
Rosemary is one of the oldest and best known herbs. Because of its meaning—remembrance—it has been used at weddings and funerals for centuries. Rosemary has thin leaves with a shape and scent resembling the fresh smell of pine. Rosemary is the traditional Christmas

herb. Its fresh leaves can be snipped and used as a garnish in your holiday punch bowl and as a table centerpiece. Rosemary is a requirement in an herb lover's kitchen. Fresh rosemary makes ordinary chicken a gourmet treat. Plain shortbread becomes a holiday tradition by adding a tablespoon of chopped fresh rosemary. My herb garden would never be complete without this plant to add to vinegar, tea, herb seasonings, jellies, cakes and cookies, and to add to potpourri and bath blends.

Unfortunately, rosemary is cold-sensitive, hardy to about 10°F, and must be brought indoors during Cleveland winters. Most successfully grown indoors is the prostrate variety of rosemary. Its low branches twist and creep to form a type of bonsai. Growing rosemary in a pot until it is potbound allows the plant's energy to go toward flowering. Tiny blue flowers bloom all winter on the plant in my kitchen window. (It is said that fairy babies live in rosemary flowers.)

Rosemary is easy to grow indoors if provided with a cool, bright location in a pot with good drainage. Never allow the soil of a rosemary pot to dry out. Rosemary, potted up and ready to be brought in, can be kept outdoors until night temperatures are consistently near 10°F. It is most happy outdoors, so move the pots out again in March when temperatures are warming.

Clove Pinks

The name clove pink describes these colorful annual flowers well. Their petals have jagged edges as if they have been cut with pinking shears and their scent is like the sweet, spicy smell of cloves. Pinks are edible flowers, which makes them a colorful, fragrant addition to salads as a garnish and to my edible flower vinegar and jelly. Their meaning, "bonds of affection," makes them appropriate to include in all tussie mussies.

Annual pinks dry well when preserved in silica gel, a commercial drying agent available at craft stores. Many pinks are grown and dried this way for use in dried tussies and potpourri.

My favorite variety of pink in the Cleveland area is Hudson pink (*Dianthus carophyllus*). The gardeners in this area say this variety originated in the cottage gardens of Hudson, Ohio. It is a dainty double variety with a shell-pink color that blooms in a prolific mound all summer long. Surrounding the mounds of pinks with stones helps to prevent root rot and encourages blooming.

A Tussie Mussie for Friendship
Roses for love and beauty
Lavender for devotion and faithfulness
Pinks for bonds of affection
Feverfew for "You light up my life"
Marjoram for happiness
Sage for esteem

Bay for glory
Rose-scented geranium for preference

Assemble herbs and flowers together in a tightly gathered nosegay. Secure stems with a rubber band. Surround bouquet with a doily and tie with ribbons. Write a card for recipient, including herb and flower meanings.

Bay

Bay laurel (*Lauris nobilis*) was one of my first herb plants. Purchased by mail from an herb shop in Maine twenty years ago, it still grows in a pot that moves from a shady area on the deck in the summer to a sunny windowsill in the winter. The scent and flavor of a fresh bay leaf is no comparison to the dried bay found on the grocery store shelf. My bay plant has been constantly shaped and pruned and the leaves added to hundreds of pots of soups, stews, and pot roasts. The trimmings have been a fragrant, pungent ingredient in dozens of bottles of bouquet garni vinegar. The leaves have even been tossed into the bathtub on a cold winter night. Although frequently thought of as a culinary herb, no fragrance is more welcome in the bath than fresh bay. Sprigs are used at Christmas to decorate wreaths and packages. The fresh scent is definitely part of my Christmas.

Bay is a popular scent in potpourri and cosmetics for gentlemen. Bay oil has been used for centuries in colognes for men. An aftershave with fresh bay leaves in the bottle makes a great gift for the men in your life!

Gentleman's Choice After-Shave

10 fresh bay leaves
1 cup distilled water
1/4 cup unscented alcohol or vodka
5 drops bayberry oil
5 drops clove oil

Add ingredients in order to glass bottle. Shake well. Allow to infuse for two weeks. Splash on face after shaving.

Lavender

Last, but never least, is lovely lavender. One of the few plants whose color has given it its name, lavender means devotion in the language of flowers. The fresh, aromatic scent is often associated with cleanliness. Lavender is said to keep one's mind sharp and clear. Colonial ladies sewed a few sprigs into their bonnets or their hems. Lavender was used in baths by the Romans and is a popular cosmetic fragrance today. 'Hidcote' is a dependable choice in the North Coast climate. It is winter hardy and grows as a compact shrub. Lavender likes a bit of lime dug into its soil, as well as a light pruning (not more than 1/3 of the bush) in the very early spring. Do not prune lavender later than early April or its flower spikes will not form. Lavender flowers in mid-June. 'Hidcote' flowers are a deep shade of purple. Flower buds should be harvested before they are open. Lavender grown organically can be used to flavor puddings, cakes, and cookies. Violet lavender tea is a popular beverage for our Fairy Festival during Mid-summer's Eve in June. Lavender can be used to flavor jelly, using apple or peach juice as the base. Lavender lemonade is refreshing on a warm summer day.

Lavender Lemonade
6 cups water
1/2 cup organic lavender flowers
1 12-ounce can of frozen pink lemonade, undiluted

Heat water to boiling. Place lavender flowers in a large tea ball or in a muslin bag. Steep lavender in hot water for 20 minutes. Remove lavender and add frozen lemonade concentrate. Chill lemonade. Serve over ice garnished with sprig of lavender.

The materials to make these recipes, as well as more detailed books on herbs, are available from the Village Herb Shop, 49 W. Orange Street in Chagrin Falls (for a Catalog and Herbal Handbook, mail $4 to 152 S. Main Street, Chagrin Falls, OH 44022.). They may also be available at herb nurseries listed in chapter 6.

An All-Access Garden

Rob McCartney, Sea World of Ohio horticulturist

Sea World's Access-for-All Garden is an exhibit that demonstrates to our guests how a landscape can accommodate people with or without disabilities. Because we are typically visited by mainstream America (and not exclusively by horticulturists, garden experts, or botanists), we had to select plants and features that looked good and let everybody interact with the garden. Once the garden was complete and guests flowed through, we discovered that the accommodations made for the disabled made the setting more pleasant for everyone. Here's how:
• A sensory walk lined with elevated planters brought annuals and perennials with unique fragrance, color, and texture up to where they were easy to see, feel, and smell.
• A garden gazebo was constructed so the work area allowed wheelchairs to move up close and fit beneath a bench-top garden. Pulleys let

seated gardeners control the raising and lowering of hanging baskets to desired levels.

• A water wall was set at the path's edge, encouraging guests to touch the cool flowing water and experience its soothing qualities.

• The path was made with a gradual elevation change that exceeds American Disabilities Act requirements, so it's easy for everyone to move through.

• Fauna was mixed with flora to create extra interest. Aviaries, home to brightly colored and talkative birds, were strategically positioned to attract attention. Hummingbirds and butterflies were attracted to feeders, pools, and appealing flowers.

"Plants possess life-enhancing qualities that encourage people to respond to them. In a judgmental world, plants are non-threatening and non-discriminating. They are living entities that respond directly to the care that is given to them, not to the intellectual or physical capacities of the gardener. In short, they provide a benevolent setting in which a person can take the first steps toward confidence."
—Charles Lewis, Morton Arboretum

Visitors enjoy the Sea World All-Access Garden.
(Photo courtesy of Sea World.)

Historical Horticulture and Our Own Gardens

By looking at early cultivation of land in northeast Ohio, we can get some eye-opening revelations that apply to what we are still doing today. Although our landscape has changed dramatically from a woodland to an urban and suburban metropolis, we are still dealing with similar soils and climate, even though both have been altered somewhat by construction, soil compaction, pavement, and buildings.

Crops

The earliest crops grown in this area remain some of the most sure-fire to grow today. The Adena Indians grew pumpkins, squash, sunflowers, and corn. The first farmers in the Western Reserve area grew corn, vegetables, and apple trees. Medina opened into a great wheat- and corn-producing district. By 1840, farmers who happened to colonize near the Lake Erie shoreline learned of its superior sandy loam soil and moderate temperatures; they began to cultivate less hardy peaches, which they used for peach brandy, and the more temperamental types of grapes. Kelley's Island soon replaced Cincinnati as the biggest wine-producing area in the state.

The Shakers, a religious sect that settled in what is now Shaker Heights, were forward-thinking gardeners. In the mid-1800s, they practiced organic gardening techniques and fruit-tree culture that we consider modern; they also sold herbs by mail.

Soil Building

The Shakers found that organic methods of soil building were essential for raising crops in the stiff clay soils of this area. "No good farmer would consider starving his cattle and swine and expect them to produce; neither should he starve his land," wrote one Shaker farmer. They enriched the soil with barnyard manure, as some present-day gardeners do.

Another early diary advised: "For a really good corn crop, begin one year ahead. . . . First spread [livestock] dung on the sward; then plow deep and harrow thoroughly—then plant the whole field in potatoes. After the potatoes are dug in fall, drag into the land 15 to 20 ox-loads of barnyard manure to the acre; then plow it thoroughly. The next spring, after the harrowing, draw on 20 or more loads of green barn manure to the acre and let it lay for a few days. Just before planting, plow this in. This last coating will hold the moisture and bring corn to maturity in the last stages while the other coats mixed with the soil will start the corn with the greatest luxuriance in the early stages of its growth." (For more on this subject, see Improving Soil with Compost, chapter 2.)

The Shakers rotated crops (growing a succession of unrelated plants in any garden location to prevent the buildup of pests or diseases specific to particular crops and to avoid depleting certain nutrients by heavy-feeding crops). The Shaker corn field was a good example of rotation. Potatoes, an underground crop, loosened the soil and did not consume large quantities of nutrients. In the season after the potatoes, the corn crop could develop deep roots and have an abundance of nutrients for good growth. In addition, the Shakers selected their own seed from superior corn plants, those with two or more ears per stalk, so they would get more food per plant.

Although the Shakers forbade ornamentation and luxury in their things, they did luxuriate in the same sense of peace that we modern gardeners enjoy when are absorbed in our gardens. A Shaker journal from June 1844 reads, "It is a perfect summer day. Not even a cloud disturbs the peace of the scene where out in the meadows the scyths of the brethren move in complete rhythm, while the sisters move quietly along the even kept rows, gathering berries and sweet smelling herbs in their well-kept gardens."

Herbs

The Shakers grew medicinal herbs for their own use and later expanded their gardens into a thriving mail-order business. It was to stock their community infirmaries that the Shakers began collecting the wild herbs of the New World, and it wasn't long before they had planted small physic gardens with imported seed of European medicinal plants. As the "outside world" (anyone who was not a Shaker) sampled the sect's herbs, demand grew. The herb gardens became larger, more varied, and more sophisticated.

When collecting herbs, the Shakers followed rigid rules set up to assure purity. Only one type of herb was picked at a time, and the harvest would be delivered to the processing area before the collection of a second herb was begun. In order to keep the herbs whole and undamaged, fragile plants were placed on 15-foot-square sheets; roots were placed in baskets. Plants were collected in season only: flowers as their buds opened or when in full bloom; berries when ripe; bark in spring, when the sap rose; roots when the plants had finished growing. Prime time for leafy plants was before the sun grew hot but after the dew dried. All of these points are good ideas, even today, if you harvest your own culinary herbs.

Fruit Trees

In 1840, Elijah Russell became head horticulturist for the local Shakers and began an aggressive fruit tree program. He planted orchards, experimented with new cultivars, grafted new forms onto existing trees, and fine-tuned pruning procedures. He wrote, "All trees in their growth seek to accomplish two things, the formation of wood and fruit buds. If too many wood buds are allowed to develop, very little fruit will mature. Pinch back the wood buds, trim apple trees from July onward; if trimmed in April or May they will bleed too freely, producing black cankers in the wound. Trimming in July and August will force the full strength of growth into the fruit buds."

Although Russell is right about thinning growth buds and fruit buds so the plant does not become overcrowded with branches or fruits, we now prune fruit trees primarily when they are dormant in early spring. Another great early fruit specialist was Dr. Jared P. Kirtland. In 1840, he bought 83 acres of land between Detroit Road and Lake Erie. Kirtland found the climate near Lake Erie ideal but saw some fault with the soil. He believed, "The evil consists primarily in a deficient quantity of lime in the soil and . . . a deficiency also of animal and vegetable matter." In other words, the soil was too acidic and low in organic matter—manure and leaf compost.

In all, Kirtland developed 30 new varieties of cherries, using an arduous technique. Collecting seed from his finest cherries, he grew the seedlings closely together so that they would hybridize. From the best 5,000 hybrid fruits on the first generation of trees, he would let only the most promising ten percent grow to maturity. And, of these, only one out of ten was deemed to be of any value. From a start of 5,000 trees, he was now down to 50 and, of these 50, only the very best would be selected for propagation by budding and grafting.

Further Reading

More information on these and other subjects related to historical horticulture can be found in back issues of *Western Reserve Magazine*. Many historical gardening volumes can be found in the rare book collection of The Cleveland Botanical Garden. Or consult the Dittrick Museum of Medical History at Case Western Reserve University, a rare book collection of herbals and catalogs housed in the Allen Memorial Library (11000 Euclid Avenue, Cleveland; 368-3648).

To learn more about the Shakers of northeast Ohio, see *In The Valley of God's Pleasure* (by Carolyn Piercy, 1951, Stratford House, NY) and various manuscripts preserved in the Shaker Historical Museum (16740 South Park Boulevard, Shaker Heights; 921-1201).

You can find out more about early landscapes in: *Treatise on the Theory and Practice of Landscape Gardening Adapted to North America* (by Andrew Jackson Downing, 1841 [original], 1991 [reprint], Dumbarton Oaks, Washington, D.C.) and *The Golden Age of Gardens* (by Mac Griswold and Eleanor Weller, 1991, Abrams Publishing, New York, NY).

And, if you're ever in Washington, D.C., check out the Garden Club of America's historical slide collection on laser disk at the Smithsonian Institution.

CHAPTER 5
A Landscape Calendar
for Greater Cleveland

Maintaining a really great garden or landscape is considerably easier when regular reminders prompt you to do little jobs around the yard or inspire you to try something fun and different when you have spare time. You'll find some such reminders in the calendar that follows. You can also look for them in newspaper gardening sections, club newsletters, and government agency fliers (see the list at the end of this section). And you can keep your own records. I have done that for the last five years and always chuckle when I go back over some of my old garden records and note interesting similarities—in weather, timing of pests, harvests, and other factors. For instance:

- In each year, snow was predicted for early October. But it only fell at that time in two of those years.
- Drought has struck in August every year except 1992.
- Bean beetles and cabbage loopers swoop into the vegetable garden every July.
- Lettuce and radishes thrive in my cold frame each March.
- I usually find time to finish cleaning up old flower and vegetable stalks in midwinter.
- My large floor plants—a rubber tree and an umbrella tree—get spider mites each February, and need regular showers to keep them healthy until they go outside in May.

- July is usually a disappointment for my annual flowers, which begin to bloom reluctantly; fewer perennials are inclined to flower.

Keeping a Record of Your Garden

When keeping your own garden records, you don't have to be elaborate—just organized. Random notes on scraps of paper can get lost or shuffled out of order and then are impossible to refer to quickly. Instead, try jotting comments in a daily calendar (my favorite method), or on index cards in a monthly file. Make it a practice to come in from the garden, wash your hands, and write down what you have done and observed that day. If you grow certain plants year after year, develop a file on each one, perhaps comparing how different cultivars grow and how they respond to changes in weather or soil. Note when you planted certain plants, when troublesome pests or diseases cropped up, when and why certain plants failed, what new projects you attempted and whether they were successful. These notes, even if they are quite brief, help you build on past successes and avoid repeating past mistakes.

To get you started, or to supplement your existing records, here is a monthly garden calendar of tasks and reminders particular to this region that may occupy your attention over the course of a year.

January

 Early January

✓ Take a break from winter bleakness and visit a greenhouse full of flowers and greenery.

✓ Take some gardening classes or check out a plant society to learn something new to spice up this long winter month.

✓ Start 'Sweet Sandwich' onion seeds indoors under lights; they need to be planted outside extra early in spring to reach a large size. 'Sweet Sandwich' onion bulbs are plenty pungent when you harvest them, but grow mild and sweet after a couple months in storage.

✓ Enjoy the look of plants topped with snow—your own winter wonderland. But be certain that evergreen shrubs growing around the house foundation are protected; heavy wet snow falling off the roof can break them open.

✓ Tune up your lawn mower and sharpen your pruning shears.

✓ Give houseplants a shower to clean the dust off their leaves, bathe them in humidity, and discourage spider mites (which like dry indoor conditions).

✓ Gather some seed catalogs and order something new and better for your garden this coming year. (For a listing of some particularly good seed suppliers,

Late January

✓ Watch for a midwinter thaw; use it to plant any spring flowering bulbs you forgot to plant in the fall or to harvest any vegetable crops that remain protected beneath the soil or in a cold frame.

✓ Bring in bulbs that were planted in pots and buried shallow in the garden last fall. Gradually increase the warmth around them to simulate spring and stimulate growth of extra-early flowers.

✓ Take advantage of times when the soil is frozen to finish cleaning up old stems and debris, which can house dormant pests and diseases.

✓ Plant some leaf lettuce, cress, or parsley seed in pots and keep them in a sunny, south-facing window. Eat the greens when they are young; then plant some more.

✓ Buy a flowering houseplant such as clivia, begonias, calla lily, or kalanchoe to cheer up the house.

Idea for January

How to Keep a Houseplant Alive

If you believe in the green thumb myth, it's time to revolutionize your thinking. Anybody can grow a houseplant. It just takes a little conscientiousness, the right soil, and enough sunlight and water.

The biggest cause of houseplant failure lies in the last category—water. A surprising number of people drown their plants as they smother them with attention. Although the motive may be good, the effect is just as bad as allowing them to die of thirst. The purple thumber keeps on watering without bothering to check if the plant really needs it. The roots start floundering in all the moisture and, as a result, the leaves begin to yellow and wilt. What does this concerned gardener do then? Waters some more. It's a vicious circle.

But there is a simple solution: wait to water until the soil is dry. Stick your finger down in the pot and see if there is water beneath the dry crust on the soil surface. Most plants grown in a peat moss-based mix will be ready for more water before this lower region dries out completely. Others, such as cacti, benefit from getting bone-dry for a short time so their roots can breathe fresh air.

If you don't feel confident making a judgment based on something as unscientific as a finger test, there are other options that are sure-fire. The least expensive is a simple Jobe's Water Spike. These are small tags printed with pictures of watering cans. When the soil dries out, the watering cans turn yellow. Although the package advises using fresh tags every three months, I have used the same ones for years and they are quite reliable.

Or, you can get serious and buy a plant water tester for about $20. These are scientific meters attached to a probe. Insert the probe deep into the pot, and it will rate the wetness or dryness on a scale of varying degrees. Then you can fine-tune the amount you water specifically to each plant. If an African violet, for instance, needs to be watered every time it becomes slightly dry, you'll notice right away.

Fragrant Plants for Winter

People who garden tend to keep close ties with the weather—the timing of the frosts, winter lows, summer highs, and periods of drought. Gardeners know that if the weather doesn't provide what a plant needs to survive and thrive, we need to do it.

But when the weather turns cold and gray in late fall and gardeners begin to spend more time indoors than out, we can lose touch with many outdoor elements. We miss the greenery, the gentle breezes, the butterflies, the colorful flowers, and the fragrances.

It may take some soul-searching to realize how much you miss the smell of warm humid air, or a freshly mown lawn, or runaway mints that you've just pulled up. What would you give to smell the fragrance of a lilac or Korean spice viburnum or honeysuckle blown on a breeze past your patio?

If, with this subtle prompting, you find you are a bit nostalgic for some garden-fresh scents, then jump in your car or get on the phone and find some fragrant indoor house plants.

Yes, there are a number of delightfully scented plants that will grow in pots in your sunny south- or west-facing window, beside a glass patio door, in a sunroom or solarium. You also can grow them under fluorescent lights—keep the plants close to a two-bulb shop fixture and use a timer to keep the lights on for about 14 hours a day.

Some house plants make you wait until they flower to enjoy their floral perfumes. Others have fragrances in their leaves that you can release anytime by brushing them with your fingers.

You can find fragrant plants locally, but it pays to call ahead to greenhouses or garden centers to see what's available. Then go shopping when the weather is above freezing, if possible, so your new plants won't be damaged by the cold. Here are a few options.

Most garden centers are carrying 'Paper White' narcissus bulbs, which produce very fragrant daffodil-like blooms about eight weeks after you plant them.

Sometimes garden centers will have gardenias, old-fashioned pot plants with intensely perfumed, white flowers and leaves that resemble azaleas. "Gardenias can be touchy to grow," said Jackie Schach, owner of Kaiser Greenhouse and Flower Shop in Rocky River. "You need to start with a fresh, good quality plant and give it bright, but indirect light. If you can get a gardenia growing after you buy it, you can keep it for years."

Gardenia flowers appear sporadically throughout the year, especially if you turn your heat down a few degrees at night, which helps keep the flower buds from dropping. Fertilize with a water-soluble, acidic fertilizer, like Miracid, once every couple weeks once the flower buds form.

A few greenhouses also have scented geraniums, which have handsome leaves scented like fruit, roses, mints, or pine trees. Give them bright light and let the soil dry out slightly between waterings.

You can find a much larger variety of plants through mail order catalogs. But since most won't tolerate cold weather, shipping can be slow and perilous. Still, browsing through a couple good catalogs may inspire you.

Check out the catalog from Logee's Greenhouses (141 North Street, Danielson, CT 06239; 203-774-8038; send $3). It includes hundreds of rare plants, including fragrant jasmine, Natal plum and datura (poisonous but sweetly perfumed).

Rabbit Shadow Farm (2880 E. Hwy. 402, Loveland, CO 80537; 303-667-5531) has a large variety of fragrant and culinary herbs, including 34 kinds of scented geraniums, Spanish lavender, chocolate mint, and topiaries of rosemary, sage, curry, and dwarf myrtle.

(For more information on fragrant plants, see Fragrant Favorites in Chapter 4.)

 ## Recipe for January

Making Bean Sprouts

Put 2 ounces of sprouting seed (alfalfa, lentils, mung beans, adzuki beans, peas, radishes, sunflowers, or sesame) in a glass canning jar; top with fine nylon mesh secured by the screw-on ring top to hold the seed inside when the jar is tipped upside-down. Use two pieces of mesh, if necessary, to contain smaller seeds. Cover the seeds with lukewarm water and soak over night. Drain the following morning and store the jar in a warm, dark location. Rinse in the evening and twice a day after that, pouring the water off after wetting the seeds. Eat the sprouts when they have emerged and elongated but before they turn green. Store in the refrigerator after seeds have sprouted. Add to sandwiches, salads, soups, or stir-frys.

February

 Early February

✓ Force flowering branches of forsythia to bloom indoors. Cut a few branches that have fat flower buds (sometimes buds are damaged by winter cold) and put them in a vase of water in a fairly cool, humid room. In about two weeks the flowers should open.

✓ Spend a little time planning this year's vegetable garden. Organize it so that each part of the garden will grow crops unrelated to what grew there last year—a technique called crop rotation. By changing the crops grown, you vary the type of nutrients taken from the soil—avoiding depletion—and discourage the buildup of pests and diseases specific to certain kinds of crops. (For more on crop rotation, see my book, *The Harvest Gardener*, 1993, Storey Communications, Pownal, VT.)

✓ Take some time to re-evaluate your landscape. Does it have something of interest to look at in all four seasons? Does it screen off less-than-pleasant views? Are the planted areas in proportion to the house and lot and are they balanced on both sides of the property? If you see room for improvement, sketch your landscape and draw in different plans for how you would revise it. This will give you some good ideas about how to proceed with improvements in spring.

✓ Browse art galleries, garden centers, and catalogs to find a garden sculpture that will give your landscape a focal point all year long.

 Late February

✓ If you have a furry-barked poison ivy vine growing up one of your trees, now is a good time to pull it off. But don't try use your bare hands—it can still give you a rash, even in the dead of winter.

✓ Start pansy seed in a light garden. Put each seed in its own cup of sterile soil-less (peat-based) mix and cover with clear plastic until the seedling has grown several leaves. If you want to grow dozens of pansies, you can start the seed by sprinkling it in a flat (a shallow rectangular nursery container), and transplant the seedlings to individual cups or six-packs when they get to be about two-thirds of an inch tall.

✓ Isolate houseplants that have been attacked by pests so the pests will not spread to other plants. Identify the pest and treat it—nontoxically, if possible. Watch out for:

• Aphids. These sucking insects with soft, pear-shaped bodies spread in great numbers along stems, leaves, buds, and flowers. They excrete sticky honeydew, which often is covered by a dark sooty mold—another easy way to identify these culprits. Kill aphids by blasting them off the plant in the shower or by spraying them with insecticidal soap.

• Mealy bugs. These sucking insects hide under leaves and surround themselves in a shield of cottony-white fluff. You can wash these off with soapy water or use insecticidal soap.

• Spider mites. Tiny (1/50th of an inch) members of the spider family, these mites suck plant juices from the undersides of leaves, making them discolored, speckled, and later brown. Spider mites can spread to infest an entire plant quickly in the dryness indoors. Rinse the plant daily and spray repeatedly with insecticidal soap or pyrethrin.

 Ideas for February

Winter Clean Up

Perennial Garden Clean Up: If you didn't remove all the old foliage from your perennial garden in the fall, it's time to do it now. Get into the garden while the soil is frozen; you can damage soil if you walk in it when its wet.

Cut off old dried stems at the base, with the exception of ornamental grasses. Leave a few inches at the bottom of those old stems; new growth will arise from them.

Put a marker in any plant clump that you want to divide or move when it begins growing in spring. Note which plants need to be trimmed back. Reset any small plants that have pushed out of the ground during winter.

Cleaning up now will reduce problems with pests and diseases in the coming summer months. And organizing now will let you tend spring tasks without spending a lot of time figuring out which plant is which.

Hardscape

Architecturally speaking, softscape is a fancy word for the growing, changing, mingling, and merging of plants. They creep, rise up, and spread, giving the landscape a more comfortable, gentle look. They delight us with their varying images, textures, fragrances, and fruits.

Hardscapes, on the other hand, look the same all the time. These are permanent structures such as walks, patios, decks, and raised retaining walls. They stalwartly provide structure and lines, angles and curves, through dreary winter, baking summer, and unexpected frosts. Hardscape may not be alive, but at least it is consistent.

Make a note to re-evaluate your hardscape. Does it look as good as the lawn, flower gardens, and shade trees? Or is there a cracking cement walk that angles stiffly and abruptly up to the brickwork of your house? Maybe this would be a good time to think about exchanging it for a slightly curved brick walk. Is that corroding deck too small to hold all the grandchildren at family get-togethers? Perhaps it is time to pave a larger space of stone, brick, tiles, or interlocking pavers.

Improvements to the hardscape will last for years. Take plenty of time now to determine what building material and structure will look and work best. Schedule a qualified contractor or landscaper (see Landscape Specialists in chapter 6), or save labor costs if you have the time and skill to do the job yourself. Either way, insist on top-quality workmanship, or the entire landscape will suffer.

Two useful books full of ideas and plans for hardscape projects are: *Stonescaping*, by Jan Kowalczewski Whitner, and *Step By Stem Outdoor Brickwork*, by David Holloway (both from Gardenway Publishing, Storey Communications, Pownal, VT).

Hardscape, or built structures, provide lines in your landscape year-round. (*Photo courtesy of Wolmanized® Wood.*)

 ## Recipe for February

Fragrant Potpourri from Scented Geraniums

Scented geraniums are smaller flowered relatives of the annual bedding geranium that have foliage delightfully scented with rose, apple, lemon, mint, pine, or other fragrances. Many people who grow scented geraniums cut the greenery back in early October and keep the plants indoors during winter. If the plant grows in a light garden or bright window, it will have resprouted, often growing quite large by February. A wonderful fragrant potpourri can be made from the leaves of these flowers.

Harvest individual leaves and dry them in a dehydrator or microwave (see the operating manual for instructions) until they are crackly crisp. Put one cup of the dried leaves in an small open bowl or basket.

Mix sweetly scented dried leaves with a half cup of colorful or fragrant plant products, such as dried flower petals, everlasting flowers, lavender, and dried lemon or orange peel.

If you have a more pungent type of scented geranium, try a half cup of small hemlock cones, pine needles, cedar chips, or pine-scented rosemary, with some flower petals for color.

Stir or heat slightly to release the fragrance. Replace as soon as the fragrance diminishes, or replenish with a few drops of your favorite essential oil, many kinds of which are available in craft and florist shops.

March

Early March

✓ Prune deciduous trees and shrubs. Shape them by cutting off overly long or dead limbs and branches that cross, rub, or shade another.

✓ Wait to prune spring flowering shrubs until after they flower. Also, wait until summer to prune maples and birches, which leak sap from spring pruning cuts. The sap does not damage the tree but certainly looks unpleasant.

✓ Start cool season crops such as cabbage, broccoli, lettuce, parsley, sweet alyssum, and calendula for planting outside in late April.

✓ Pot tender tubers (which do not survive frost), such as tuberous begonias, elephant's-ears (*Caladium*), tuberose, and calla lilies. Keep them in a sunny location indoors until the danger of frost passes.

✓ Enjoy the maple syrup produced by the many sugar maples in our area. Learn how to tap your own trees.

✓ Find out how fertile your soil is: have it tested by the County Cooperative Extension Service. Call to receive a test packet (Cuyahoga: 631-1890, Geauga: 834-4656, Lake: 357-2582, Lorain: 322-0127, Medina: 725-4911, Summit: 497-1611).

Late March

✓ If you want to save money on new plants and experiment with new and different cultivars, you can start eggplant, tomato, and pepper seeds indoors under lights. Also try perennial coneflowers, flax, English daisies, columbine, Shasta daisies, petunias, and salvia from seed.

✓ Watch for the tiny flowers on maples, oaks, and other deciduous trees. They create a blushing halo around the leafless trees, and are especially lovely to see—a cascade of color—when you view a woodland hillside from afar (for example, the Cuyahoga Valley National Recreation Center area from I-271).

✓ There is often a dry spell during this month when you can begin preparing the soil for flower or vegetable gardens or for new landscape beds—even when it is still too cold to start planting. If you need to order topsoil, do it now if conditions are dry. Landscapers are not as busy as they will be later in the season, so you may be able to get some help fast.

✓ When the weather is dry but cool, you can do hardscape work, such as building a rock garden, a rock retaining wall, a brick walk, or patio. Any construction must be completed before you can safely plant around the area—first things first!

✓ Look for areas with poor drainage. These are easy to spot after the snow melts because water puddles there. Since most plants can't grow in saturated soil, raise the lawn or garden with more topsoil and route the excess water out of the yard with a drainage ditch or underground drainage tiles.

✓ If you order a truckload of topsoil to raise an area, look for soil that is pre-mixed with organic matter like leaf compost or decayed horse manure. This is fluffier and more fertile than plain clay topsoil and makes growing ornamentals or turf easier.

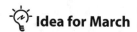 **Idea for March**

Proper Pruning

There are some new thoughts on the best way to prune naturally. Because early spring is an ideal time to prune shrubs and trees (except leaky maples and birches and flowering shrubs), here is something to ponder as you clean and sharpen your pruning tools.

The idea behind natural pruning is to use a plant's growth habits to your advantage; it makes the pruning job easier and your landscape more attractive. Shrubs will flow into clusters or masses that blend into natural-looking screens, backdrops, and islands of interest.

On the other hand, when you shear an evergreen into a box or barrel shape you set it apart from the rest of your yard. And you make more work for yourself. When you clip with hedge shears, you leave stubs above the slightly swollen nodes where leaves, twigs, and buds arise. This interrupts normal growth patterns and encourages many new shoots to race for the sun. The cluster of young shoots will need shearing again very soon. And the shrub will become a shell of greenery with a barren interior.

If instead of shearing you would thin out long, weak, or undesirable branches one at a time by cutting back to a node, you could prune just once a year and maintain the soft, natural shape of the shrub. The process is simple but requires you to deal with individual branches. Use hand-held pruning shears to cut off overcrowded twigs, long-handled loppers for branches between an inch and two inches in diameter, and a pruning saw for larger limbs. (Save hedge shears for hedges.) If a branch is too tall, cut it back to a side branch that is at least two-thirds of its diameter, or remove the branch where it emerges at the ground. A new shoot will take its place, keeping the plant young as well as short.

It's hard to begin this kind of thinning on an evergreen that has already been sheared. You can renovate some healthy broadleaf evergreens by cutting off one-third of the oldest branches every year and thinning the new ones that take their place. In three years, the shrub will look like new. Narrow-leaf evergreens such as junipers and yews will not resprout from wood that has no greenery. Either cut them back to actively growing shoots or remove very old branches entirely.

On trees, remove damaged branches or limbs that hang too low or rub each other or the house. Call an arborist if the branches are large and heavy, or are located anywhere near power lines. For smaller branches that you can handle yourself, cut outside the swollen branch collar that connects the branch to the trunk or parent limb. Don't cut flush with the branch; this leaves a larger wound and removes the collar, a powerhouse of chemicals that seal off the rest of the tree from pests and diseases. First, cut upward from the bottom of the branch until the saw reaches about one-third of the way through. Finish the cut from the top, placing it just outside the first cut. This allows the branch to fall without tearing healthy bark on the trunk.

For more on pruning, see *All About Pruning* (1989, Ortho Books, San Francisco, CA), which I co-wrote with Fred Buscher, professor emeritus at Ohio State University.

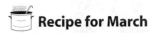 Recipe for March

String Bean Casserole

This is a good time to use up the rest of the beans you froze from last year's garden. Try them in this casserole, which is reprinted with permission from *Nature Center Cookery* (edited by Kathy Heffernan and Carol Provan, 1981, Shaker Lakes Regional Nature Center).

1/4 cup flour
2 cups milk
1 cup cream
1/8 teaspoon hot pepper sauce
3/4 pound American cheese
4 teaspoons soy sauce
1 teaspoon salt
1/2 teaspoon pepper
3–4 packages (10 ounces each) frozen French-style string beans, thawed and drained
2 cans (4 1/2 ounces each) mushrooms
1/2 cup onions, minced
2 tablespoons butter
1 can (8 ounces) water chestnuts, halved
3/4 cup almonds
1/2 cup bread crumbs

Mix together the flour, milk, cream, hot pepper sauce, cheese, soy sauce, salt, and pepper. Add the string beans and mushrooms. Sauté the onions in the butter. Add to bean mixture. Add the water chestnuts. Place in buttered 3-quart casserole.

Mix almonds and bread crumbs, and sprinkle over casserole. Dot with butter. Bake at 350°F for 40 to 45 minutes. Yield: 10 servings.

Note: for an interesting flavor variation, cook the beans with 1 1/2 teaspoons of savory (either summer or winter).

Coltsfoot announces the arrival of spring in March.

April

Early April

✓ Look for wildflowers, such as coltsfoot, blooming along the roadways on warm days. Forsythias also are coming along now.

✓ Spring flowering bulbs are coming up. Leave their foliage on until it yellows to recharge the bulb with energy so it will perform well next year.

✓ Sow seeds of leaf lettuce, spinach, Swiss chard, arugula, parsley, and radishes outdoors every two weeks during spring for plenty of fresh salads before summer heat sets in. Protect the young plants under a floating row cover. The first crop may or may not thrive, depending on the weather, but will be wonderful if it does. The next succession you plant is sure to succeed.

✓ Invest in a cold frame or make your own. This is a large box (6 to 12 inches high in the front, 12 to 18 inches high in the rear). Top it with a clear, sloping lid (which will catch the sun's rays most efficiently) that you can open for access and ventilation. To make your own, build the box of wood or cement blocks, and the lid of an old glass window. Use it to grow perennials, hardy herbs, lettuce, endive, and pansies from seed.

You can also protect early crops with low plastic tunnels, hot caps, Wall O' Water protectors, or similar translucent-walled insulating structures.

Late April

✓ You may be receiving bare rootstock from catalog orders now—perennials, strawberries, and roses that are grown in fields and then dug, freed of soil, and shipped directly to you while they are still dormant. Plant these outside in a prepared bed as soon your shipment arrives. Or transplant them into a large nursery container and keep them in a protected outdoor location until you can get a garden area ready.

✓ Start peas early if you have a raised bed that is warmer and drier than the surrounding soil. (If the soil is too cold and wet, the seed will rot.) You can pre-sprout the seed in peat pots indoors and set the small seedlings out under floating row covers (and plastic in severe weather).

✓ New shrubs and trees will be arriving at nearby garden centers. This is a good time to browse around and pick out the choice plants that will enhance your landscape.

✓ If you want to plant vegetables extra early, lay a sheet of clear or green infrared transmitting (IRT) plastic (a new type of plastic developed to warm soil up fast) on the soil for several weeks before your anticipated planting date. Both types intensify sun warmth; only the green blocks weed growth.

✓ Apply a lawn fertilizer containing slow-release nitrogen now. This causes less pollution from fertilizer run off, encourages the grass to grow slightly slower, and needs to be applied only once a year.

✓ Plant grass seed on new lawns or on bare spots in existing lawns, taking advantage of spring rains and leafless trees to provide young grasses with extra water and light.

✓ Start seeds of cucumbers, melons, squash and pumpkins, marigolds, basil, and nasturtiums in peat pots indoors in a light garden or a sunny south-facing window. You can transplant them outdoors after the last frost.

✓ If your yard is so shady that few plants grow well, this is a good time to call an arborist and have your shade trees limbed up (the lower limbs removed), or thinned (some of the branches removed to let filtered light through). You might even remove a few trees altogether.

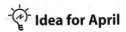 **Idea for April**

Gardening in Containers

Sometimes the most successful garden is the smallest one, especially if it's grown in a container. Making a garden in a pot or planter puts you in the driver's seat. You will control elements of nature's domain, variables such as soil, water, nutrients, and even sunlight. Set a concrete planter in a sunny gap in a shady yard; put a plastic-lined peach basket on the balcony of an apartment; edge a patio with open-end-up clay drain tiles of various heights. Or invest in redwood window boxes or similar containers made of long-lasting fiberglass.

Whether you spend a bundle or nothing on a container, remember these tips:

• Wood inevitably will rot, but redwood, cedar, and pressure-treated lumber last longest.

• Fiberglass may crack.

• Clay and terra-cotta pots will also crack, especially if you leave them outside in the winter.

• Ornamental vases may lack drainage holes. Put a layer of stones in the bottom and water carefully so the plants don't drown.

• Metal containers transmit winter cold and summer heat. To moderate both extremes, line the container with a layer of plastic foam.

Fill your planter with a good soil, usually a soil-less professional mix rather than potting soil, which will pack too densely for good root growth. Allow plenty of rooting depth or the plant is likely to fade in midsummer. Fertilize regularly with a diluted, balanced, water-soluble fertilizer.

Your plants will need extra water—as often as twice a day if you put smaller pots out in summer sun and heat. You'll also find that porous clay pots dry out faster than plastic or metal. To slow water loss, add a water-holding gel (see Proper Planting in chapter 2) to the soil and grow drought-tolerant plants such as ageratum, cockscomb, marigold, geranium, and portulaca. Or double-pot: put one pot inside a larger one and fill the gap between with moist peat moss or vermiculite. Or buy a planter that is set above a reservoir of water that is pulled up into the pot with a wick.

Recipe for April

Spicy Mesclun Salad

Grow the following greens in spring and snip off the tender young leaves when they are about two inches long.

4 cups assorted leaf lettuce, including one kind with red leaves
2/3 cup French sorrel
2/3 cup arugula
2/3 cup Mizuna Japanese parsley

Wash and dry greens. Add 1/2 cup radish seedpods, halved. (Harvest them from radish plants that have flowered and set seedpods that are beginning to swell.) Serve with vinegar and oil dressing to taste. Yield: 4 servings.

May

 Early May

✓ Wildflowers are going strong; take a walk through the Metroparks to enjoy them and consider planting some of the showier ones—such as liverwort, jack-in-the-pulpit, Dutchman's-breeches, and wild geranium—in your garden. For more information, see *Wildflowers* (by Rick Imes, 1993, Rodale Press, Emmaus, PA).

✓ Take note of which trees and shrubs are in flower simultaneously and surround them with complementary bulbs, perennials, and bedding flowers.

✓ Weeds will be growing quickly at this time of year. Be sure to hoe or pull every one out so they cannot reproduce. If you clean out garden weeds early in the season, you will not have to weed as much later in the summer, fall, and following year.

✓ A frost may still strike just when flowering trees and shrubs are at their peak. If it does, cover small trees and shrubs with plastic, burlap, or paper to protect their flowers.

✓ If you want to have more of a particular kind of perennial flower, or if you want to shuffle a perennial to a different part of the garden, dig and divide now while the shoots are emerging from the ground. You can divide nearly any species now except spring blooming plants, which are best divided when they fall dormant in summer or fall, or plants that resent disturbance, such as peonies, monkshood, and gas plant.

✓ Watch for borers on bearded irises. If you have a problem with them, spray from the time the eggs hatch in spring, suggests Dorothy Willott, a breeder in Beachwood. If you find the off-color trails borers make in the foliage, follow them and squash the wormlike borer when you find it. Cut off the flower stalks after blooming so borers can't tunnel down them and bore into the rhizomes.

✓ Support floppy perennials such as certain peonies, Shasta daisies, and asters with wire grid supports. Plants can grow up through these grids and then fill out to hide the wire. For perennials with long stems and large flowers, such as delphinium and dahlias, tie the rising stems to green bamboo stakes. If you wait until the plants are flopping, you may break the stems or destroy the natural character of the plant by forcing it upright in a corset of twine.

Late May

✓ Take out some books or attend classes on basic flower arranging so you can use the flowers you grow to decorate your dining room table.

✓ Plant potatoes and corn a couple weeks before the last frost date—they can take a slight chill, and with an early start they sometimes escape attacks by pests like Colorado potato beetles and aphids.

✓ After the last frost date, plant tender crops such as bedding annuals (marigolds, ageratum, petunias, zinnias), vegetable plants (tomatoes, peppers, eggplants), vegetable seeds (beans, cucumbers, squash), and annual herbs (basil, sweet marjoram, summer savory).

✓ Harvest asparagus while the heads are still tight and before the spears get long and tough.

✓ Take houseplants outdoors to a shady location for the summer. Most perk up dramatically given this extra sunlight and drenching rain. Remember to remove the drainage pan beneath the pot so rainwater can drain freely.

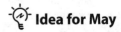 Idea for May

Be Sure Soil Is Dry Enough Before You Start to Work

Since most of the soil in these parts is a stiff clay (see Dealing With Clay in chapter 2), it tends to stay wet well into the planting season. Wet soil is not only difficult and mucky to work in, it is also vulnerable to compression. Even though you are brave enough to enter a mud pit of a garden, you could do serious damage to the soil. Wait to till the earth or to do a lot of walking in your garden until a ball of soil breaks easily in your fist. Any earlier and you may have a garden of bricks rather than plants.

If you want to be able to get into a garden earlier in spring, raise it 6 to 12 inches above the surrounding soil, so the water will drain off. And amend it with sharp sand and compost, which loosen the soil and let water escape.

 ## Recipe for May

Super Savory Sugar Snap Peas

Sugar snap peas, which are eaten pod and all, are extra delicious if you eat them just moments after picking. The best sugar snaps contain peas that are swollen, but not full-sized, in a glossy-skinned pod; these are at their sweetest. Try them in this easy recipe.

3 tablespoons butter or margarine
1 teaspoon fresh summer savory, chopped
1 pint sugar snap peas

Sauté one teaspoon finely chopped summer savory in 3 tablespoons butter over medium heat. When the savory has wilted, set the pan aside for 15 minutes to let the flavors steep. Go outdoors and harvest a pint of prime sugar snap peas. Rinse them, and remove strings and tops. Sauté the pods in the savory butter for two minutes, stirring once. Eat immediately. Yield: 4 servings.

June

 ## Early June

✓ Rhododendrons are just finishing their prime-time bloom. Visit some rhododendron gardens and nurseries—but remember that rhododendrons need well-drained soil. Don't bother to plant them unless you are willing to create the proper conditions.

✓ Strawberries are at their peak. Keep a close eye on your own, or on the pick-your-own strawberry farms, so you can harvest them when they are perfectly ripe. These strawberries are sweeter (and more perishable) than anything you buy at a store.

✓ Old-fashioned roses are at their peak of bloom. Look in rose display gardens and at nurseries for some of the roses that fashioned history.

✓ Get in the habit of weeding and hoeing once a week or more, because the weeds will be rocketing up. If you can get rid of weeds before they set seed, you'll eliminate most of your weed problem.

✓ If you hate to stake perennials upright but also dislike how some droop when in flower, consider placing a self-supporting plant nearby for the droopers to lean on. For instance, you could put droopy frikart's asters next to sturdy boltonia, or droopy red yarrow near sturdy iris leaves.

Late June

✓ Cabbage loopers (green caterpillars spawned by the small white moths that flutter around vegetable gardens) will demolish broccoli, cabbage, Chinese cabbage, and cauliflower plants if you're not alert. Spray with Bt (a bacterial disease of caterpillars) to control them without using poisons.

✓ Those cute little baby bunnies you saw in spring are getting bigger, and so is their appetite for anything green. Encourage them to leave by cleaning up their hiding places—old sheds, log piles, weedy corners—and fencing in your vegetable garden. Use a fine wire mesh fence about three feet high and buried at least six inches below the ground so they cannot tunnel under.

✓ If you usually have problems with insect pests, you could try buying an army of beneficial insects from a mail-order insect farm. (There are many of these nationwide; you can find their catalogs in the library of The Cleveland Botanical Garden.) Beneficial insects prey on, or parasitize, pests—there are dozens of them to choose from. Ladybugs are one kind that lives naturally around here, though they are not worth ordering, because they will just fly away. Other types, though, such as spined soldier bugs (for beetles and other pests), mealybug destroyers, fly parasites, and tiny parasitic wasps that attack caterpillars can do a good job. The best bugs tend to get sold out fast, so order early.

✓ Deadhead perennials (remove the faded blooms) to give the plants energy and vigor they would otherwise have spent in seed production. Cut off the old flowers individually if more buds remain ready to bloom, or cut off the whole stalk at the base if the flowers are gone for the season. Plants such as yarrow, Shasta daisies, delphinium, and coreopsis usually rebloom after deadheading.

✓ Plant more bean seed so you have fresh beans all summer long. Inoculate the seed or the trenches you set the seed in with powder-like, nitrogen-fixing bacteria, often sold as legume inoculant. These bacteria help beans, peas, and other legumes grow by pulling nitrogen out of the air and fixing it in a form plants can use. Once you apply inoculant, the bacteria will stay in the soil for years.

 **Idea for June**

Edibles Can Be Ornamental, Too

Your garden can look as good as it tastes. If you're short on space, time, energy, or enthusiasm, conserve your resources by planting ornamental edibles.

One of my favorites, which you can plant now, is red-stemmed Swiss chard, a salad green that's also good for steaming. It grows in upright clumps, an interesting variation when planted among annual bedding flowers. If you complement its red stalks with low-growing annual flowers such as pink petunias or blue pansies, the effect is stunning.

Other vegetables are earning a place in flower gardens. Pepper plants, especially bred to be compact and bear yellow, orange, red, and purple upright pods, are popular for edging or using in masses. Use ornamental cabbages and kale, with blue, white, pink, purple, and blue foliage, for a lovely fall display. Kale usually will stay pretty until late into December. (But don't forget to control cabbage looper caterpillars or they will deform the showy head.)

Some flowers are also edible. Peppery-flavored nasturtium flowers, leaves, and seeds are wonderful in salads or herbal vinegars. Calendula, or pot marigold, which you can plant now or in the late summer, has an interesting bitter flavor. Don't forget sunflowers, which are available in a two-foot-tall form—wonderful for small sunny spaces.

Take caution, though: when you mix ornamentals and edibles, don't spray herbicides, fungicides, or pesticides that are not safe to eat.

Enjoying Basil

Pick a few leaves of basil and smell its sweet, pungent fragrance on your fingertips—it's wonderful. Then chop the leaves, blend them with a little oil and vinegar, and drizzle them on tomatoes for a complex taste treat. Far different from what you'll experience if you buy the musty dried herb that often passes for basil in grocery store canisters.

Many herbs taste better when fresh, but with basil the difference is astonishing. Basil, like most herbs, is full of essential oils that give it aroma and flavor. But the essential oils in basil are particularly volatile. They evaporate whenever the herb is heated over 85°F, chopped, cooked, or allowed to age. By the time commercial basil is processed and put in a can to sell, it's gone through all of those experiences and lost essential oils every step of the way.

So if you like to cook with herbs, it's a great idea to grow your own basil, including cultivars such as the following:

- traditional sweet basil, which includes extra ruffled types and Italian heirlooms;
- large or lettuce-leaf basil with foliage broad enough to wrap around meat rolls;

- bush basil, with tiny leaves and tender, compact stems, which forms neat mounds in the garden;
- purple-leaved basil, which has burgundy-colored foliage that makes a pretty pink herbal vinegar;
- lemon basil, which combines the flavors of both of it's namesakes and makes great herbal tea.

All of these basils are easy to start from seed. (You may find seed at garden centers; otherwise you can get it from mail order catalogs.) Just put a couple seeds in a six-inch-wide pot of sterile grower's mix (a blend of peat moss, vermiculite, and perlite). Keep the soil moist and warm; in a week or two the plants will begin to come up. Choose the strongest growing one to keep, and cut off the other seedlings.

You can grow your pot of basil outdoors as long as the weather stays warm. But bring it in when the temperature drops down to 45°F; basil can't take much cold.

Keep the soil evenly moist, not soggy or dry. Fertilize potted basil every four weeks with a water-soluble fertilizer while it is in bright sunlight. And keep pinching off the top growth to use in your cooking. This makes the plant bushier and more productive.

When you bring the plant in for the fall, put it in a bright south facing window or under plant lights. Cut back on how much you fertilize and pinch the plant often to keep it about six inches high.

Sometimes basil will fade indoors, especially when the furnace comes on and the house gets dry or when the days get short and cloudy. That's when to start some new seeds so you'll always have fresh plants coming on.

I kept basil going in my basement under fluorescent lights all winter long last year. It was refreshing to leave the snowy world behind to go downstairs and harvest basil. And the aroma filled the house with scents of summer, which we enjoyed immensely. Give it a try!

Recipe for June

Basil Bean Salad

    1 pound French-cut green beans
    1 large onion, sliced thin
    5 tablespoons olive oil
    3 tablespoons vinegar
    pinch of dry mustard
    1/4 teaspoon dry basil
    salt and pepper to taste
    3 tablespoons sugar

    Place cooked beans in a serving container. Add onion. In a small bowl, combine oil, vinegar, mustard, basil, salt, pepper, and sugar until well blended. Pour dressing over beans and onions and toss gently. This is best made the day before serving. Yield: 4 servings.

Adapted from *Nature Center Cookery* (edited by Kathy Heffernan and Carol Provan, 1981, Shaker Lakes Regional Nature Center).

July

Early July

✓ If the weather is dry, red spider mites may show up on mums, roses, cucumbers, annuals, delphiniums, phlox, and even some shrubs and trees. As soon as you detect their presence, call a horticultural hotline to find out how to take preventive action. (See Other Answer Sources in chapter 8)

✓ Annual flowers may begin to slow down after their first riotous burst of bloom. Cut them back by about one-third, then water and fertilize to rejuvenate them.

✓ Mulch your vegetable garden with straw to keep the soil moister and cooler. You can also mulch your trees and shrubs, but don't layer shredded bark on too thickly.

✓ You may have the pleasure of picking your first zucchini and beans now. They will be succulent and delightful. Keep harvesting both crops; if the pods or squash mature on the vine, they will stop producing new edibles.

✓ Keep pulling out crops that have finished producing, as well as the weeds. Compost them all, as long as they do not carry seeds or diseases. Some disease spores and weed seeds will survive despite the composting process and attack again when you use the compost.

✓ Fewer perennial flowers bloom at this time of year, so the perennial garden may be looking a bit shabby. Clean up the flowers that have already bloomed by cutting back faded blossoms. Then find room for several clumps of a plant that will bring color to the midsummer garden, such as coneflower, 'Moonbeam' threadleaf coreopsis, late Shasta daisies, balloon flower (*Platycodon grandiflorus*), or speedwell (*Veronica spicata*).

Late July

✓ Even though the weather is getting hot, you can still plant container-grown shrubs, trees, and perennials. Just be sure to keep the area moist for the next three or four weeks.

✓ Look into lighting your garden so you can enjoy it more at night. You can install lights along a walk, near the patio, or on a specimen tree to show it off like a piece of art.

✓ Beans, squash, and even a few tomatoes will begin ripening. Make a point to pull out a few recipes that feature these crops so you can make the most of them.

✓ If Japanese beetles become a problem, treat your lawn with milky spore disease, which, in a few years, will kill beetle grubs as they emerge from underground. Don't bother with Japanese beetle traps—they may attract more beetles than they capture.

✓ Wouldn't a water garden with water lilies, fish, or a trickling waterfall be soothing right now? You can make a small water garden in a plastic-lined half barrel, antique bathtub, horse trough, or other deep watertight container to see if you like gardening with aquatic plants. If all goes well, you can expand to an in-ground water garden next year.

 Idea for July

Give Perennials Some Attention

In springtime, perennial flower gardens are like a beautiful tapestry of colors and textures. But in summer, many a garden begins to fray. When springtime bloom is through, you will be left with barren stems and browning pods. Don't worry. Just get out your pruning shears and start trimming.

Many plants suffer in midsummer, but perennial gardens are most notorious for their bleakness. Once they are through flowering, they channel all their remaining energy into seed production, a wasted effort from most gardeners' perspectives. Get rid of those seed heads and you'll benefit twice. Plants will look much neater and some will put out another small show of flowers.

Before cutting, look at the flowering stem of your perennial flowers. Some are simply a stalk with all the flowers at the summit. When these are done blooming, shear off all the stems. This may bring about a second bloom in plants such as sea pinks and coral bells.

On perennials such as phlox, Shasta daisies, yarrow, and delphinium, old brown flower clusters are noticeable at the top. But at the junction of leaf sets below, there may lie a small cluster of flower buds waiting for an opportunity to sprout. Cut off the old flowers and let the new take their place. This type of pruning takes a little more time and care, but it's worth the trouble. When the stem is finally through blooming, it may begin to yellow. This is the time to cut it out entirely at the base.

Some perennials, such as Shasta daisies, lobelia, and mountain bluet, revert to a low-growing rosette form for winter. It's natural for all tall stems to die back as the plant reverts to this state; remove the old stems when you see the rosette is established. Other perennials, like peonies, maintain attractive foliage long after flowers are gone. Cut off these seed heads so that plants use all their energy for good health and growth rather than seed production.

A few perennial flowers look good with seed heads attached. Astilbe, butterfly weed, coneflowers, *Sedum* 'Autumn Joy', and ornamental grasses are just a few. Leave the pods and capsules on these unless the plant seems to be suffering.

Others, such as columbine, bellflower, and violets, produce seed that is worth keeping. You might let these seed heads stay to maturity and sprinkle their offspring through the bed.

 ## Recipe for July

Yellow Squash with Fresh Thyme
When you have a lot of squash coming in from the garden, try some innovative ways of serving it to make the rich garden-fresh flavor a treat. Here's one of my favorites.

1 tablespoon butter
1 teaspoon fresh thyme leaves
4 young yellow squash, sliced
salt and freshly ground black pepper, to taste

Melt the butter with the thyme in a large skillet over medium-low heat. Add the squash, stirring to mix well. Cook covered, stirring occasionally for 5 minutes. Season with salt and pepper to taste. Yield: 4 servings

(From my book, *The Harvest Gardener*, 1993, Storey Communications, Pownal, VT.)

August

 ## Early August

✓ Because we often have a drought in midsummer, prepare for the worst. Use leaky hoses or trickle-irrigation to provide water slowly at ground level. This minimizes water loss to evaporation and discourages leaf diseases, such as black spot, which get started on wet foliage.

✓ If you cannot keep your lawn watered, it may turn brown. Fortunately, grasses are capable of going dormant during stressful times. Unless the drought is prolonged, they will green up again in fall (or when rain resumes).

✓ Plan a picnic now because you won't have to mow as often.

✓ If you see that trees and shrubs (especially newly planted ones) are struggling in dry conditions, let a hose trickle on them for up to several hours at a time. It should soak the soil deeply so that tree roots will continue to dig deeper and stay moist for some time.

✓ Humidity is often high even during our usual August droughts. Expect to see an increase in plant diseases such as mildew on roses, phlox, zinnias, asters, lilacs, and bee balm. You can prevent mildew with protective sprays of fungicides, but only if you're persistent. Or look for disease-resistant forms of these plants—they're out there if you're willing to search.

✓ Replant some fall crops, such as lettuce, radishes, and beets, in the shade of tomatoes and beans. The shade will help them get started in the heat; then you can pull out the faded tomato or bean plant to give the fall crops full sun.

✓ Move and divide summer-dormant perennials such as iris, Oriental poppy, Virginia bluebells, and bleeding heart.

Late August

✓ This is a good time to pick and dry herbs and flowers. Herbs dry best in a dehydrator or near a dehumidifier or air conditioner. They often mildew if left out in high humidity. Everlasting flowers, including strawflowers and statice, dry much more easily; just hang them in an airy dark closet. Other flowers—roses, for example—will dry if you work them into a sealed container of desiccant such as silica gel.

✓ Stop pruning hardy trees and shrubs (with the exception of hybrid tea roses). Pruning now could stimulate them to put out new growth, which will not be hardened enough to survive winter.

✓ Give hybrid tea roses their last dose of fertilizer so they can begin to wind down before cold weather comes.

Idea for August

Plants that Tolerate Drought

As August clouds roll over my garden without dropping a single hint of moisture, the sugar maple foliage begins to droop. The leather-leaf viburnums become tinted with autumn red and the sweet woodruff wilts flat on the ground. The lawn falls dormant and turns brown.

Since drought can be expected nearly every summer, we need to identify which plants require special attention when rainfall is scarce and which can hold their own. Most plants that we commonly grow, especially bluegrass, vegetables, and roses, require one inch of rainfall per week. If moisture does not come naturally, it must be provided through irrigation (if there is not a watering ban in the area).

Soak the soil deeply, encouraging the roots to dig down where they will have access to more moisture. Try to avoid watering by hand, especially trees and shrubs; most of us just don't have the patience to stand there holding the hose long enough to wet soil thoroughly. And sprinkling is not particularly efficient either. Most of that moisture evaporates into the air from leaf surfaces or goes to feeding weeds between plants. The best option is a trickle system. This delivers moisture directly to plant roots. Simply run a small stream of water out of a hose onto tree roots, or buy a canvas or perforated plastic hose that will release gentle droplets of water. You can also invest in a permanent underground irrigation system.

To minimize the garden's dependence on water, plant species that can go for long spells without rain. They may develop deep root systems; they may store water in leaves, stems, or roots; or they may protect their foliage from water loss with waxy, leathery, bristly, or hairy coatings. Some even vary their method of photosynthesis to minimize water loss through leaf pores. Here's a shopping list of plants that will tolerate future droughts:

• Annual flowers: Annual phlox, portulaca, California poppy, morning glory, annual pinks
• Perennial flowers: Yarrow, yellow and purple coneflowers, perennial sunflowers, blanketflower, coreopsis, daylilies, hosta, sedums, sweet William, Oriental poppies
• Herbs: Perennial thyme, rosemary, sage, savory, oregano, santolina
• Vegetables: Swiss chard, purslane, Good-King-Henry, sorrel
• Shrubs: Junipers, Japanese and Mentor barberry, flowering quince, smoke tree, privet, potentilla, Amur maple, Russian olive, witch hazel, St.-John's-wort, Nannyberry viburnum, yucca, staghorn sumac, buckthorn
• Trees: Osage orange, juniper, golden-rain tree, bur oak, locust, sassafras, Siberian elm

 **Recipe for August**

Tomato-Onion Pie
    8 medium onions, peeled and sliced
    5 cups soft bread cubes
    8 medium-size tomatoes, peeled and sliced
    1 tablespoon sugar
    1/2 teaspoon salt
    1/8 teaspoon freshly ground black pepper
    2 tablespoons butter or margarine

Preheat oven to 350°F Boil onions in 1/2 cup salted water until they are almost tender. Drain. Heavily butter a 2-quart casserole dish. Line the bottom of the dish with 4 cups of the bread cubes, reserving 1 cup for topping. Layer onions and tomatoes over bread cubes. Sprinkle sugar, salt, and pepper over tomatoes. Top with reserved bread cubes. Dot with butter. Bake in a preheated oven for about 30 minutes. Yield: 8 to 10 servings.

(From my book, *The Harvest Gardener*, 1993, Storey Communications, Pownal, VT.)

Let your mature storage onions dry for a week in a warm, dry place before storing them in a cool spot.
(Photo courtesy of the National Garden Bureau.)

September

 ## Early September

✓ Use some dried herbs and garden flowers, plus wild roadside flowers to make everlasting wreaths. Wire small bunches of flowers and herb sprigs onto a framework of wire, grapevines, or straw, all of which are available at most florists.

✓ Plant some evergreens to screen out unpleasant views, muffle traffic sounds, or give a view of solid greenery this winter. Look for conifers that are not sheared for a more natural look. Keep new plantings moist through the fall.

✓ Sow seeds of hardy annuals such as sweet alyssum, pansies, Shirley and California poppies. These can pass the winter while quite small and will flower very early next year.

✓ Plant cold-tolerant greens such as spinach, endive, and winter lettuces like 'Arctic King', 'Brune d'Hiver', and 'Winter Density'. Grow them to a small size in a well drained bed and cover with a floating row cover and straw when the weather turns cold in November or December. They will stay small during winter and begin growing extra early in spring.

✓ Buy some ornamental kale plants for your garden. These colorful-leaved plants will stay beautiful well into December.

Late September

✓ Prepare houseplants to return indoors. Evict crawling bugs that have crept into the drainage holes in the bottom of the pot and any pests on the leaves or stems. Move the plants gradually into dimmer, warmer locations until they are acclimated to household conditions. Once indoors, they will begin a period of rest and need less water and little fertilizer.

✓ Look for some late crops to be abundant now, such as bush lima beans, hot peppers, and eggplants. You can freeze eggplant after dipping peeled slices in egg, then breading and baking. Roast, dry, or pickle hot peppers.

✓ Garden chores slow down a bit at this time. If you've been planning to put in a new garden bed, this is a good time to do so. Since nursery stock often is picked over at this time of year, you may have to wait until spring to find the best cultivars and specimens.

✓ Admire wild goldenrod and purple New England asters that spread across meadows and roadways all around town. You can move some of these wild prairie plants into large gardens or naturalized areas near your home so you are sure to have lots of fall color.

Idea for September

Choreographing Bulbs

Are you planting more bulbs and enjoying them less? It may be difficult to imagine a less-than-attractive daffodil or tulip, but colors mixed unknowingly can look polka-dotted and chaotic. Be certain any investment you make in bulbs and planting time is well spent. Study what is available at garden centers. Pick different types of bulbs that will come into and go out of flower the entire spring season.

Henk Koster, chief garden architect of the Dutch Keukenhof Garden where millions of bulbs are put on display from February to June, explained the concept. "It's like dance choreography," he said. "You plan blooming so that everything happens when you want it to, in sequence. It's also important to consider the blooming times of flowering shrubs and other perennials."

Furthermore, plan to blend handsome color combinations that look good with other bulbs, as well as your landscape and home. "Color is really the key," Koster said. "Bulbs are color. If you put masses of color together, you achieve a more stunning effect."

Ellen Henke, California-based botanist and gardening spokesperson, writes in *Flower and Garden* about techniques she uses to create movement. She combines no fewer than 12 bulbs of a single cultivar into a mass, not a straight line. She puts the tall bulbs in a triangle toward the back of the bed and matches their color to shorter bulbs in the front. The color flows back and forth, side to side. You also can match bulb colors with low-growing perennials or annuals such as violas, pansies, English daisies, or forget-me-nots.

Once you have the color coordinated, pay attention to smaller details: flower shapes, foliage colors, and the overall form of the plant. "What makes a planting impressive from a distance might be sharp contrasts of color or patterns of contrasting or complementary colors," Koster said. "Up close, the shape and textures of the flowers and leaves become important." You might consider using varied flower types, such as lily-flowered tulips or double-flowering daffodils, or species tulips that have interesting patterns on their leaves.

 ## Recipe for September

Harvesting and Drying Herbs for Teas

1. Be sure that sprays and pesticides have not been used.

2. Pick plant materials on a sunny day, ideally after two consecutive days of sunshine. The flavor will be stronger.

3. Discover the prime time for each plant. Usually this is just before flowers form. When herb flowers are used, pick them in bud or early bloom.

4. Immediately after picking, wash plant material in lukewarm water. Use a large container filled with water. Change water three or four times for a thorough cleaning. When clean, place herbs in a terry towel and gently pat dry.

5. Dry herbs on screens in an area away from light and where air circulates. Dry until *crisp*.

6. Before drying scented geranium or large basil leaves, use scissors to remove the large center vein in each leaf.

7. Strip dried leaves from stems before storing. For evenly dried leaves, place in a shallow pan and put in a warm oven (150°F) for up to 10 minutes. Keep oven door slightly open.

8. To create tea blends, rub the leaves through a coarse sieve. A food processor may also be used to crumble herb leaves; use quick on/off pulses to achieve uniformity. Guard against over-processing or powdering the leaves.

9. Store material in glass jars, tightly capped, in a dark, cool cupboard. Label and date the containers. Refresh supply each year.

Note: Follow these same steps for harvesting and drying herbs for culinary uses.

(Reprinted with permission from *Cooking With Herb Scents*, edited by Donna Agan, 1991, the Western Reserve Herb Society.)

October

Early October

✓ Harvest pumpkins and squash before they are hit by frost or sit on the wet soil too long. In either case, they will not keep very long. Store them at about 50°F, if possible, for the longest shelf life.

✓ Plant fall bulbs. Make groups of the same varieties, five, seven, or more per group. These larger bunches of flowers provide more impact when seen from a distance. (See Choreographing Bulbs in the September section for more details.)

✓ Put extra bulbs into flowerpots, sink them in holes in the garden, and surround the pots with sand. Give them from 8 to 15 months outdoors (depending on the type of bulb), then bring the pots indoors for an extra-early bloom.

✓ Protect flowers and vegetables from early frosts by covering them with sheets of plastic or burlap, or bags, buckets, or bins. Remove the protection when the weather warms up again.

✓ Dig up small annual flowers such as impatiens, and herbs such as basil, sweet marjoram, and chives to keep on your windowsill or in a light garden. They will not grow as well as they do outdoors, but they will be okay for a month or more and will provide garden-fresh flavor and color all the time.

✓ This is your last chance to plant perennial flowers safely. They need several months to develop roots before the soil freezes in winter.

✓ Evergreen trees with needles will lose some now. Don't worry about this natural occurrence, unless needle loss is extreme. In that case, call an arborist to see if there is a problem with the tree.

✓ Enjoy the beautiful fall colors and be certain you have some of the best plants for autumn displays in your yard. Among them are burning bush, maples (especially cultivars such as 'Autumn Flame'), *Enkianthus*, oakleaf hydrangea, sweet gum, red oak, and cut-leaf staghorn sumac.

✓ Plant a witch hazel tree so you can enjoy its spidery yellow flowers, which emerge around now.

Late October

✓ Fertilize deciduous trees and shrubs once the leaves fall but while the roots are still growing. Bury tree spikes or small pockets of a complete granular fertilizer down below turf roots and all around the perimeter of the branch canopy.

✓ Rake up fallen leaves and compost them (see Leaf Composting in this section). Or shred them with a lawn mower and put them on garden beds as a mulch. If you leave piles on the lawn they will make the turf rot.

✓ Look through some of the photos you took of your garden during the summer. Is there one that would make a nice holiday greeting card or a competitive entry in a photo contest? Note the cultivar names on pictured plants for future reference.

✓ Protect evergreen shrubs growing near the house by surrounding them with burlap to support the branches against snow sliding off the roof.

 Idea for October

Leaf Composting

Since leaves are no longer welcome in landfills, many homeowners are starting their own compost piles. This is a double blessing: it saves landfill space and produces a great soil amendment that is free of weed seeds. The organic matter released when leaves decompose helps aerate and drain our heavy soils. It also holds nutrients and just enough moisture to nourish plant roots. Soils rich in organic matter shelter a community of beneficial microbes that protect against plant disease. Making your own compost also saves you the expense of buying compost, peat moss, or composted cow manure to condition the soil.

If you have only a few leaves, you can chop them up finely with your lawn mower; they will decompose and fertilize the lawn with no further effort on your part. Some lawn mowers are fitted with mulching mechanisms that distribute the chopped leaves evenly over the lawn.

But if leaves fall thickly enough to mat down on the grass, rake and compost them. An easy but less efficient way is to sheet-compost, by layering leaves over a garden bed, then rototilling them in spring. A layer of leaves, however, will keep soil wet much later than ordinary and may not decompose rapidly.

It's better to pile leaves in a long row and chop them with a lawn mower. The smaller the pieces, the faster they will turn into organics. Add some nitrogen fertilizer or compost accelerator (bacteria that break down leaves), then turn the pile once or twice in the winter to provide air to the inside and speed up the decomposition process. To spare your neighbors from sharing the view, you can make your compost pile in a shallow pit in a well-drained area. This will keep leaves warmer so they decompose actively.

Recipe for October

Quick Pumpkin Muffins

Halve a small pumpkin and scoop out the seeds. Set on a cookie sheet, with the cut sides down, and bake in oven at 350°F for about 30 minutes or until tender. Scoop out the pulp and mash it. Add between 1/2 and 1 cup of the mashed pulp to an instant blueberry muffin mix and prepare according to package directions. You can freeze any excess pumpkin to use at another time. Yield: 4–6 servings.

November

Early November

✓ Plant tender bulbs such as 'Paper White' narcissus for bloom during the holidays. Larger and more expensive amaryllis bulbs may take longer to flower, but their colorful, mammoth blooms are spectacular enough to warrant the wait.

✓ Protect hybrid tea roses for the winter. Remove the overly long canes that would be damaged if they whip around in the wind and cover the graft at the plant's base with a thick layer of leaves and burlap or a styrofoam rose insulator.

✓ Tidy up the garden by edging the beds to give them sharp clean lines.

✓ You can still plant lily bulbs, but give them especially well drained soil because they rot easily.

✓ Notice trees that have interesting bark, a point of beauty you can enjoy all winter. Some of the best include paperbark maple, blood-twigged dogwood, lace-bark pine, and river birches. White birches, though their bark is lovely, are pest-prone.

✓ Resolve next year to plant trees and shrubs with fall and winter fruit that attract birds and brighten up the yard. These include crab apples, viburnum, sumac, fire thorn, cotoneaster, and barberry.

✓ Move all containers of hardy plants into protected locations. If you take them into the garage, water them occasionally. To give evergreens some light, sink them into the soil near your foundation plantings.

Late November

✓ Make a planter in an interesting basket or heirloom pot or bowl; it will become a conversation piece for the upcoming holidays. Line the container with plastic so it will not be damaged by the moist soil. Then do something different; plant it with a small red poinsettia and red-leaf rex begonia, or a white poinsettia and silver-leaf aluminum plant and dangling white marbled pothos. Or use gold-dust dracaena with a golden flowered mum and Swedish ivy.

✓ On a warm day, spray an antidesiccant on your rhododendrons to keep the leaves from drying out during winter.

✓ Cut your lawn fairly short so the grass blades won't pack down during winter and encourage fungus diseases to attack.

✓ This is your last opportunity to plant deciduous trees and shrubs. Water them well to help them get established.

 Idea for November

The Three Ps for Indoor Gardening Success

Just as the Three *Rs* are the foundation of education, three *Ps*—pinching, pruning, and potting—are the basis of successful indoor gardening.

Pinching is a simple but important technique used to make annuals or bush-type houseplants grow full and handsome. Nip off the shoot tips on a plant to stimulate side buds to grow into branches.

Pruning involves removal of larger branches and often requires pruning shears or loppers. Prune to remove dead or diseased branches or to encourage resprouting from older, often threadbare, plants. Most indoor trees will require some pruning to prevent them from growing through the roof. Both the shoots and roots can be pruned back by 20 percent every year to maintain a tree at the same size.

Potting is a good task for renewing houseplants. If a plant is pot-bound and its roots slip easily out of the pot or creep out the drainage hole, move it up to a pot an inch or two larger in diameter. Untangle any roots that are tightly matted around the perimeter of the root ball. Replant into fresh soil, using great care not to bury the plant any deeper or set it any shallower than it had been. Firm the fresh soil and water well.

Recipe for November

Golden Autumn Soup

Crisp, early fall apples and tart cider provide good flavor in this squash soup. It may be prepared ahead and reheated.

1 1/2 pounds buttercup squash (substitute butternut or acorn)
2 tablespoons butter or margarine
1 large onion, chopped
1 rib celery, chopped
3 medium carrots, scraped and diced
2 tart apples, peeled, cored and diced
3 cups chicken broth
1/4 teaspoon grated nutmeg
1 teaspoon rubbed sage
1/4 teaspoon ground cumin
1/4 teaspoon crushed rosemary
2 tablespoons butter or margarine (additional)
2 tablespoons all-purpose flour
1 1/2 cups tart apple cider
1/4 teaspoon ground cinnamon
Garnishes: 1/2 cup grated sharp cheddar cheese, 1/2 cup toasted chopped walnuts.

Cut squash in half, remove seeds. Place squash in a shallow baking pan and bake in preheated 375°F oven until tender, about 40 minutes. Remove from oven and set aside.

In 4-quart Dutch oven or soup pan, melt butter over medium-high heat. Add onions and celery: cook until soft.

Remove pulp from squash and place in soup pan. Add carrots, apples, broth, and seasonings. Reduce heat and simmer for 30 minutes. (For a smoother texture, soup may be puréed in food blender or processor.)

In small saucepan, melt additional butter. Whisk in flour and let cook over medium heat for 4 minutes. Gradually whisk in apple cider; add cinnamon. Cook and stir until smooth and slightly thickened. Stir into soup. Taste for seasoning; salt and pepper may be added. Let simmer about 5 minutes.

To serve, ladle soup into bowls and sprinkle with grated cheese and walnuts. Yield: 4–6 servings

(Reprinted with permission from *Cooking With Herb Scents*, edited by Donna Agan, 1991, Western Reserve Herb Society.)

December

 Early December

✓ Prune your evergreen shrubs now to get some fresh greens for holiday decorations. Try this with holly, taxus, rhododendrons, and junipers—but leave pines, spruces, and firs alone.

✓ Spray holiday greens with an antitranspirant (a product that seals plant leaves to reduce moisture loss) and move them outdoors when you are out of the house during the day to keep them fresh longer.

✓ Buy some poinsettias. They come in red, white, pink, yellow, and combinations, and last for months if you keep their soil constantly moist and the plant in reasonably bright light.

✓ Look for pine cones, seedpods, and dried flower heads to use for holiday decorations. Let your imagination run wild for especially creative holiday displays.

✓ Check out the many holiday garden shows around town. (Among the biggest and best are those at the Cleveland Botanical Garden and the Rockefeller Park Greenhouse.)

✓ If you are buying a live Christmas tree, dig the hole for it now, before the soil freezes. Move it indoors for as brief a time as possible to give it a better chance of survival outdoors.

✓ Look for Ohio-grown Scotch and white pines, which are fresher than those cut in early fall and shipped in from out of state.

✓ Keep houseplant soil from building up accumulated salts that come in water and fertilizer. Drench the pot and let the extra water run out the bottom to carry salts away. Or when you see a white crust on soil or on the outside of a clay pot, soak the pot, plant and all, for a few minutes to remove those salts.

 Late December

✓ When the soil freezes, cut the boughs off your Christmas tree and use them to mulch perennials that are prone to frost-heaving (shifting out of the ground when the soil freezes and thaws during winter). These include strawberries and coral bells.

✓ If your garden soil is fairly heavy, most other perennials will survive winter best without mulching. Mulch keeps winter soils wetter when they are not frozen and will encourage perennial roots to rot.

✓ Don't salt walks near gardens, especially if all the salt runs off into nearby garden soil or if salt-sensitive rhododendrons are close. Try cat litter or wood ashes instead.

 **Idea for December**

Garden Resolutions

Since the time to make New Year's resolutions is getting close, let's resolve to have more fun and better results in our gardens. These will be vows that you can look forward to carrying out. Unlike past vows you may have made, you can approach these resolutions cheerfully.

I'll let you in on a little secret right here at the start. By concentrating on your garden, you may inadvertently tackle some of the difficult personal resolutions that you haven't been able to deal with in the past. Let's look at some of the unexpected advantages of making garden resolutions this year.

1. If you get out and mow, weed, hoe, prune, or harvest in your garden at least half an hour a day, you can get many of the cardiovascular and toning benefits of a regular exercise routine.

2. This same amount of outdoor puttering can burn off a couple hundred excess calories a day. Over time, this becomes an easy way to lose unwanted pounds.

3. If you suffer from low self-confidence or self-esteem, grow a mammoth pumpkin, a tall patch of sweet corn, or a fragrant, graceful, prize-winning rosebush. You'll find hidden reserves of pride growing within yourself as you see your achievements bloom.

4. If you often get too tense and have trouble unwinding from work, you have many ways to relax in the garden. Take a shovel and hoe and vigorously attack the earth to relieve your aggressions; sit outside in the cool of the evening to drink in the beauty of what you've created and grow mellow.

5. If you want to make more friends, you'll find striking up conversation easy when you're with other gardeners. You can discuss your lawn maintenance techniques, share divisions of perennial flowers or annual seeds, or lend your gardening books or magazines. You also can join a garden club or horticultural society to begin making friends in a big way.

When you work out in the garden, you get the courage and means to take on other personal challenges. You may not even realize how far you have come, until you are already on top of your goals. How's that for a great way to enter the new year?

 **Recipe for December**

Marinated Brussels Sprouts
A piquant and tasty way to eat your sprouts.

1 pound Brussels sprouts
2 tablespoons sweet pickle relish
2 tablespoons chopped pimiento or red bell pepper
2 tablespoons finely chopped scallions
1/4 cup dry white wine
1 tablespoon vinegar
1 teaspoon Dijon mustard
2 tablespoons vegetable oil
1 clove garlic, finely chopped
1/2 teaspoon salt
1/4 teaspoon pepper

Trim and clean Brussels sprouts. Steam or boil them in a small amount of water until tender but firm; drain and cool quickly in ice water to stop the cooking process. In a medium bowl, combine the rest of the ingredients and mix together. Add the drained Brussels sprouts and toss lightly. Cover and refrigerate for at least an hour to let the flavors blend. Serve chilled or at room temperature. Yield: 4 to 6 servings.
(Reprinted with permission from *Recipes from a Kitchen Garden* by Renee Shepherd, 1990, Shepherd's Garden Publishing, Felton, CA.)

Where to Find Current Gardening Reminders

Newspapers
  • *The Plain Dealer* (Wednesday Food section; Friday; Saturday Real Estate magazine; Sunday)
  • *Sun Newspapers* (Thursday)
  • *Akron Beacon Journal* (Wednesday)
  • *Elyria Chronicle Telegram* (Friday)
  • *Lake County News-Herald* (Friday)
  • *Lorain Journal* (Friday)

Magazines/Newsletters
  • *Bulletin* of the Cleveland Botanical Garden
  • *Ohio Gardening*, Cuyahoga County Cooperative Extension Service

Other Media
  • Northcoast Gardener, Alan Hirt's radio show, 10 a.m.–noon Saturdays on WWWE.
  • Compuserve Garden Forum. Managed by the National Gardening Association, this online forum offers interesting discussions, a library of information, and expert advise. (For information on obtaining a Compuserve account, call 800-848-8990.)
  • On the Internet. A gardening mailing list is maintained by the University of Kentucky at listserv@ukcc.uky.edu.

CHAPTER 6

Landscape Professionals & Suppliers

Even if you are a dedicated do-it-yourselfer, you may eventually run out of time or expertise. Very few of us can do everything we would like with our own bare hands; we sometimes need help. For example, I do most of my own garden work, designing and tending my landscape and starting most of my vegetables and flowers from seed. I even build stone walls and rock gardens. But when it comes to heavy work like hauling soil and trees, intricate stuff such as building a stone patio, or exacting tasks like grafting evergreens, I call in professional help. Whether it's brains, brawn, or supplies you need, there are a wide array of horticultural professionals to choose from.

Evaluating the Project and the Professional

Once you recognize that you need help, you have to figure out who can handle the job. For nearly every task that needs doing around a yard, there are several kinds of professionals you can employ, from highly skilled specialists to day laborers. The hard part is finding the right balance of skill, education, versatility, and cost.

For example, to build a stone patio or walk you can use a stonemason who specializes in stonework or a landscape contractor who does some construction in addition to planting, pruning, mowing, and other jobs. Your decision here may depend on the complexity of the project, the size of your budget, how long each company will take to do the job, and whether the contractor has the right experience.

If you are looking for someone to handle your lawn maintenance, you can use a landscape maintenance company, a lawn-care service, or neighborhood kid with a lawn mower. Each may approach the task from a slightly different perspective and complete the job in different ways. For instance, the neighborhood kid may be the least expensive but usually is also unskilled and won't know when to apply certain products, when to let the grass grow longer or when to cut it shorter, or when pests and diseases may be causing problems. A turf specialist from a lawn-care service will know all of these things but may not be able to help you with your flower garden or shrub pruning. A landscape maintenance company can tend to the other jobs around the yard but may not be as up-to-date on turf technology.

Once you decide the kind of service you need, check the qualifications of suppliers before giving them a deposit or setting them free in your yard. Learn what it is that a certain company does best, find out if they stand behind their work, and ask for several references. Look at some of the work they have done and be sure you like it. Also, will they stick to the price they quote you? Do you need to be at home to supervise, or is there a project supervisor who understands what you want and will see that it is done to your satisfaction? Has the company been in business long or might they disappear overnight? Is the company certified to sell you nursery stock or apply pesticides? Are their workers insured in case accidents happen? Does the company belong to a professional organization that keeps them informed of new developments? Ask these questions when the company salesman comes to call and before you sign a contract. And, finally, it is wise to get several estimates whenever you are contemplating major projects.

Local Professional Organizations

One sign that horticultural professionals are serious about what they do is membership in one or more of the dozens of national horticultural organizations. Three major groups that have active local chapters in the greater Cleveland area are:

Ohio Landscapers Association
P.O. Box 170, Richfield, 44286; 659-9755

Probably the most visible local association for horticultural professionals, the Ohio Landscapers Association includes landscapers, nurserymen, and designers, most of whom are from northeast Ohio (all the current officers and board of directors are in the 216 area code). OLA members come from large and small companies, but all must be recommended by another member of the association and all must prove they hold the necessary licenses for spraying or for buying nursery stock wholesale and selling it retail. Representatives of some of the top local landscaping companies hold positions on committees or as officers.

The OLA provides plenty of opportunities for members and nonmembers to learn more about the field. The association sponsors a landscape design short course that gives new designers the fundamentals they need to begin designing landscapes. Other programs focus on new plants, new techniques, new products, and employee management methods. The OLA puts out a sophisticated monthly magazine, *The Growing Concern*, in which members share ideas, technology, and problems. The also install a garden of Preferred Plants at Floralscape garden festival.

Design Network
1506 Maple Rd., Cleveland Heights, 44121

Many of the area's independent landscape designers belong to the Design Network, an idea-swapping organization that is loosely allied with the Association of Professional Landscape Designers. The group meets bimonthly in members' homes for programs and round-table discussions about plants, drawing techniques, construction, lighting, and garden products.

The Design Network is one place to find an independent designer, most of whom do not advertise. For a listing of designers' names and specialties, send a self-addressed, stamped envelop to the address above.

Western Reserve Section, Ohio Chapter
American Society of Landscape Architects
1069 W. Main St., Westerville, 43081; (614) 895-2222

This organization brings together landscape architects from the greater Cleveland area for dinner meetings, instructional programs, and workshops at architecturally interesting locations around town. "Joining ASLA is not mandatory for a landscape architect, but a lot of landscape architects do belong because that is how you keep in touch with what's going on," said Bill Boron, former secretary of the Ohio Chapter of the ASLA. ASLA members can keep up with design trends, new materials, and creative alternatives used locally and nationally.

Landscape Specialists: Who Does What?

While most people would not consider making a long-term investment without the advice of a stockbroker or financial counselor, few are as organized when it comes to their own landscape. Like a closet, a yard can become a collection of random but costly odds and ends without function.

Imagine that instead of looking like an outdoor flea market, your yard could effectively increase your home's living space. You could entertain, swim, barbecue, play, and relax in comfort outdoors. Your landscape could also make your time indoors more enjoyable by giving you a pleasant view or more privacy. In addition, should you decide to sell your home, an attractive yard will help it sell more quickly and for a better price.

Obviously, making the most of your yard requires careful planning. It can involve as much strategy as investing in the stock market or preparing for retirement, and can require major amounts of time and money—good reasons to consider getting professional advice.

The cost need not be prohibitive. A landscape plan can be free, provided you pay for the installation. Or a plan can cost over $1,000. The cost depends upon the complexity of the job, which, in turn, will influence whether you should call upon a landscape architect, designer, or contractor.

Landscape Architects

Landscape architects must be registered with the state of Ohio and have a college degree in landscape architecture. Their academic training emphasizes architecture, urban planning, and civil engineering. Many landscape architecture firms concentrate on large residential, commercial, institutional, and government design. Some landscape architects, however, work on more modest projects as well. Some full-service landscape companies, those that design as well as build, have landscape architects on staff to work on hardscape such as roads, pools, bridges, and fencing. Design fees can range from $40 per hour, for an unregistered landscape architect, up to about $100 per hour.

Unless your yard needs a lot of grade changes or major construction, you may not need a landscape architect. If what you want is a good planting plan, a landscape architect may not fill the bill; most are not as well versed in plants as designers (though there are always exceptions).

Landscape Designers

Unlike landscape architects, landscape designers often come from horticultural backgrounds or have a two-year associate degree in landscape design. They tend to be knowledgeable about plants and have a good feel for aesthetics. Anyone can call himself a designer, however, so it is wise to check an individual's background before you sign a contract.

Designers' fees are easier on the budget than those of architects. They range from about $35 to $80 per hour. A simple plan may take only a few hours. On the other hand, a landscape carefully tailored to fit your lifestyle now as well as ten years in the future will require more frequent sessions with the designer. Irrigation systems, lighting, drainage, patios, decks, and other construction will also take time to design. Some designers also will consult for a fee without drawing an actual plan. They will walk around your yard with you and help you decide which plants should stay and which should go. You can do the actual planting yourself or hire a landscape contractor to undertake the designer's suggestions.

Landscape designers work either as part of a design/build team or independently. Independents may provide you with a plan with no further commitments or help. They also may put it out to bid. Many prefer to oversee construction, a form of quality control that is worth paying for. Some specialize in specific types of projects, such as herb or perennial gardens. Others will plan the entire yard.

Landscape Contractors

The third type of landscape service to consider is the landscape contractor, who can install from existing plans. In some states, a landscape contractor must have a degree in landscape architecture, but in Ohio that is not necessary or common.

Sometimes, a landscape contractor's crew may be certified as landscape technicians by the Ohio Nursery and Landscape Association. "Everyone in our landscape division takes the certification test," said Richard Kay, owner of Breezewood Gardens. "It brings a certain amount of professionalism with it. Before taking the test, a person gets a detailed book and six months to study. Those employees who have passed the test take more pride in what they do."

In the next few years you also may see landscape contractor managers and owners certified by the Association of Landscape Contractors of America, a national group in which a few of the more successful local contractors participate.

Legally, certification is not necessary to install or maintain gardens, nor is any background in design required. Anyone with a truck or a lawn mower can go into landscaping. Consequently, not all contractors are qualified to design. Some prefer to install an independent designer's work; others specialize in maintenance only.

"Having landscape contractors design a landscape can be a real shot in the dark," says Lee Behnke, a landscape architect. "They may use things in their inventory they want to move out, or they can overdo on colored or variegated foliage and weeping habits."

"Everyone needs to know their own limits," agrees Steve Pattie of the Pattie Group, a full-service landscaper.

Landscape contractors traditionally have been the labor end of a landscape. Today, however, many larger contractors also have their own design departments. Design/build firms may design for an additional fee or for the price of installation. Others will design for "free." This is a

sales tool, and, though it may sound like a bargain, many design professionals warn that you should not expect to keep the plan unless you sign
up for installation. The design costs may be hidden in the labor fee or
the markup on plants.

Affiliated Professionals

A variety of affiliated horticultural professionals exist to fill a range
of gardening and landscape needs, including:

Compost and Soil Supply

There are bulk suppliers of soil, compost, mulch, and sometimes
stone and brick. From them, you can buy by the truckload. Look under
topsoil or stone in the Yellow Pages for commercial sources. Or, you can
buy leaf compost from the independent and nonprofit Greater Cleveland Ecology Program (687-1266), which collects landscape and garden waste from several communities and markets the resulting Cuyahoga Leaf Humus. Also, several cities and townships offer their own
compost: the city of Solon (248-1155) gives finished humus away free to
its residents; Westlake (871-3300) and Bay Village (871-2200) jointly
sell and deliver finished compost within their city limits.

Garden Lighting

You can have garden lighting installed by electricians, landscapers, or
garden lighting specialists. Rick Tomko, owner of Site Illuminations in
Newbury, is a landscape architect who specializes in site lighting. "My
background lets me combine design capabilities with the technical and
engineering experience of electrical contractors. Usually you get one or
the other. The electricians might give you more functionality with little
design; the landscaper might give you all design without current lamp
technology. Since the lighting field changes on a daily basis, a company
has to focus only on lighting to stay abreast of those advances."

Tomko recommends including lighting in the master plan for new
homes and landscapes so the underground wiring can go in before the
finished grading is done. Then you can put the lighting fixtures in after
the plants are installed. Likewise, he suggests, run the wires indoors
before the drywall is installed so the switches are properly placed.

Interior Plantscaping

To install a few planters in a sunroom, develop an indoor atrium at an
office, or maintain indoor plantings in a commercial atrium or a mall,
you can get help from a specialist: an interior plantscaper.

"Interior work uses a different skill set for plant identification, maintenance, and care," says Nancy Silverman, owner of Plantscaping, Inc.
"Even diseases are totally different from outdoors. It's a unique industry
in its own."

A few universities offer horticulture programs specializing in interior plantscaping, and some community or technical schools, such as the Agricultural Technical Institute (see Adult Education in chapter 8), offer a two-year associate degree in interior plantscaping.

Beyond university training, many companies train their own maintenance staffs. "We have good luck training horticultural technicians who maintain plantings. Since Hurricane Andrew damaged most of the plant nurseries in Florida, we are really working on maintenance because some plants are just unavailable, especially the big stuff for the malls," Silverman said.

Mary Blaha from Interior Green Corporation said, "Most of our technicians are not horticulture graduates but are trained in-house by a manager who has a degree. I've trained a lot of people—enough to know it takes a special kind of person to work with plants. They have to recognize when a plant is failing and to know what to do."

Company-trained interior landscape technicians and, through a separate test, interior landscape professionals can be certified by the Interior Landscape Division of the Association of Landscape Contractors of America (the same certification previously available through the National Council for Interior Horticulture).

Irrigation

Curtis Straubhaar, designer for Irrigation Supply, Inc. in Warrensville Heights, says irrigation specialists can consult with the landscape contractor who will be designing an irrigation system and install it with specialized machinery that leaves minimal disturbance in existing landscapes.

"Compared to landscape contractors, irrigation specialists are better versed in water conservation and application rates for different soils and plants. They can adapt the systems, using microsystems for small beds, or adjust the watering schedule according to the weather. We can tell contractors which irrigation nozzles to apply for the most efficient water application in the least amount of time with the least cost," Straubhaar said.

Some irrigation specialists are certified by the national Irrigation Association, which gives different tests to certify workers for residential, commercial, or golf-course irrigation.

Stone and Brick Work

If you want to build an elaborate patio or walk that will require a specialist, you can look for stone- or brick-masons, who are part of the building trade and not commonly used for home landscapes. Because union bricklayers seldom take on smaller home landscaping projects, according to Solon-based stonemason Sal Fusco, only a few freelance stone- and brick-masons in this area are available to make patios and walkways.

The alternative to which most people turn today is landscape contractors who will work with brick, stone, or prefabricated interlocking paving blocks. These contractors may not have a background in stone and masonry work and may therefore lack some of the knowledge and skill of the specialists. "Furthermore," said Fusco, "most have to start from precut stone, which is less efficient than stone that is cut to fit the job."

Tree Care

Arborists specialize in woody plants and may be the only kind of garden professional you can get to climb up in a tree or use a power saw, because of the high insurance costs of doing either. "Tree work is a specialty. Landscape crews who work on the ground are the artists; the guys in the trees are the daredevils—a breed of their own. Most of them would rather be up in the trees, even though they have to hold on with one hand and saw with the other—a dangerous job," said Fred Robinson, consulting arborist in Kirtland. You may want to use arborists to prune or remove a large tree, shape rare or disease-prone woody plants, help you select or plant trees and shrubs properly, control insects, or do other jobs that require a solid background in woody plants.

Some of the larger landscape contractors or maintenance firms may have a crew of arborists as well as landscape crews; other companies specialize only in tree care. In either case, anyone can call themselves an arborist. To be sure skill lies behind the name, look for a crew that has at least one member certified by the International Society of Arboriculture.

Under certain circumstances, you also may need to use a consulting arborist. Consulting arborists are members of the American Society of Consulting Arborists, which admits new members only after they are approved by two existing members. ASCA arborists are qualified to provide advice; they study problems, make plans and diagnoses, hazard assessments and appraisals—seldom climbing into trees themselves. You can find consulting arborists at some large firms that handle tree care. Or you can hire independents and have the actual work done by the lowest or most qualified bidder.

To locate arborists in the Yellow Pages, look under Tree Care.

Turf Care

If you like an emerald-green lawn of beautiful turf, then you know that keeping a lawn manicured takes considerable time and skill. For that reason, some horticulturists specialize in this field, taking care of golf courses, public parks, and baseball and football fields in addition to serving with lawn-care companies.

Dr. Bruce Augustin, the agronomist who handles education programs for Lesco, Inc., a lawn products supplier in Rocky River, says some turf specialists have horticulture or agronomy degrees. "There is a wide range of backgrounds in the lawn-care business, from trained agronomists to business people from other backgrounds," Augustin said. "In most big companies, there is a Ph.D. on staff, but some smaller companies also are run by Ph.D. horticulturists. The quality of the service they supply depends a lot on the individual."

Some people working in lawn care have two-year associate degrees or attend short courses to get some background. Any of them who apply pesticides must be tested and certified with the state of Ohio. Some companies belong to the Professional Lawn Care Association of America or the Ohio Turf Grass Association, which are not selective about their membership but provide members with up-to-date information on new practices.

In addition to lawn specialists, some landscape contractors (who mostly install plants) will mow lawns, too. And the middlemen—grounds maintenance crews—can apply lawn chemicals, mow, and maintain plantings.

Plant Sources

In spring it seems as though everywhere you turn, people are selling plants. Pot after pot is lined outside of department stores, discount houses, and grocery stores, as well as the more traditional garden centers, nurseries, and greenhouses. Rather than buy the first plant that you see, find out what to expect from these vendors. Take possible limitations into account so you can be sure you get a healthy plant and good advice for keeping it healthy.

Grocery Stores, Discount Houses, Department Stores

These vendors do not specialize in plants, so don't expect them to answer your questions knowledgeably. You may, however, be able to find lower prices here because such chain stores buy in bulk. But the pressure is on you to know which plant will work well and whether it is healthy before you buy.

The plants may be of decent quality, if they were good plants to start with and have been tended well during shipping and stocking on shelves. But sometimes they have suffered a bit.

Always look closely at plants such as these before you buy. Be sure you know what cultivar you need; do your homework before you shop so you don't end up taking home something that will grow too big or flower in the wrong color. Then check to be sure the plant is labeled with the cultivar name; many are not and may be something less desirable. Be sure the leaf color is bright and appropriate for the type of plant, which shows that it has not suffered major setbacks in earlier life. Look under the leaves and along the stems to be sure insect pests are not clustered in hidden nooks.

Roots are harder to evaluate unless you remove the plant from the pot, a practice most stores frown upon. A plant will grow more vigorously if the roots are not overcrowded; ideally they will not be emerging through the pot holes and they certainly shouldn't be wound around and around inside the pot, a condition called root-bound. It's hard to get a plant to recover and grow when its roots are old and tangled.

Garden Centers

These full-service establishments are convenient because most carry supplies, fertilizers, tools, and may even offer landscape services. Better yet, they specialize in plants and related items so you know the management and buyers have thought about the kind of plants they carry and offer only cultivars that they feel are good for this area.

Many garden centers also offer sound advice on planting, pruning, or fertilizing to accompany your purchases. During the spring rush, however, or during off-hours the salespeople may not be trained horticulturists. If you need advice, look for the most reputable garden centers or call ahead and drop in at a time the manager or horticulturist is in and available.

Unlike nurseries and greenhouses (described in the next section), garden centers buy plant stock from wholesale growers, although a few growers also have garden centers at their production facility (see Specialty Growers in this chapter). When plants come from different growers, they may vary. For instance, I once was trying to find a couple of 'Blue Girl' holly bushes, the kind with blue-green leaves and red berries. At one garden center, I saw three very different looking shrubs all called 'Blue Girl'. I thought the labeling had to be wrong because one was quite short with few leaves but many berries, one was tall and lanky with leaves that were more green than blue, and another was shorter with darker leaves. Upon inquiring, I learned they all were 'Blue Girl' but from different growers. They were of different ages and had been fertilized in different ways; some were grown indoors and others had been kept outdoors; some were in containers and others were field dug and balled and burlapped. All of these factors changed their appearance and might affect their garden performance.

When you don't know who grew the plants offered at a garden center, try to find out if they come from local sources or are shipped in from the South or West Coast. Plants propagated from stock that grows naturally in warmer climates can be less hardy than the same species that grow in USDA zone 5 (see Climate in chapter 1) or cooler climates.

Despite the variations in origin of the plants, some garden centers will warranty their plants for a season or a year after purchase—if you keep the receipts. You can save yourself replacement costs on big purchases if you seek out these places.

Nurseries

Establishments that grow their own plants know how to make them grow well. And most growers are delighted to share what they know with you—as long as you don't ask during the busy spring season. Some will seek out the hardiest, or the showiest, or the newest cultivars for certain locations or certain purposes; they take pride in the plants they can present to you. Since anyone can legally grow and sell plants, however, you will have to choose nurserymen who know what they're doing. Some smaller or backyard nurseries may have limited plant selections and may not be able to advise you as well as an educated garden center salesperson. You also may have to travel elsewhere to buy tools or accessories.

Greenhouses

Indoor growing facilities are geared mostly to growing houseplants and holiday and annual flowers or to propagating hardy plants indoors. They are excellent places to find flowering plants or houseplants without working through middlemen. Some greenhouses, however, do not grow their own plants but merely keep them going after they are shipped from Florida or some other warm place. Also, some nurseries have greenhouses; some greenhouses have outdoor garden beds, too—so you occasionally can get the advantage of homegrown greenhouse items from vendors who do not necessarily call themselves greenhouses.

Mail Order

In addition to buying locally, you can order a great variety of plants—including many unusual ones—through the mail. There is nothing wrong with this, as long as you buy from a reputable company, but the plants usually are smaller and have to endure shipping (and you have to endure the shipping and handling costs). For more information on mail-order nurseries, see the huge catalog file at the Cleveland Botanical Garden library and *Gardening By Mail* (by Barbara J. Barton, 1994, Houghton-Mifflin, Boston, MA).

Specialty Growers

A number of local plant growers are situated in northeast Ohio, though you may have to travel some distance to reach them because few remain in Cleveland. Some growers will save you the drive and let you order what you want from a catalog and then ship the plants by mail.

But if you have the time, it's fun and informative to drop in and inspect, or be inspired by, the plants. Here is a list of my favorite local (or nearly local) nurseries where you can also find:

- Breeders, who produce their own cultivars
- Display gardens, with plants in garden settings so you can see what a small potted plant will mature to look like
- Specialists, who concentrate on certain kinds of plants

Also, some growers will give tours and some have plant lists available. Beyond the growers mentioned here, there are many general and wholesale growers. A few of these wholesalers may sell a small percentage of their plants retail, but they prefer not to deal with individual customers and are therefore not listed.

Art Form Nurseries
15656 Rte. 306, Bainbridge, 44023; 338-8102; display gardens

Art Form specializes in growing perennials outdoors in one-gallon containers that are larger than most mail-order plants. They carry a large but fluctuating stock, including many of the popular newer cultivars. You can get inspired as you drive in beside the long perennial border that extends down to an interesting rock garden at the sales yard.

Barco Sons, Inc./Liberty Gardens
935 Rte. 18, Medina, 44256; 722-3038

Liberty Gardens, a garden center, is the retail outlet for bedding plants produced by the wholesale growers Barco Sons, Inc., a family who have been in the greenhouse business for three generations.

Betzel Greenhouse
3225 North Ridge Rd., Lorain, 44055; 277-4470

This wholesale greenhouse grower dabbles in retail sales, devoting half of one greenhouse range to tempt us gardeners. They grow seasonal flowers, such as poinsettias and Easter plants, foliage plants for the house, and annual flowers for springtime. A second greenhouse range located in Avon is strictly wholesale.

Bittersweet Farm
1720 Rte. 60, Millersburg, 44654; 276-1977; closed January and February; tours and talks by advance reservation

This is a new site for Bittersweet Farm, which was formerly located in Medina County. Now, the farm is surrounded by nature on 190 acres of land. As in the past, they specialize in growing everlasting flowers and also have herbs and perennials plus gardening supplies and topiaries.

If you take the trip to Bittersweet Farm, be sure to save time to wander through the 20 display gardens, which feature a kitchen garden, butterfly garden, everlasting garden, scented geranium garden, bog area, and waterfall pond. Call to see if the Farmhouse (now under renovation) is open for lunch; it will feature meals served with homegrown herbs and flowers. Come in late September for the fall harvest open house with herbs, flowers, Indian corn, gourds, demonstrations, and refreshments.

Bluestone Perennials

7211 Middle Ridge Rd., Madison, 44057; (800) 852-5243 or 428-1327; freer catalog

This nursery specializes in selling young perennial plants produced in a high-tech greenhouse, and at low prices. They sell by catalog but have reasonable shipping fees, and the plants are guaranteed to arrive in good shape and grow, or they will be replaced. Such plants may not bloom on time the first year—and will be slower to claim their rightful position in the garden—but they catch up with larger plants fast.

Borlin Orchids

9885 Johnnycake Ridge Rd., Concord-Mentor, 44060; 354-8966 or (800) 284-9518; delivery available in Cuyahoga County

Borlin's is the only greenhouse in this area that specializes primarily in orchids, both potted plants and cut flowers. Although the owner, Lou Borlin, does not start his own orchids, he often keeps plants for years and has a lifetime of experience to share. Borlin has a display area that features all the orchids that are in bloom at any particular time and a separate garden center and florist shop. In November, he has a holiday Premier open house—call for details.

Burton Floral & Garden, Inc.

13020 Kinsman Rd., Burton; 834-4135

This greenhouse is a bit of a haul for some, but it's worthwhile if you are looking for new and different cultivars such as ivy geraniums, trailing dusty-miller, felicia daisies, as well as perennials, poinsettias, chrysanthemums, and Easter flowers.

Cattail Meadows

P.O. Box 39391; Solon, 44139; 248-4581; plant list available; open by appointment

If you are looking for native North American wildflowers, look no further. This small, family-run nursery stocks your favorites plus more unusual plants. Send a postcard with your name and address to get a free catalog.

Chagrin Valley Nurseries

1370 River Rd., Gates Mills, 44040; 423-3363; tours available for garden groups with advance reservation—contact Victor Mastrangelo

This is a favorite east-side nursery; it is inclined toward chemical-free growing and carries 400 different kinds of plants—about 50 percent homegrown. You can tag the plant you want in the field and have the nurserymen custom-dig it for you while you enjoy a view of the wooded Chagrin River Valley from the nursery.

Chestnut Herb Farm
35335 Chestnut Ridge Rd., North Ridgeville, 44039; 327-5857; open Tuesday through Saturday, 10 a.m. to 6 p.m. from May to October and at Christmastime; classes held other times; call for more information

This is a small nursery with developing display gardens. They carry about 250 types of herbs, 60 types of scented geraniums, and also miniature roses, heirloom flowers, and everlastings. The herb shop features over 200 kinds of bulk herbs plus herb wreaths and herb blends for teas, potpourri, and other uses. They also have fresh cut trees at Christmas.

Champion Garden Towne
3717 N. Ridge Rd., P.O. Box 21, Perry, 44081; 259-2811

Champion Garden Towne is the retail outlet for Lake County Nursery, Inc., one of the area's largest wholesale nurseries. You can find or order anything from the catalog at Champion Garden Towne, including new plants like the Meidiland roses and Lake County Nursery's own cultivars of crab apple 'Harvest Gold' and seedless *Acer* 'Celebration' (a hybrid between red and silver maple). Champion Garden Towne also sells annuals, perennials, ornamental grasses, fresh produce, cut flowers, gifts, gourmet foods, and statues.

Just down the road, you can enjoy Lake County Nursery's plants in the Mary Elizabeth Garden.

The Cleveland Botanical Garden
11030 East Blvd., Cleveland, 44106; 721-1600

The Cleveland Botanical Garden has local growers custom-grow a wide assortment of the best cultivars of flowers—annual and perennial—for their annual May plant sale. They also stock other garden items for this fun-filled sale.

Corso's Flower and Garden Center
3404 Milan Rd., Sandusky, 44870; (419) 626-0789

If you're visiting Cedar Point, drop in to find some unusual perennials at this good grower's facility. Corso's propagates over three hundred varieties of perennial plants, mostly sold in four-and-a-half inch or one-gallon pots (a few are bigger). Some of the best finds here are hard-to-get hardy ferns; hostas; tetraploid daylilies; bearded, Japanese, and Siberian iris; and monkshood. Check out the perennial border that edges the parking area for new ideas to use at home. Corso's also propagates bedding annuals and grows aquatic plants.

Crintonic Gardens
For a catalog, send $1 to County Line Rd., Gates Mills, 44040

This is the breeding facility of Kurt Hanson, who sells his daylily hybrids through a mail order catalog.

Daisy Hill Greenhouses, Inc.
34050 Hackney Rd., Moreland Hills, 44022; 247-4422

This was the estate greenhouse in the old Daisy Hill estate of the Van Sweringen brothers, who developed much of Shaker Heights. The greenhouse was originally used to grow fruits, vegetables, and flowers for Hotel Cleveland (now Stouffers Tower City Plaza Hotel). Now you will find the greenhouse hidden in a lovely and exclusive residential area. The staff continues to do an excellent job of growing herbs and perennials, topiary, indoor flowering and foliage plants, and annual flowers in hanging baskets. Once a month, you can come for a Saturday program combining art and flowers. Christmas and Valentine's Day open houses include tours and refreshments.

Dean's Greenhouse and Flower Shop
3984 Porter Rd., Westlake; 871-2050

This greenhouse is devoted primarily to growing geraniums and it is complemented by a garden center and florist shop, and a small herb garden that you can wander through. There are new gardens of everlasting flowers and classes on dried flower arranging.

Forgotten Thyme Gardens
6253 Norwalk Rd., Medina, 44256; 723-1948; open May and June, 10 a.m. to dark; July to September, 10 a.m. to 5 p.m.; display gardens

Beyond offering good plants such as herbs, unusual and hard-to-find perennials, cottage garden flowers, David Austin roses, old-fashioned roses, hostas, and peonies, this nursery is truly unique. It has a train garden, with model trains that pass through a garden setting all year round. The Little Blue House, an herb and everlasting shop, also sells these model trains. Joanne Myers, the co-owner, collects unusual seeds from overseas botanical gardens and international seed collectors, making her plant collection truly outstanding.

Garden Place
6776 Heisley Rd., Mentor, 44060; 255-3705; catalog available for a small fee

This mail-order retailer (which also grows wholesale for many national mail-order nurseries) offers over a thousand varieties of perennials, including many of the newest and best types. They are shipped bare root in spring, which makes them a bit trickier to plant than those grown in containers.

Garden Village

33911 Center Ridge Rd., North Ridgeville, 44039; 327-6007; open year round; call for hours

Go to Garden Village for bedding plants, poinsettias, and cut flowers grown in the huge R. B. Minute and Son wholesale greenhouses. Garden Village also has a full-service garden center.

Girard Nurseries

Box 428, 6839 North Ridge [East Rte. 20], Geneva; 44041; 466-2881; free catalog available; display gardens

The Girard family propagates and grows many types of trees and shrubs; they also breed evergreen and deciduous azaleas, rhododendrons, dwarf conifers, and evergreens, such as the patented juniper 'Saybrook Gold'. They also offer bonsai starts, small grafts of rare species like weeping Nootka cypress, silver noble fir, Gentsch white hemlock, and Japanese dragon-eye pine. You can order small items by mail or go there and pick up larger plants.

If you make the trip, visit the display gardens. You can walk grass paths between mixed island beds of perennials, shrubs, and trees (especially lovely and large specimens of rare nursery stock), and stop at a gazebo and sunken arbor. You are welcome to visit their 64 growing houses that are open to the public.

Gilson Gardens, Inc.

3059 U.S. Rte. 20, P.O. Box 277, Perry 44081; 259-4845; free catalog available

This nursery, with a large attached garden center and florist shop, specializes in ground covers—over a hundred different types, including European ginger, Bethleham sage (*Pulmonaria* species), hardy cactus (*Opuntia*), lamium, epimedium—and low-growing perennials such as 'Palace Purple' coralbells, coreopsis 'Moonbeam', and hosta. You can buy their homegrown plants at their garden center or order small plants from a mail-order catalog.

Granger Gardens

1060 Wilbur Rd., Medina, 44256; 239-2349; plant list available if you send a self-addressed, stamped envelope; tours by advance reservation

This greenhouse has been hybridizing standard and pinwheel African violets for decades and now sells their cultivars internationally. You will be surprised by the diversity available in African violets today, which you can see as you wander through the Granger greenhouse range. Owner Jim Eyerdom says the most sought-after varieties include powder-blue flowered 'Wonderland', which has been voted most popular several years running by the African Violet Society of America, and the Fantasy series, violets with different-colored speckles on their flowers.

Hansen's Greenhouse

8781 Columbia Rd., Olmsted Falls, 44138; 235-1961

Look in this three-quarter-acre greenhouse range for floral crops such as poinsettias for Christmas, flowers for Easter and Mother's Day, and for herbs or flats of annual flowers.

Hirt's Greenhouse and Flowers

13867 Pearl Rd., Strongsville, 44136; 238-8200

Hirt's is propagating many of its own plants to provide hard-to-find cultivars of vegetables, herbs, and perennials. You will find over 50 different kinds of herbs, including 15 cultivars of basil alone, 75 varieties of seed-grown tomatoes (many of which are heirlooms), and over 100 types of perennials. Beyond what is grown in-house, Hirt's offers a range of garden center goods.

Holden Arboretum

9500 Sperry Rd., Kirtland, 44060; 946-4400; call for sale dates

Holden Arboretum offers some homegrown wildflowers during their spring fund-raising sale, usually held in late April. In past years these native plants have been propagated from Ohio wildflowers; more recently, the arboretum has been buying some plants from out-of-state propagators, which natural-areas coordinator Brian Parsons says can be even better quality than Holden's own plants. You will also find cultivars of wildflowers such as *Tiarella* 'Oak Leaf', a distinctive form of foam-flower, and 'Fuller's White' woodland phlox. The Holden staff, however, will continue to stock some local plants, especially seedlings or divisions taken from their wildflower garden. They also have trees, shrubs, and perennials on hand.

Holly Ridge Nursery

5925 South Ridge Rd., Geneva, 44041; (800) HOLLY01 or 466-0134; open by appointment year-round

This young nursery has the largest selection of hollies in America on four cultivated acres of prime nursery land. Their hollies include many cultivars of species such as American holly, possum haw, and winterberry, and also azaleas, boxwood, and Caryopteris. You can buy small rooted cuttings or plants as large as three feet.

Kaiser's Greenhouse and Flower Shop

2157 Northview Rd., Rocky River, 44116; 333-5650

A one-acre greenhouse area of poinsettias, annuals and geraniums, plus a garden center and florist area.

Kridler Gardens

4809 Homeworth Rd., Homeworth, 44634; 525-7914; open mid-April through Christmas; display gardens; call for class information

Here's another source of great garden plants—perennials, bedding plants, bulbs, trees, shrubs, conifers, unusual hanging baskets, and bonsai—all grown in nine greenhouses. You'll enjoy the 15 acres of display gardens abounding with daffodils, crabapples, perennials, conifers, and hostas (over 600 varieties). Come when you can stay for a class—water gardening and bonsai classes are popular. Call for a class schedule.

Lafayette Greenhouse
6323 Lafayette Rd., Medina, 44256; 725-7442; open daily April 20 to July 20; Monday through Saturday, 9 a.m. to 8 p.m.; Sundays 1 to 5 p.m.; open by appointment in August and September

Here's a nursery every plant lover should visit at least once. It has over 1-1/2 acres of perennials, displayed in pots in beds that wind through woods and meadow areas in a parklike setting. There's 600 cultivars of perennials, 100 varieties of tomatoes, including heirlooms, also hundreds of kinds of heirloom and hard-to-find annuals, such as a variegated dwarf morning glory and giant marigolds, and natural dye plants.

If you are looking for a plant—and haven't been able to find it anywhere, ask here. They take pride in locating and growing lost plants. Check out the unique underground pit greenhouse, a unique concept in the nursery business, and ask about the L. L. Designs computer software for perennial garden design, which is available here.

Lake Erie Nature and Science Center
28728 Wolf Rd., Bay Village, 44140; 871-2900

This privately operated nature center, located in the Metroparks' Huntington Reservation, has a spring plant sale, the Spring Thing, which offers annual and perennial plants and wildflowers, some of which are local. Call in early spring for the sale date.

Landscape Creations Nursery
13040 Chillicothe Rd., Chesterland, 44026; 729-1374; open March 1 to Christmas but hours adjusted according to the weather; display gardens; tours by advance reservation

This nursery, which sells retail and wholesale, carries about 460 varieties of great landscape plants, including choice dwarf conifers, dwarf flowering shrubs, perennials, and special rock and water garden plants. Be sure to call ahead so you can tour the 2 1/2-acre display gardens, with a covered bridge, old-fashioned building replicas, and a stone gristmill and water wheel (which is currently under construction). The gardens are most lovely from April to June when the spring flowers are out and the five waterfalls are active.

Leeland Greenhouse
24377 Royalton Rd., P.O. Box 1057, Columbia Station, 44028; 236-5891

This four-and-a-half acre greenhouse range sells annual flowers, poinsettias, and Easter flowers wholesale and retail.

Lily of the Valley Herb Farm

3969 Fox Ave., Minerva (actually closer to Louisville), 44657; 862-3920; display gardens; tours by reservation

Lily of the Valley Herb Farm stocks 1,000 kinds of plants, including herbs, perennials, everlastings (flowers for drying), scented geraniums, ornamentals, grasses, roses, and woodland flowers—a great variety of each. For example, they have 20 different cultivars of basil and artemisia.

For prime plant selection, visit during greenhouse season from April to July. Or come September to March to take herb, craft, and garden workshops. Special open houses are scheduled in December for Christmas, in April for planting season, and in fall for dried flower season. In mid-June, you can find bargains during the plant clearance sale.

There is an herb shop with books, potpourri, botanicals, and dried flowers that's open year-round. They also have display gardens with beds of roses, herbs, perennials, everlasting flowers, and a country pond with water-garden plants. You can take a garden tour by advance reservation for a $15 fee.

Lowe's Greenhouses and Gift Shop

16540 Chillicothe Rd., Chagrin Falls, 44023; 543-5123; plant list available

Lowe's grows unusual perennials, such as purple-leaved black snakeroot (*Cimicifuga racemosa* 'Atropurpurea') and toad lilies, and unusual annuals like poor-man's orchid (*Schizanthus*) and several types of strawflowers. You are welcome to walk through the one-acre greenhouse, where you will see these and other flowers, including cut flowers such as lisianthus and blue Queen Anne's lace that are used in Lowe's florist shop. They also have a garden center area.

Maria Gardens Greenhouse

20465 Royalton Rd., Strongsville, 44136; 238-7637 and 10301 W. 130th St., North Royalton, 44133; 582-4750

Maria Gardens uses their own garden centers as retail outlets for the on-site greenhouses. The Strongsville location has a two-acre greenhouse; the North Royalton range has one-half acre under glass. They specialize in popular and traditional types of seasonal flowers, annuals, perennials, and foliage plants.

Moldovan's Gardens

38830 Detroit Rd., Avon, 44011; 934-4993; catalog available

Steve Moldovan, a former high-school horticulture teacher, his mother, Mary Moldovan, and Roy Woodhall sell their own hybrid daylilies and hosta, plus miniature daylilies from other breeders, through a mail-order catalog. Among their many hosta listings is Moldovan's 'Leprechaun' with yellow-chartreuse leaves that are only two by three inches long, and 'Monitor', with almost black-green leaves that grow nearly three feet high and six feet wide. Among daylilies, Moldovan lists new lines of tetraploid (having twice the normal number of chromosomes, which can make flowers bigger and bolder) daylilies with purple, lavender, and pink flowers. The new hybrids cost between $100 and $150; earlier introductions can be less expensive.

Musial's Greenhouse
5913 Avon-Belden Rd., North Ridgeville, 44039; 327-8855

This greenhouse entices retail and wholesale customers in spring with hundreds of impressive hanging baskets of unusual plants. They also carry more than twenty-five different kinds of geraniums, plus other bedding annuals, herbs, and perennials. You'll see these if you take the North Ridgeville Growing Arts Tour.

Naturally Country Dried Flower and Gift Shop
845 Lais Rd., Norwalk, 44857; (419) 668-4340; open daily 10 a.m. to 5 p.m.

If you like dried flowers, you'll want to check out this shop. Roses, peonies, carnations, and other flowers grow in about three acres of outdoor gardens, while indoors a freeze-drying machine is preserving their blossoms. Freeze-drying preserves the size, shape, and, in most cases, color of the flowers so they look almost fresh.

The shop sells bulk flowers for arranging and country gifts; they'll make custom designs for weddings. Come on the weekend before Easter for the spring open house, on the third weekend in August for the garden party, or on the weekend after Thanksgiving for the Christmas open house. Call ahead to confirm special events.

Old Brooklyn Greenhouse
4646 W. 11th St., Cleveland, 44109; 351-9338

Talk about convenience, right in the heart of the city you'll find an acre of greenhouse filled with holiday plants and bedding annuals. In December, you'll also find Christmas trees and Christmas cacti. They sell about half of their crops retail and the other half wholesale.

Perennials Preferred
8360 Rte. 6, Kirtland; 285-2720; call to make appointments during spring.

This small retail nursery specializes in unusual perennials, miniatures, and alpines, including rare species of phlox, veronica and gentians, as well as trough gardens (small rock-like tubs used to grow tiny ornamental plants). A small display garden winds around a nearby pond, showing off the interesting textures and flower forms of the tiny creepers, plus a few bigger perennials. There is a variegated *Phlox* x *procumbens*, a sought-after 'Ballerina' hardy geranium, a dwarf *Inula*, and many others. Even though the garden is small, you can see a lot if you look closely.

Piazza Floral Greenhouse

35638 Detroit Rd., Avon, 44011; 937-6888

Piazza's two-acre greenhouse, which sells wholesale and retail, specializes in growing geraniums but also carries a variety of annual flowers in flats as well as holiday floral crops. They have a large selection of blooming plants and cacti.

Quailcrest Farm

2810 Armstrong Rd., Wooster, 44691; 345-6722; plant list available; workshops and programs avail. for garden-oriented groups

This nursery/garden center (they don't grow everything themselves) is well known for its gift shops and display gardens, but also offers homegrown herbs, unusual indoor plants, and perennials. One growing field is devoted to perennials that you may select yourself and have the staff dig—an old-fashioned practice that is almost unheard of today. Other plants come in contemporary containers.

Quality Nursery

U.S. Rte. 6 and Clay St., Montville, 44064; 968-3990

This nursery, an eclectic one-man-operation, though out of the way for many, is worth visiting if you're looking for unusual plants. During daylily season in July, owner Hal Boesger, Jr., holds a festival featuring hybrid daylilies of his own breeding and about three thousand other varieties. One especially notable cultivar is Boesger's 'Around in Black', a lemon-colored dark-throated rebloomer developed from 'Stella d'Oro'. Boesger also collects a large assortment of variegated plants and unusual species, such as eight-foot-tall late-flowering daylilies and bush clover (*Lespedeza thunbergii* 'Gibralter'), a perennial herb that displays a shrubby wall of flowers in mid-October.

Richardson's Farm Market and Greenhouse

369 Tuxedo Ave., Brooklyn Hts., 44131; 661-7888

A garden center and farm market back up to greenhouses that hold unusual indoor plants such as night-blooming cereus cactus, Cape primrose (*Streptocarpus* species), variegated hibiscus, and angel-wing begonias, succulents such as weeping notonia, and bedding annuals, including geraniums and impatiens. Chickens and cats roam the range, making a visit fun for kids.

Rock Bottom Farms

7767 Parkman-Mesopotamia Rd., Middlefield, 44062; 693-4126; catalog: $2.50; open Monday through Saturday, 10 a.m. to 5 p.m., from April 15 to September 15; other times by appointment

Here's an easy way to get some new daylilies. Rock Bottom Farms offers about 500 daylily cultivars, which are nicely described in their catalog and will be shipped mail order. Or you can go out and visit the farm (in the heart of Amish country), see the daylilies, and pick your own strawberries and blueberries in season. Stop in at the greenhouse to see owner Jonathan Ford's Cape primroses. He has developed nearly 70 new hybrids, including some spectacular types with doubled flowers and unusual colors.

Rosewood Farm
13768 Lisbon St. SE, Paris, 44669; 862-3120; open from the last Monday in April until the Saturday before July 4; by appointment July to October; display garden

If you've been hunting for old-fashioned roses and cottage garden perennial varieties or flowering vines, check out this resource. You can get ideas for how to use these plants by checking out the mixed beds located around the nursery.

Rosby Brothers Greenview Greenhouse
42 East Schaaf Rd., Cleveland, 44131; 351-0850; tours available

This old Schaaf Road greenhouse grows annuals, perennials, and poinsettias as well as pick-your-own strawberries and red raspberries. There is a garden center and compost facility that you can tour with advance reservations.

Shaker Lakes Regional Nature Center
2600 South Park Blvd., Shaker Hts., 44120; 321-5935

This nature center holds a spring plant sale, sponsored by the Friends of the Shaker Lakes Nature Center, that features annual flowers, vegetable plants, and homegrown perennial flower divisions, most of which can be ordered in advance of the sale. Contact the Center for an advance order form in early spring.

Silver Creek Farm
7097 Allyn Rd., P.O. Box 254, Hiram, 44234; 562-4381, or 569-3487; group tours, talks, slide shows available with advance reservations

This is an organic market garden where you can buy produce that has never been touched by garden chemicals.

Sunnybrook Farms and Homestead Division
9448 Mayfield Rd., Chesterland, 44026; 729-7232; catalog avail.

This is a large garden center area with a greenhouse range devoted to growing about two hundred types of herbs, including many kinds of scented geraniums and mints, plus dozens of different ivies and hundreds of hosta. It's fun to combine browsing in the greenhouses and garden center with a stroll in the hosta garden.

Sweet Bay Gardens
9801 Stafford Rd., Auburn, 44023; 543-9396

This small nursery is one of the few commercial enterprises to grow native plants for woodlands, wetlands, bog, and meadow gardens. They also have a fair number of exotic species that will do well in these habitats, too. Visits to the nursery are by appointment only.

Thibo Greenhouses
7691 Avon-Belden Rd., North Ridgeville, 44039; 327-8151

This 3.5-acre greenhouse sells primarily wholesale but will accept retail customers in April and May. It specializes in bedding plants, including 10 kinds of geraniums, and in hanging baskets.

Warren Road Nursery
3206 Warren Rd., Cleveland, 44111; 251-2221

You may not realize how many different kinds of daylilies, hostas, and ornamental grasses are available today until you see them at Warren Road Nursery. Come in late June to see the daylilies bloom. Check out the big-big specimen plants that grow in extra large containers to give you a feel for how mature plants will look.

The nursery brings in new hybrid daylilies from top national breeders, including Steve Moldovan from Avon. They have collected close to 500 named cultivars, many of which are spectacular new cultivars that will rebloom, or which have ruffled petals or unique colors. But they also have thousands of mixed tetraploid daylilies sold inexpensively in collections for naturalizing or large gardens.

Hosta enthusiasts can find about 70 named cultivars of hosta, as well as other great perennials for shade. If you're looking for ornamental grasses, you will find close to 40 cultivars. They also have over 50 types of unusual annual flowers for cutting and drying.

In addition to these specialties, Warren Road Nursery carries a broad selection of other perennial flowers and has a full service garden center. They have display gardens that show how to use daylilies, hostas, and other plants in rock gardens and sun or shade. They keep detailed cultural information sheets on most cultivars in stock; be sure to ask for them.

William Tricker, Inc.—Water Garden
7125 Tanglewood Dr., Independence; 524-3491

If you want to see something different, visit this greenhouse of water plants and animals, a well-kept secret in Cleveland. Although Tricker's was founded in 1895, the company has a low profile because they don't advertise locally. Instead, they sell most of their stock by mail. But it's lots of fun to browse through the beds of water lilies that feature some of Tricker's own hybrids, such as pink-flowered 'Independence', rose-flowered 'Cleveland', and deep purple-flowered 'Blue Bird'.

Vanderbrook, Don
Newbury; 371-0164

Don Vanderbrook holds a spring plant sale of unusual flowers, many of which he grows in his own garden. The sale happens during one weekend in May. Call the office number listed here to find out the date and directions to his garden-plant sale.

Wade and Gatton Nurseries
1288 Gatton Rock Rd., Bellville, 44813; (419) 883-3191; perennials sold retail—other nursery stock is wholesale only; display garden

This nursery is the farthest from Cleveland in this listing, but if you like hosta and other unusual perennials it is worth the drive. You can take I-71 south to Route 13 and follow charming country roads over rolling hills to this nursery, said to have the world's largest collection of hosta. Thousands of hosta plants are spread across several acres of gardens, nestled beneath a high canopy of oaks and pines. Grass paths and a trickling stream wind between the beds, which often are devoted to hosta cultivars developed by a single breeder. The soil in the beds is astonishing—rich in peat and perlite, which may account for the lush way the hosta grow.

In a sunnier area on a nearby hill, you also can see extensive collections of daylilies and an impressive bed of ornamental grasses. These and the hosta are interplanted with other perennial flowers, including such rare plants as Scotch thistle, variegated rhubarb, variegated phlox, and iris.

The perennials you can buy are divided out of these gardens or grown in one gallon or larger containers. Write to ask the nursery about the availability of cultivars you are looking for, and they will write back with the price and how they can ship it. Tell them if you are a member of a garden club or plant society to receive a small discount.

Wildwood Gardens
14488 Rock Creek Rd., Chardon, 44024; 286-3714; plant list available; will ship UPS

In the midst of rural Geauga County lies one of the area's few bonsai nurseries and display gardens. They also grow alpine and rare plants. The nursery was begun over thirty years ago to finance the plant collection of Anthony Mihalic, who is still active in the business. The nursery is operated by his son, Frank, who travels to Asia to import bonsai every year. Mihalic also propagates and trains his own bonsai plants and teaches others to do the same. Some of the most interesting older bonsai plants and some intriguing alpines are displayed around a large tufa-rock garden behind the bonsai studio. For more information on how to take care of bonsai plants, look for Frank Mihalic's book, *The Art of Bonsai*, which is sold through the nursery. Check out the classes on bonsai, including the all-day seminars in spring and fall.

Willotts, Dorothy and Tony

26231 Shaker Blvd., Beachwood, 44122; 831-8662; catalog sales only; can give slide lectures on irises

·These veteran breeders of irises specialize in dwarf types that bloom earlier than most bearded irises. They sell only by mail. Their list includes over a hundred of their own introductions. Some familiar sounding dwarfs include raspberry, amber and orange-flowered 'Falconskeape', light to full violet-blue flowered 'Geauga Lake', and yellow and brown striped 'Landerwood'. In the taller types, you can find cream, gold, and orange-yellow flowered 'Cedar Point' and ruffled cream, gold and brown flowered 'Pepper Pike'. The irises are shipped bare root in late summer.

Wood and Company, Inc.

2267 Lee Rd., Cleveland Hts., 44118; 321-7557

This garden center may be the only one in the area that imports its own flowering bulbs. The Brumbaugh family, owners, deal with some of the smaller bulb growers in Holland, Israel, and other bulb-growing areas and buys only their best. They can tell you nearly anything you want to know about bulbs and will special order.

To find more local retail growers or generalists, look in area Yellow Pages under Nurseries or Greenhouses.

Other Horticultural Suppliers

Specialists

In addition to fields directly linked to horticulture or landscaping, you can find goods for gardens at places you might not expect. For:

• Outdoor sculpture, Japanese lanterns, or weather vanes: look at art galleries and studios or museum shops
• Terra-cotta pots and planters: consult pottery shops
• Benches or tables: look at furniture and patio stores
• Fountains: try plumbing dealers
• Gazebos and garden houses: check at lumber stores
• Gates or plant stands: look for wrought-iron blacksmiths

Mail-Order

If you can't find what you want locally, check the many speciality catalogs.

Catalog shopping—for plants, gifts, clothes, or toys—can make our lives so much easier; you don't have to go out and hunt around for what you need. The biggest problem with catalog shopping is that you can't always be sure you'll like what you get when it finally comes in the mail.

But when it comes to buying plants, you can't go wrong by browsing through a few nursery catalogs. It's a great way to start planning and deciding which plants would be perfect for your yard. You can order from large catalogs with color pictures or more simple catalogs with plant names alone or with descriptions. Some may have extensive collections including rare and unusual plants that may be hard to find locally. Others offer fairly ordinary plants.

Order only from catalogs that are put out by reputable companies. You want established businesses that will send you the right plants and stand behind their merchandise if there is a problem with it. Here are some of my favorite catalogs:

Nursery Catalogs

White Flower Farm: (203) 496-9600
Wayside Gardens: (800) 845-1124
Logee's Greenhouses: (203) 774-8038
Andre Viette Farm and Nursery: (703) 943-2315
Native Gardens: (615) 856-0220

Seed Catalogs

Thompson and Morgan: (908) 363-2225
Garden City Seeds: (406) 961-4837
Johnny's Selected Seeds: (207) 437-4301
Shepherd's Garden Seeds: (203) 482-3638; 6116 Highway 9, Felton, CA 95081
W. Atlee Burpee and Co.: Warminster, PA 18974
The Cook's Garden: P.O. Box 535, Londonderry, VT 05148; small fee for catalog
Park Seed Company: Cokesbury Road, Greenwood, SC 29647-0001
Pinetree Garden Seeds: Box 300, New Gloucester, ME 04260

Catalog Shopping Tips

Read the descriptions—the color, height, season of bloom, and best growing conditions. Note the plants that interest you most, then compare the descriptions with a couple other catalogs and a good gardening book. You may find that some catalogs are more honest or more thorough in how they depict the plants they sell.

When you think you're ready to order, take a minute to consider the details and decide if it might be better to buy that plant locally.

You'll have to pay a handling and shipping charge, which could be anywhere from $2.50 to over $15, depending on the company and the amount of plants you are ordering.

And you may find that although you're paying premium prices, you receive lightweight plants in small pots or dormant bare-root plants which are stripped of soil.

Because someone has to pay for transportation, it's hard to get large, mature plants through catalogs. If you want a tree or shrub that has some substance to it or a big hosta or astilbe that will be instantly magnificent, you'll have to shop locally. But if you order quick-growing perennials or annuals or have the patience to wait a year or two for results, mail order plants may be fine.

Sometimes, when you open a box of mail order plants, they'll look a bit scrunched from the trip to your house. But if you take them out right away and give them some light and water, if they need it, they should perk up. If any die right away, call the mail order company and ask for a replacement.

If you receive bare-root plants, which is common when ordering perennials, strawberries, and asparagus, plant them right away. If you can't put them in the ground immediately, put the roots in a trench in the ground and cover them with soil.

For more catalogs, see the book *Gardening By Mail* (by Barbara J. Barton, 1994, Houghton-Mifflin, Boston, MA) or check the catalog files in the library at The Cleveland Botanical Garden.

You can start impatiens and hundreds of other flowers from seed.
(Photo courtesy of the National Garden Bureau.)

CHAPTER 7

Horticultural Organizations

There are hundreds of local garden clubs, plant societies, and horticultural institutions that welcome new members. Gardeners join them for a variety of reasons: to make new friends who share common interests, to learn from veteran members or outside speakers, or to swap experiences—a therapeutic way to learn and grow.

There is great diversity in club organization and purpose. Some, like the Western Reserve Herb Society, are working clubs dedicated to learning, maintaining a display garden, and fund-raising throughout the year. Others mix service projects with planting talk, crafts, and events such as home tours and flower-arranging or fashion shows. Some are devoted to studying a certain kind or group of plants in depth; others touch on a wide range of related topics. Some include members from all across greater Cleveland; others are concentrated in a certain region. Some include a variety of different kinds of people; others cater to men or women, or younger or older members.

To give an idea of what kinds of organizations are out there, here is a lengthy list of those known to welcome new members. Not included are groups that get new members by invitation only or clubs that grow only by bringing in friends and acquaintances of existing members.

In nearly every case, visitors are welcome to attend club meetings and shows to meet the group and see how they operate before joining. You may not be able to attend special events or parties, however, until joining. Fees for plant society memberships tend to be very reasonable; they pay for the club operations and often a newsletter. As might be expected, horticultural institutions charge considerably more because they have to pay for their facilities and staff.

General Horticultural Organizations

Cleveland Waterfront Coalition

401 Euclid Ave., The Arcade, Room 462, Cleveland, 44114; membership: $10 student/ senior, $20 individual, $50 organization, $100 corporation; newsletter; 771-2666

Although not strictly a horticultural organization, the Waterfront Coalition has attracted members from among local gardeners. They are working to give the public access to the ten miles of Lake Erie shoreline and create a bike path between Euclid Beach and Edgewater Park. There are about fifteen hundred members involved in fund-raising and activist aspects of this group.

Cleveland Zoological Society

P.O. Box 609281, Cleveland, 44109; annual membership fee: $30 individual, $40 family, $25 senior couple, $22 senior single, $55 contributing, $100 sustaining, & up; quarterly Zoo News; contact Carol Olson, 661-6500

Membership in the Cleveland Zoological Society, a fund-raising and support group for the public zoo, brings discounted rates for rain forest admittance and free zoo admittance, invitations to special zoo parties, discounts at zoo shops and programs, and free admission to 100 other zoos nationwide. The quarterly *Zoo News* includes insights into how the zoo works, what's new, and educational articles on the zoo exhibits—stressing animals of course.

Clean-Land, Ohio

1836 Euclid Ave., Suite 800, 44115; annual membership fee: $30 individual, $75 treemendous member, $150 branch benefactor, and on up; contact 696-2122

Clean-Land, Ohio, a nonprofit agency, is dedicated to improving the physical environment of the Cleveland area and teaching people to become environmentally responsible. They have developed City Side Gardens on vacant city lots and planted urban mini parks called Clean-Land Commons. They are currently undertaking to reforest the city—they'll be planting 10,000 new trees by 1996 with the Trees for Tomorrow program.

In addition to greening up Cleveland, they are cleaning it up. Crews in CleanScape's litter-pickup program gathered 25,000 bags of garbage in 1994. To reduce overflowing garbage problems, Clean-Land devised Wise Buys, a program that teaches consumers how to reduce household waste. Clean-Land, Ohio also provides environmental education for kindergarten to 12th graders—they reached over 5,000 students in 1994. There's also a new state-wide forestry educational program.

Cleveland Botanical Garden

11030 East Blvd., Cleveland, 44106; 721-1600; annual membership fee: $30 individual, $40 family, other levels available; monthly *Bulletin*; 721-1600

You can view the gardens, attend the shows, and look at the library books without joining the Botanical Garden, but by joining you help finance all the good things that go on there. You also can borrow library books, get discounts at the Trellis Shop, receive the information-packed Bulletin, and invitations to previews, art shows, lectures, and other events. Members get a discount on classes and can can get gardening advice.

Community Gardening

People without space for a garden at their home, office, or apartment can lease a plot at a community garden. These occupy otherwise vacant land throughout much of greater Cleveland and give garden access—and a chance to socialize with other gardeners—to anyone who is interested.

Most of the community gardens are vacant-lot-sized and contain two to four gardens. Some of the larger ones are in Cleveland Heights, in Cleveland at 104th and Sandusky, and in Old Brooklyn at Ben Franklin Elementary School. The size and cost of community garden plots vary, said Dennis Rinehart of the Cooperative Extension Service, but the average cost is between $5 and $25.

Although community gardeners may form their own garden clubs, there is no community gardeners' society. Instead, they are supported by government organizations such as Seed to Shelf and the Summer Sprout Program (both included in this listing).

Friends of the Greenhouse, Inc.

Don Slogar, Rockefeller Park Greenhouse, 750 E. 88th St., Cleveland, 44108; 664-3103; meets the 2nd Wednesday of each month, 10 a.m. at the Greenhouse; annual membership fee: $20 student/senior, $25 individual, $30 couple, $40 family

This fundraising group organizes horticultural classes and garden parties that members can attend at discounted rates. There are at least three major events and seminars each year. The biggest project the Friends are tackling is raising enough money to expand the greenhouse lobby and make other renovations.

Gardenview Horticultural Park

16711 Pearl Road, Rte. 42, Strongsville, 44136; 238-6653; annual membership fee: $25 to $49 for single or family, other levels available; 238-6653

This nonprofit organization supports the extensive gardens and the horticultural library at Gardenview. Members may visit at any time free of charge and may use the library with advance reservations. Sustaining members may bring 10 free guest visitors.

Hiram Community Gardens

Box 402, Hiram, 44234-0402; annual membership fee: $15; spring newsletter; no phone

This organization started in 1978 as a way to raise funds to maintain the network of public gardens in Hiram. The members are mostly residents of Hiram but others are welcome to donate and join. The funds allow the organization to hire college students who are trained by Jim and Jamie Barrow. "It's become a community effort rather than public or private," Barrow explained. "It's especially unique in such a tiny village, but people could easily see the improved quality of the environment and recognize its value."

Holden Arboretum

9500 Sperry Rd., Kirtland, 44094; 946-4400; annual membership fee: $40 family, $25 seniors, $75 contributing, $100 rare-plant testing program; $150 sustaining, and up; Arboretum Leaves quarterly newsletter; 946-4400

Membership in this nonprofit arboretum includes use of the grounds free (including fishing and cross-country skiing), discounted rates for programs, and members-only parties. It also includes *Arboretum Leaves*—which always brings news of developments in the gardens and woodlands around Kirtland—a 10 percent discount at the gift shop, and a free guest pass.

Summer Sprout Program, Cleveland Dept. of Redevelopment

Contact Jack Krumhansel, assistant commissioner, 664-2045

This city-sponsored institution, funded by Community Development Block Grants, supplies soil amendments, seeds, bedding plants, and soil tilling for people who want to garden on vacant land in the city of Cleveland. They also can arrange reduced price permits for gardeners who want to irrigate from nearby fire hydrants. All sites have a volunteer garden coordinator who serves as contact between the city and the garden.

Plant Societies

Camera Guild of Cleveland

Usually meets weekly, 8 p.m. Thursdays at The Cleveland Botanical Garden, except in summer when meetings are twice a month; annual membership fees: $25; monthly newsletter; contact Robert Schroeder, 449-1331

Many gardeners like to capture what they have grown in photographs. Since good photography takes very different skills from growing roses or herbs, you may find you need to turn to more experienced photographers, like members of the Camera Guild, for help. There are approximately thirty members of this fifty-year-old group who meet regularly to critique photos and slides of nature and travel.

They hold monthly competitions, field trips, instruction sessions, and sometimes sponsor group photography exhibits at places like the Cleveland Botanical Garden.

Chagrin Valley Herb Society
Meets at 1 p.m. on the 3rd Thursday of most months at Bainbridge Library, Geauga County; annual membership fee: $10; contact Kathy Catani, 338-3986

This group was organized to develop a public herb garden in eastern Geauga County. Presently, there are about forty members who tend the garden and have monthly programs and workshops—including one workshop for the public. They also hold a plant sale on the Saturday before Mother's Day.

Cleveland Bonsai Club
Meets at The Cleveland Botanical Garden at 7 p.m. on the 4th Wednesday of most months; annual membership fee: $15; monthly newsletter; contact the Cleveland Botanical Garden, 721-1600

This club is restricted to 100 members who are practicing the Oriental art of bonsai (growing trees in shallow containers). "In the creation of bonsai, there are aesthetic principles which must be taken into consideration. Tree and container must be compatible as to size and shape and color; the tree itself must adhere to certain rules of proportion; it should appear as it does in nature but in miniature. By careful pruning and trimming, the tree is shaped to show its own essential beauty, to bring into harmony its trunk, branches and foliage," Club literature explains.

The Cleveland Bonsai Club was founded in 1956 by the late Viola Briner, librarian at the Cleveland Botanical Garden, and Arthur Leudy, Cleveland nurseryman. Meetings are devoted to advice on potting, pruning, and general care plus practice sessions and demonstrations by recognized authorities. The club holds the Great Lakes Bonsai Show in June at the Cleveland Botanical Garden.

Cleveland Cultural Garden Federation
Meets usually on the 2nd Tuesday of the month, 6 months a year, at 2 p.m. at Cleveland City Hall mayor's office or dining room; no annual membership fee; contact Richard Konisiewicz, 341-3553

The Cleveland Cultural Gardens Federation governs the Cultural Gardens. An associate member of University Circle Incorporated, the federation includes about twenty delegates and their substitutes. But D'Emilia says anyone interested in the Cultural Gardens is welcome to attend the meetings and contribute to their efforts to raise money, maintain the gardens, and preserve the cultural heritage that the gardens reflect. The federation also works with newly organized ethnic groups who want to apply to put in their own cultural gardens.

Cleveland Ikenobo Society

Lessons twice a month on Saturday mornings from March to November in Parma; annual membership fee: $18; each lesson is $3 plus materials; contact Dorothy Kansaki, 888-3482

This 30-member, ten-year-old chapter of the oldest school of Ikebana (Japanese flower arranging) is devoted to teaching the Ikenobo methods. The society also hosts workshops with internationally known instructors and holds public displays twice a year. The school's forty-fifth headmaster, Senei Ikenobo, who is headquartered in Kyoto, Japan, explains the school's background in a society brochure: "We try to arrange so there is harmony between the arranger and the plants—so the arrangement is in harmony with the environment."

Cleveland Rose Society

Meets on the 2nd Wednesday of most months, 7:30 p.m. at The Cleveland Botanical Garden; annual membership fees: $10 per household; monthly newsletter The Thorn; [The Rose, a monthly magazine of the American Rose Society, is available with ARS membership]; contact Jim Wickert, 696-5729

This 150-member society was founded in 1932; members have been planting roses and consulting ever since. The society brings in well-known speakers and has two annual rose shows. They host garden tours, lectures, and guest speakers of all kinds related to rose growing; they also demonstrate rose growing and pruning at the Cleveland Botanical Garden's Rose Garden (see Gardens Open to the Public in chapter 9). Members who belong to the American Rose Society and like to share information can earn the rank of ARS consulting rosarians; those who show successfully can be trained as ARS judges.

Other rose societies have similar programs but concentrate their activities in different parts of Cleveland and the surrounding areas. They include:

- Akron Rose Society; contact Bob Choate, 235-2751
- Euclid Rose Society; contact Cal Schroeck, 585-0506
- Forest City Rose Society (a predominately west-side group); contact Bob Choate, 235-2751
- Northeast Ohio Rose Society (serves the Lake County Area); contact Ray Wickert, 428-2929
- Parma Rose Society (mostly south side); contact Helen Purcell, 251-3057

Cultivating Our Community

Ohio State University Extension Program; 3200 W. 65th St., 44102; newsletter:r $6; contact Dennis Rinehart, 631-5588

Since 1978, this program (formerly called Seed to Shelf) has helped Cuyahoga County residents organize and maintain community vegetable gardens. The staff provides information on planting, cultivating, and harvesting vegetables. They also train volunteer leaders to coordinate garden groups. In addition, the program uses Master Gardeners to plant and maintain demonstration gardens of perennials, herbs, and vegetables at the Extension Service office and some community sites.

Dahlia Society of Ohio

Meets on the 1st Friday of most months, 7:30 p.m. at the Cleveland Botanical Garden; annual fee: $7; Dahlia Digest monthly newsletter; contact Tim Slade, 232-6714

The Dahlia Society is composed of people devoted to growing this wonderfully diverse class of native American tubers—with flowers ranging in size from half dollars to dinner plates in every color but blue. Just as there are a lot of dahlias available, there are a lot of people who grow them locally. Overall, the society has 200 members, making it larger than any other dahlia society in the Midwest (partly because it attracts dahlia enthusiast members from neighboring cities and states).

"People often join societies outside of their own region to get the newsletters and show announcements," said Monica Rini, 1992 president. "They also join ours because we give outstanding prizes at our shows."

The Dahlia Society holds a large dahlia show at a shopping mall in late summer and a second smaller show at the Cleveland Botanical Garden on the first weekend in October. Many members also exhibit their flowers at the Cuyahoga and Geauga County fairs. Besides showing what they grow, the society holds auctions of dahlia tubers, hosts a July picnic and an August garden tour, operates a lending library of dahlia videos and books, and sells dahlias at the Cleveland Botanical Garden's spring plant sale. Dahlia Society members are available to lecture to other groups.

Dahlias are available in an incredible range of colors.

Greater Cleveland Orchid Society

Meets one evening a month, usually at a restaurant; annual membership fee: $10 single, $12.50 family; monthly newsletter; contact Cleveland Botanical Garden, 721-1600

The Greater Cleveland Orchid Society, a group that's about fifty years old and 170 members strong, is concentrated on the east side of town. Their meetings usually include a well-known speaker—some nationally and internationally prominent—who talks about a certain kind of orchid and who often sells plants. They sometimes bring in top speakers for combined meetings with other local orchid groups. In August, the meetings adjourn for a summer picnic and plant auction. In spring, the club puts on a plant show at the Cleveland Botanical Garden. Members can borrow from the club's small library of orchid books and videos.

Growing Together Organically (GTO)

Meets the 3rd Wednesday of the month at varying locations; no annual membership fee; contact Alanna Meyers, 631-3233, or Don Bryant, 237-0673

This five-year-old group is a project of Northeast Ohio Greens, dedicated to developing healthy environments and growing organic food in urban areas. They spend meetings discussing projects, exchanging organic gardening tips, and eating dishes made with organic foods. With grants from the Federal EPA, GTO helps groups and organizations set up organic gardens. Volunteers provide information on organic gardening techniques, as well as small garden equipment and volunteer assistance. You can see the results of their efforts in gardens at Zelma George Women's Shelter, St. Herman's Monastery, and several other schools and institutions. Their volunteers also helped Tree Source, an Ohio-based group that planted over 1,700,000 tree seedlings last year.

The Herb Guild

Meets 2nd Wednesday of most months at Porter Library in Westlake; workshops begin at 10 a.m.; annual membership fee :$25; newsletter; contact Sandra Zanders, 777-9562

This guild, which is almost 30 years old, does all kinds of great things with herbs. They maintain the herb garden at Rosehill Museum at Cahoon Park and hold a fundraising plant and tussie-mussie sale, usually in June. An August luncheon boutique helps finance scholarships given to college students who want to study horticulture or a related field. Membership is limited to 60; a waiting list is available.

Ikebana International, Cleveland Chapter 20

Meets on the 1st Wednesday of several months, during the daytime; annual membership fees: about $50; for information, contact the Cleveland Botanical Garden, 721-1600

Ikebana International, headquartered in Tokyo, Japan, is a worldwide group that includes the many schools of Japanese flower arranging. The group's goal is to encourage friendship through the study of flower arranging and other cultural arts of Japan. The Cleveland Chapter, founded in 1959, includes primarily the Ohara, Sogetsu, and Ikenobo styles of arranging, each of which has a structured curriculum and ranks of achievement. The group has workshops from different Ikebana schools, annual public demonstrations, and internationally known speakers.

Ikebana International members also created, financed, and continue to support the Japanese Garden at the Cleveland Botanical Garden; they also organize periodic festivals.

Ichiyo School of Ikebana

Monthly group lessons on the 2nd Monday of each month at Community Center of Highland Heights; fees vary; contact Louise Taylor, master, 442-6769

Students of the Ichiyo School of Ikebana use imagination to develop creative designs that reflect the nature of the designer, working through a simplified, but still structured, lesson program. Ichiyo is the only school of Ikebana to offer a correspondence course.

Indoor Gardening Society of America, Cleveland Chapter

Meets on the 4th Monday of most months, 7:30 p.m. at the Cleveland Botanical Garden; annual fee: $5; monthly newsletter; contact Tom Sampliner, 321-3702

The 110-member Indoor Gardening Society is devoted to exchanging ideas, methods, and experiences related to growing plants indoors. Meetings include local speakers, book reviews, demonstrations, and occasional nationally known experts for a special Sunday lecture or field trip. In October and March, the society holds Sunday plant sales.

"It's a great group—we all get a big kick out of putting on the two plant sales. Members donate all the plants, and we all work together for two days. Beyond that, the holiday party is a knock-out. We fill up the Duncan Room with about sixty festive people," said Jack Keller, a 10-year member who has five floral carts full of plants at his home.

The society also encourages indoor gardening by leasing floral light carts (at no charge) to nonprofit groups and giving scholarship grants to students of indoor gardening or making donations to the Cuyahoga Soil and Water Conservation District's forestry camp program.

Midwest Cactus and Succulent Society

Meets at members' homes on the 3rd Sunday of each month; annual membership fees: $5; contact Penny Chaikin, 381-2515

This 60-year-old society of approximately thirty members sponsors potluck dinners and programs about cacti and succulents, shares slides, and holds a show and sale (usually on the first Sunday of March at the Cleveland Botanical Garden). Several members have greenhouses but most grow cacti and succulents on windowsills or in light gardens.

The Midwest society is affiliated with the Cactus and Succulent Society of America, which is devoted to studying and appreciating this unusual group of plants. Membership in the national group ($35) gives access to the seeds of rare plants, field trips to exotic places, show-judge training, and a subscription to the bimonthly *Cactus and Succulent Society Journal*, a scholarly research and reference resource.

"Cactus and succulent societies are especially big in Germany, Britain, and many of the Slavic countries," said Penny Chaikin, local secretary/treasurer and national liaison. "You really don't know how many people are involved in these areas worldwide until you join a club. Last year, the national conference brought succulent growers from Europe, Japan, and Madagascar. It's just fantastic," Chaikin said.

Native Plant Society of Northeastern Ohio
Meets on varying weekends and evenings; annual membership fee: $10 active, $15 family, lifetime memberships available; On the Fringe quarterly magazine; contact Tom Sampliner, 321-3702

This plant society was formed by a handful of people who attended a 1982 wildflower symposium held at the Holden Arboretum. The group now has about a hundred members. Its name reflects this society's broad range of interests, which include native trees, grasses, flowers, ferns and fern allies, mosses and liverworts, fungi, lichens, and algae. (Native plants are separated from more recent introductions by the fact that they were growing in Ohio at the time of European settlement.)

The group may canoe an isolated lake identifying plants, learn to propagate wildflowers and ferns or to identify plants in winter, and they sometimes hear local and national speakers. The monthly meeting dates vary: many are weekend field trips that range across northeast Ohio; some are lectures on weekday evenings. The group also plants wildflower gardens at the Cuyahoga County Library in Chagrin Falls and assists with the wildflower garden at the Cleveland Botanical Garden.

"Our members include professional biologists and interested lay people—anyone who wants to see rare plants or wildflower gardens. I notice on our field trips that some of us are more partial to flowering plants, like carnivorous pitcher plants, wild orchids and gentians, but as long as we find something that is rare and endangered—flowering or not—it's pretty exciting," said Tom Sampliner, president.

Like the interesting programs, their *On the Fringe* newsletter includes club notices and informative articles, like what you might find in a winter walk through a bog or how society members plant and maintain Metropark's wildflower gardens.

Northeast Ohio Iris Society
Meets 6 times a year, usually the 2nd Friday of the month, at Busch Funeral Home Community Room in Parma; annual membership fee: $3; yearly calendar of events; contact: Douglas Fuhrmeyer, 467-4788

This society was founded in the 1950s and includes about 30 active iris enthusiasts. Meetings feature guest speakers and programs by members. Sometimes the society joins with other iris society chapters for special events or conventions. They hold an iris show at the Cleveland Botanical Garden around the end of May. The annual picnic is in July and a fundraising iris sale is held in August in Independence.

Northern Ohio Perennial Society

Meets 4 times a year on the last Monday of the month, 7:30 p.m. at The Cleveland Botanical Garden; annual membership fees: $10 for Botanical Garden members, $12 for non-members; monthly newsletter in season; contact Eva Sands, 371-3363, or Judith Siegel, president, 831-4320

The Northern Ohio Perennial Society began more than a decade ago when founder Eva Sands organized a perennial swapping group. It has grown into an active society of 240 members that sponsors lectures, information sharing, and garden tours. The society designs and maintains two perennial beds at the Cleveland Botanical Garden.

"We love perennials because with them we know the joy of witnessing the rebirth of nature year after year. What gives more pleasure each spring than recognizing and welcoming each little familiar shoot as it valiantly reappears, having survived even the severest of winters," writes Sands.

This society also has sponsored publication of a handbook, now in its fourth printing: *Growing Perennials in Northern Ohio: Gardener to Gardener* (available from Dorothy Bier, 2672 Derbyshire Road, Cleveland Heights, 44106). "These are all perennials we have grown, so we know they are hardy and do well here. We give examples of ways to use and combine these perennials," said Bier, 1992 president.

Ohara School of Ikebana, Northern Ohio Chapter

Meets on Fridays during the day, approx. 5 months each year; annual fee $7.50; contact the Cleveland Botanical Garden, 721-1600

This is an evolving school of Ikebana that is intimately inspired by nature. The Ohara School uses traditional Ikebana containers and shallow bowls or containers designed by Unshin Ohara, founder of the Ohara School in the late 1800s. This alternative container expanded the possibilities for different classes of arrangements and for the use of different flowers.

Workshops are given by local teachers and occasionally by international masters. Many members also study Ikebana from one of several local masters.

Ohio Daylily Society

Meets at Kingwood Center in spring, summer and fall; annual membership fee: $5; newsletter; contact James Biaglow, 238-8294

This organization, which has about 130 members from northern and central Ohio, holds an annual show the 3rd week of July at Kingwood Center. They also participate in other societies' shows and conventions in different states. Members receive free daylily plants to grow for two years and return (all but one) for a plant sale and auction, held the 3rd week in August. In summer, members' gardens may be open for tours.

Ohio Lily Society

Meets at Kingwood Center on 4 Sundays in spring, summer, fall, and late fall; annual membership fee: $4; newsletter; contact Larry Diehl, 779-7643

If you like lilies, you'll enjoy this group, devoted entirely to these queenly flowers. The Society of about 100 members has a lily show in July and bulb sales, the profits of which are donated to Kingwood Center. At meetings, growers exchange tips and bulbs, and combine lily orders to get group rates.

Oldest Stone House Herb Society

Meets on the 4th Monday of every month, 7:30 p.m. at the Oldest Stone House, Lakewood; annual membership fee: $10 to join the Lakewood Historic Society plus $5 for the Herb Society; contact Oldest Stone House, 221-7343.

This is one of the newest local plant societies, developed to maintain the herb garden at Lakewood's Oldest Stone House and to promote interest and knowledge of herbs. The group has workshops and lectures plus meetings devoted to using herbs. They also maintain the Oldest Stone House Herb Garden.

Quail Hollow Herb Society

Meets on the 1st Sunday of every month, 2 p.m., at Quail Hollow State Park; annual membership fee: $10; contact: Virginia Gamble, 877-2223

As with other herb societies, the membership (about 60-strong) is dedicated to developing and maintaining a public herb garden and developing interest in herbs. They have speakers and special events such as a craft show and herb sale, held the first weekend in May, which help finance garden upkeep.

Town and Country African Violet Society of Painesville

Meets on the 1st Wednesday of every month except January at member's homes; annual membership fee: $6; contact Gertrude Morabito, 352-9119

This 35-year-old society specializes in African violets and other gesneriads. They hold programs and slide shows at meetings and exhibit prize violets at the Ohio State African Violet Society Show at Kingwood Center (usually held the last week of September). They have their own flower show and sale at the Great Lakes Mall on Mother's Day weekend.

West Shore Arrangers

Meets on the 1st Tuesday of the month, mornings,; annual membership fees: $15; contact the Cleveland Botanical Garden, 721-1600.

This group, limited to 35 members, is devoted strictly to studying flower arranging, following the system given in the *Handbook of National Council of State Garden Clubs*. Members design and critique flower arrangements and give programs on this artistic process to other groups. Prospective new members must demonstrate flower-arranging abilities and apply for future membership openings.

West Shore Orchid Society

Meets on the 3rd Wednesday of every other month, evenings, at restaurants; annual mem-bership fee: $10 per couple; newsletter; contact Mary McAtee, 166 Carolyn Dr., Elyria, 44039

This is a west-side group of 116 members devoted to growing orchids. The society originated in 1945 and includes some folks who have been members for ten or more years. Many have greenhouses; at least half grow orchids in light gardens. Meetings include lectures or slide shows featuring different kinds of orchids or different aspects of orchid growing. The group usually has a fall show or occasional orchid seminar with prominent national speakers—often commercial growers who offer specially-priced plants.

Western Reserve Herb Society

Meets several Wednesdays each month in varying locations; annual membership fee: $45 active; $50 associate; monthly newsletter; contact The Cleveland Botanical Garden, 721-1600

This 125-member organization recently celebrated its fiftieth anniversary. Its members have created a world-class herb garden and raised public consciousness about herbs through an annual herb fair and regular programs and activities. They also hold herb symposia, luncheons with speakers, and Summer Herbal Affairs.

They meet several times a month, with unit meetings for business and speakers; other regular monthly meetings focus on using herbs in cuisine or horticulture. During the growing season, many more work meetings are devoted to harvesting and blending herbal creations that are sold in the October fund-raising herb fair. In addition, many members meet on Tuesday and Thursday mornings to maintain the garden.

"Come down to the Garden on Tuesdays and you will be greeted with open arms," said Jean Ingalls, membership chairman. "That's how we get most of our members. In the Herb Society, there are lots of ways to express your own skills and interests. It is frowned upon to sit on your hands and only come to meetings. People are very ambitious about learning and disseminating information. And they are very generous in providing scholarship funds for horticulture students."

The society publishes a series of herbal handbooks and cookbooks, including new booklets: *Thyme* ($6.00) and *Herbs and Children* ($4.00)—both available (add 75 cents postage) if you write to Western Reserve Herb Society, 11030 East Boulevard, Cleveland 44106. The Society also publishes cookbooks, including *Cooking with Herb Scents* ($16.95 plus $2.50 postage and handling) and *Herbs: A Cookbook and More* ($7.50 plus $2.00 postage and handling)

Finding a Garden Club

In addition to the many plant societies, there are hundreds of garden clubs in our area. Some are devoted to younger or older women, a few are just for men, and some attract people from certain communities. Some are devoted exclusively to gardening or flower arranging; others expand into home, fashion, and related fields. Some meet in the day; fewer meet in the evening. Some are affiliated with the Garden Club of Ohio; others are associated with the National Council of State Garden Clubs.

You can find out a bit about many garden clubs by calling The Cleveland Botanical Garden (721-1600), which keeps a list of over seventy garden clubs that are affiliated (a percentage of the club membership are members of the Cleveland Botanical Garden, so they are entitled to use the meeting rooms). But there are other groups that are not affiliated and prefer to meet in homes, libraries, or town halls. You can find out about them by asking around your neighborhood, looking in the meeting section of your community newspaper, finding out who is planting flowers in community centers or village squares (which your mayor's office or chamber of commerce would know), or attending flower shows at nearby malls.

Plant Shows: What Are They? What Do They Mean?

Plant societies often stage shows of their best plants or cut flowers; flower arrangers may display arrangements that fit a certain theme. Whether the shows are exhibitionary or judged, they provide a chance for the group to show off what they can do and a chance for you to see the best specimens, be it orchids or Ikebana arrangements. You can read about fabulous flowers all you want, but their beauty will not be as real to you as if you see them in person.

The Rose Society and Dahlia Society members exhibit cut flowers— each carefully labeled—hoping to earn a ribbon or trophy. In these kinds of shows, flowers are judged according to very specific criteria established by the national organization. A prize winner is an example of perfection; it doesn't necessarily mean that the plant is easy to grow or is good for using in the landscape. If you see a flower you cannot live without in your own garden, take the time to learn the ins and outs of growing it from society members who are manning the show.

Other societies, such as the Bonsai Club and Ikebana International, display their plants in a noncompetitive fashion. Think of these displays as works of art; stand back and admire the concepts, shapes, colors, and combinations. You may someday become so entranced that you will decide to take up these avocations.

CHAPTER 8
Gardening Education, Information, and Events

Maybe you made a few mistakes in your early gardening efforts and now want to rework them. Or perhaps you find yourself redesigning your gardens or landscapes as your tastes and needs change over time. Because there are so many different plants that can be grown (34,000 are listed in *Hortus III*, a dictionary of cultivated plants) and at least as many combinations of microclimates, soil variations, and uses for vegetation, the gardening field offers limitless possibilities. You could garden, read, and study your entire life and never learn everything there is to know about growing plants. Though you certainly can get a good idea of how to plant and tend your own yard, gardening is an art you can continue to learn and grow with in every passing year.

Gardeners have different needs and interests, and those needs and interests can change with time. A young couple with children and a small suburban lot may want to keep their landscaping simple. But later on, if they find themselves with more space and time, they might want to begin perennial gardening or try raising their own vegetables. Perhaps this couple will need a break from the pressures of work and will decide to make their yard into a hidden retreat with a patio, waterfall, and waterlily pool. Someone who has given up house and yard for a condominium might spend time once reserved for mowing the lawn on growing bonsai on the patio or tending an indoor light garden full of orchids. Another person, tired of working behind a desk or counter, may decide to return to school and become a landscape architect or tackle a certificate program to become a nurseryman.

The bottom line is, each of us can keep learning. You can let your yard evolve to reflect your own lifestyle or let the way you earn a living reflect the kind of life you want to live. Learn so you can try something new. Learn so you can do any job right the first time. As you will see in the following educational listing, you are not limited by educational opportunities and should never suffer from lack of available gardening knowledge.

You can choose among all-encompassing, formal college programs or shorter, more focused community, garden center, or arboretum classes. Mix pleasure with learning by visiting horticultural festivals or taking garden tours. Pick up the phone and call one of several horticultural hotlines to resolve a specific garden problem. Join a plant society or horticultural organization. Or simply select a good book at a nearby library to find your answers in peace and solitude.

Adult Education

Organized by Less-Formal, Intermediate, and Formal programs; listed alphabetically by sponsoring organization.

Less-Formal Programs

Chestnut Herb Farm
35335 Chestnut Ridge, North Ridgeville; 327-5857

This nursery offers a wide range of gardening, herbal, and spiritual programs. They also have classes for kids.

Community Education Programs

Many local community education programs offer gardening, landscaping, or flower-arranging classes, especially during the spring. Contact your local school system, recreation board, or community center for information. If your community does not offer a topic that interests you, check with neighboring communities.

Cleveland Botanical Garden
11030 East Blvd., Cleveland, 44106; 721-1600

Besides holding many plant shows and seasonal extravaganzas, the Cleveland Botanical Garden offers short classes and more extensive symposiums on a variety of horticultural subjects. Recent programs included a day-long kitchen gardening symposium co-sponsored by

Horticulture Magazine and an evening with perennial expert Pamela Harper co-sponsored by the Northern Ohio Perennial Society. Lectures let both groups benefit from the expertise of national authorities. Staff and instructors also hold short (one- to several-session) classes in landscape design, flower arranging, and gardening.

Great Lakes Herb Symposium
Contact Jamie Barrow: P.O Box 402, Hiram, 44234-0402

A three-day symposium with programs, tours, and top speakers in the field of herbs comes every few years to the Hiram College Campus; watch for it, because it is well worth attending. Past themes have focused on herbal cuisine, fragrant herbs, and garden design in medieval and Victorian times.

Holden Arboretum
9500 Sperry Rd., Kirtland, 44060; 946-4400

Holden sponsors short (one- to several-session) programs that are nature- and gardening-oriented. Holden staff and a few outside experts teach about native and cultivated plants (as well as wildlife such as bald eagles, marsh wrens, and black terns). In the classroom, they get down to complicated topics like plant taxonomy and the use of plant keys, or practical issues like landscaping, planting window baskets or using herbs.

Ivy Tree Bed and Breakfast
195 S. Professor St., Oberlin, 44074; 774-4510 after 5:30 p.m.

This Oberlin bed-and-breakfast features occasional weekend workshops given by Steve Coughlin, landscape designer for Barnes' Nursery in Huron. The late 1800s Colonial Revival and Victorian home features a garden that Coughlin is developing. Call for information about his occasional Garden Gathering Weekends, featuring lectures, tours, and the company of other gardeners.

Lake County Farmpark
8800 Chardon Rd., Kirtland, 44094; (800) 366-3276

Take a regularly scheduled tour to learn how the park has re-created gardens of history. Or enjoy special events that will show how gardens and farms were handled in bygone years.

Lake View Cemetery
12316 Euclid Ave., Cleveland, 44106-4393; 421-2665

During the spring and early summer blooming season, Lake View offers occasional guided walks that teach about the unusual plants at this cemetery. Call for information.

Lakeland Community College
7700 Clocktower Dr., Mentor, 44060-7594; contact: Nursery Production Coordinator: 953-7213; Community Education: 953-7116

Lakeland Community College offers one- to six-session community education programs in perennial gardening, herb gardening, home landscaping, floral design, and the art of bonsai.

Lily of the Valley Herb Farm
3969 Fox Ave., Minerva; 862-3920

This nursery offers workshops and lectures on arranging flowers and using herbs in many ways.

North Coast Pruning
P.O. Box 0428, Oberlin, 44070; 774-1556

North Coast Pruning owner, Mark Long, specializes in teaching people how to prune properly. He offers educational programs for garden clubs and other groups, training sessions for grounds crews, pruning workshops, and one-on-one instruction for homeowners.

Sea World
1100 Sea World Dr., Aurora, 44202; Head Horticulturist: Rob McCartney; 995-2156; Tour Booking: 562-8101 ext. 2525

Sea World staff horticulturists occasionally hold gardening lectures and tours of their grounds. They also are available to give group tours that emphasize a variety of subjects and then let you enjoy the other pleasures of the park at discounted admission rates.

Sunnybrook Farms
9448 Mayfield Rd., Chesterland, 44026; 729-7232

Tim Ruh, owner of Sunnybrook Farms, sometimes invites nationally known landscape designers, book authors, garden experts, and herb crafters to speak at nursery festivals or day-long symposiums at the Cleveland Museum of Natural History. Call the nursery to see what he has in store during the growing season and ask to be placed on their mailing list.

Intermediate Programs

The Cleveland Botanical Garden
11030 East Blvd., Cleveland, 44106; 721-1600

In addition to their less-formal educational offerings, the Cleveland Botanical Garden also has a horticulture certificate program, which includes such classes as botany, plant identification, pruning, bed preparation, and plant selection. Participants must take a total of 12 core classes and three electives within a one- to three-year period.

Holden Arboretum
9500 Sperry Rd., Kirtland, 44094; 946-4400

Holden offers a landscape certificate program that awards certification after attendance at 12 core classes and other electives in plant science, plant materials, and design.

Master Gardener Program
Varied locations; organized by the Ohio Cooperative Extension Service of Ohio State University; County offices: Cuyahoga: 631-1890, Geauga: 834-4656, Lake: 357-2582, Lorain: 322-0127, Medina: 725-4911, Summit: 497-1611

Residents can train with their County Extension Service to be Master Gardeners and acquire the basics of most aspects of horticulture. The classes, held between February and April (actual dates change every year) include eight full-day sessions. They are taught by Extension professionals, university professors, and specialists. On finishing the course, Master Gardeners must complete 50 hours of volunteer work in gardening fields. The class is limited to about thirty people per year, so sign up early. Material costs run about $75.

Formal Programs

Agricultural Technical Institute
1328 Dover Rd., Wooster, 44691-9989; 264-3911 or (800) 647-8283

The Wooster-based Agricultural Technical Institute of Ohio State University offers two-year associate of applied sciences degrees in floral design and marketing, greenhouse production and management, grounds management, landscape construction and contracting, nursery and garden center management, and turf-grass management. Programs in agriculture and animal industries are also offered.

Horticulture students take general college courses in science, math, communications, and social science. The remaining 60 percent of their studies are concentrated on courses in their chosen field that include hands-on experience in campus greenhouses, outdoor display gardens, and floral shops, as well as an internship.

Cleveland State University
CSU Department of Community Education; Applied Technologies; 2344 Euclid Ave., Room 103, Cleveland, 44105; 687-4850

The CSU Department of Continuing Education offers a popular two-year certificate program in landscape/horticulture. There are six required classes, held one evening a week for eight weeks. They include introductory horticulture and landscape operations, turf grasses, integrated pest-management, landscape design, trees and shrubs, and flowers. They also have other short courses on specialities such as landscape construction and landscape lighting.

Cuyahoga Community College

Plant Science Program, Eastern Campus, 4250 Richmond Rd., Highland Hills, 44122; 987-2035

This two-year plant science technology degree has been developed to train skilled personnel to work in greenhouses, landscaping, nurseries, and horticultural sales.

Cuyahoga Community College also offers a two-year associate of applied science degree combining classroom, laboratory, and field studies in soils, plant pathology, plant production, identification, landscape design, general contracting, entomology, and related business and social sciences.

Kent State University

Department of Biological Sciences, 256 Cunningham Hall, Kent State University, Kent, 44242; 672-2444

Kent offers a degree in biology and college-level classes in plant anatomy, systematic botany, morphology of lower plants, local flora, genetics, plant physiology, and organic evolution—any of which might be of interest to serious students of horticulture or nature.

They also have a new Horticultural Technology Program at the Salem Campus (332-0361) that provides an Associate of Applied Science degree, helpful for most horticultural industries. The curriculum includes technical, business, and general studies courses with outdoor labs and summer internships.

Lakeland Community College

7700 Clocktower Dr., Mentor, 44060-7594; contact Nursery Production Coordinator: 953-7213; Community Education: 953-7116; see also Informal Programs in this section

Lakeland Community College offers a two-year certificate in nursery production taught by industry professionals and geared toward developing supervisors or middle-management staff for nurseries. It requires students to take 17 five-session practical and business-related courses in plant science, supervisory management, effective communication, pest management, plant nutrition, water management, nursery equipment, maintenance, and operation, plus six months of field experience in a horticulture work site.

Ohio State University

College of Agriculture, 100 Agricultural Administration Building, 2120 Fyffe Rd., Columbus, 43210; (614) 292-1589;

Dept. of Urban Forestry, School of Natural Resources: 379 Kottman Hall, 2021 Coffey Rd., Columbus, 43210; (614) 292-2265;

Dept. of Landscape/Horticulture: 152 Howlett Hall, 2001 Fyffe Ct., Columbus, 43210-1007; (614) 292-0281

The horticultural college for the state of Ohio is well respected but has recently suffered from budget cuts. Students can earn four-year bachelor degrees and advanced degrees in horticulture and related areas. In the landscape/horticulture program alone, students can specialize in commercial landscaping, production and sales, fruit crops, or vegetable crops. Graduates work in jobs in a variety of fields, including greenhouse management, landscape design, horticultural sales or teaching, interior plantscaping, nursery or farm management, or pest management.

Vocational Schools

High-school students interested in a career in horticulture can get a head start by attending their district's vocational school. In the evenings, most of these facilities also offer continuing education for adults.

Cuyahoga Valley Career Center
8001 Brecksville Rd., Brecksville, 44141-1294; 526-5200

This large vocational school serves communities to the south of Cleveland, including school systems in Brecksville-Broadview Heights, Cuyahoga Heights, Garfield Heights, Independence, Nordonia Hills, North Royalton, Revere, and Twinsburg. It has an extensive adult education listing; over 16,000 adults attended these classes during the 1991-92 school year.

In addition, there is a two-year horticulture program for high school juniors and seniors; it's also offered tuition-free to adult residents or employees of businesses in the affiliated school districts. The horticulture program consists of eight nine-week classes—540 hours of instruction per year.

Gates Mills Vocational Horticulture School
Gates Mills Horticultural Center, 390 County Line Rd., Gates Mills, 44040; 423-4631; open houses: December sale of holiday decorations and May sale of annuals, perennials, and vegetables

High-school students from Mayfield, Aurora, Beachwood, Chagrin Falls, Orange, Richmond Heights, Solon, West Geauga, Bedford, and Cleveland Heights can take a half-day junior- and senior-year program at the horticultural center. Instructors teach classes in landscape design, construction and maintenance, greenhouse and garden center management, floral design and crops, turf- and golf-course management, nursery stock, and small-engine maintenance. Students also can co-op, working in a horticulture-related job two days a week, and attending the center three days a week.

Mentor Vocational Program

6477 Center St., Mentor, 44060; 255-4444 ext. 370.

The horticultural vocational program at Mentor High School (available to students in the Euclid, Brush, Willoughby South, Eastlake North, and Wickliffe school systems) taps the wealth of nurseries and landscaping operations in Lake County to enrich the students' education. It also stands apart from other programs because up to 60 percent of the graduating class go on to two- or four-year college programs in horticulture. "Kids need a competitive advantage to be successful in today's society and we bend over backwards to give it to them," said Karl Hagedorn, horticulture instructor.

The curriculum includes an introduction to horticulture for tenth grade Mentor students. Juniors from all the participating Lakeshore schools can attend three hours of daily laboratory and classroom learning in floriculture, landscape-turf, plant identification, plant and soil science, floral design, equipment operation, and greenhouse, garden center, and golf course management. Seniors combine classes that touch on business and management, with three hours of daily on-the-job experience.

Polaris Career Center

7285 Old Oak Blvd., Middleburg Hts., 44130; 243-8600

Juniors and seniors from Berea, Strongsville, North Olmsted, Olmsted Falls, and Fairview Park can spend half the day in horticultural vocational training and the other half at their home school. Juniors take a comprehensive overview of floral design, landscaping, greenhouse and nursery production, and turf maintenance, then go on to take a summer job in the field. Those students who maintain an A average for 95 percent of their classes can continue working in horticulture as part of their senior year laboratory. Other students are placed in internships for the last nine weeks of the school year.

"We have a special advantage here because every kind of horticultural industry is within driving distance—large nurseries, wholesale houses—you name it, we have it. It's a great opportunity for the kids," said Tom Evans, horticulture instructor.

Washington Park Horticulture Center

3875 Washington Park Blvd., Cleveland, 44105; high school program: 441-8070; adult education: 441-8075

This horticulture center, operated by the Cleveland public schools, has the largest public school greenhouse in the state of Ohio plus 57 acres of park land with an arboretum and sports fields. These facilities house a high-school vocational program that emphasizes landscaping involving sports turf and equipment—a program that is undergoing restructuring. Classes are offered in landscape and sports turf, landscape mechanics, small animal care, floral design, and interior plantscaping.

Washington Park also offers adult vocational programs for residents of northeast Ohio; it's the largest adult vocational agribusiness program of its kind in the state. The staple among these offerings is a commercial floral design certificate program that consists of 96 hours of hands-on classroom instruction. Classes in recreational flower arranging and day-long floral workshops on special holiday themes and interior plant identification and care are also offered. Periodically, the Center gives classes in gardening, mechanics and small-engine repair, and beginning and advanced bonsai.

West Technical High School
2201 W. 93rd St., Cleveland, 44102; 634-2215

The vocational program at West Tech serves the Cleveland public school system but offers a different program from Washington Park. In this one-year program, students study garden center management and floral design, and learn maintenance, sales, and plant production skills such as propagation.

A two-year program concentrates on landscape design and construction, teaching identification and use of plants as well as estimating and installation.

High-school freshmen and sophomores can take a one-year course in diversified agriculture. It offers an overview of horticulture, including plant identification, landscape design, small animal care, and small engine mechanics.

Children's Gardening Programs

Cleveland Botanical Garden
11030 East Blvd., Cleveland, 44106; 721-1600

The Cleveland Botanical Garden offers its own programs for kids, including seasonal library story times and fun classes that feature planting or crafts focused around a plant or holiday theme.

School or church classes, Scout troops, and similar groups with fewer than 35 children can arrange classes or tours with children's specialists.

Green Thumb Club
Contact the Cleveland Botanical Garden, 721-1600

School kids throughout greater Cleveland can buy inexpensive flower and vegetable seeds, fertilizer, and gardening instructions through the Green Thumb Club, a program jointly sponsored by the Cleveland Botanical Garden, the Cleveland Public Schools, and the *Plain Dealer*. At the end of the growing season, kids are rewarded for their gardening effort with certificates, buttons, pins, ribbons, and free admission to the Cuyahoga County Fair.

Green Thumb groups must have five or more children and be sponsored by an adult or group of adults who can pick up supplies, supervise the gardens, and organize a garden fair or fall display.

Holden Arboretum
9500 Sperry Rd., Kirtland, 44060; 946-4400

Holden offers an extensive children's program, including such classes as Insects Through a Toddler's Eyes (ages 2 and 3 with adult) and Monster Rock Walk (ages 7 to 10).

Indoor School Garden Program
Contact The Cleveland Botanical Garden, 721-1600

With the aid of a GrowLab light garden, elementary schoolchildren can grow plants indoors year-round in their classrooms. The kids think it's fun; teachers use it as a laboratory of hands-on activities to accompany science, math, art, and other curriculums. The program, which began in 1986, has placed over 45 GrowLabs in Cleveland Public School classrooms.

Lake County Farmpark
8800 Chardon Rd., Kirtland, 44094; (800) 366-FARM

Lake County Farmpark offers educational tours for school classes and other children's groups.

Lake Erie Nature and Science Center
28728 Wolf Rd., Bay Village, 44140; 871-2900

Kids can learn about nature and science during daytime preschool classes, after-school programs for schoolchildren, and through hikes, field studies, and classroom observations at the Lake Erie Nature and Science Center. The Nature and Science Center also offers programs for children's groups.

Shaker Lakes Regional Nature Center
2600 South Park Blvd., Shaker Heights, 44120; 321-5935

Kids from ages 2 to 9, and sometimes 10- and 11-year-olds, can participate in environmentally oriented programs, including plant identification and seed growing, held once a week during the school season or daily during the summer. The Nature Center also offers programs for children's groups.

Horticultural Therapy

Two area programs, sponsored by the Cleveland Botanical Garden and Holden Arboretum, use plants to help young, old, disabled, and disadvantaged people feel better about themselves and develop physically, intellectually, and socially. The programs are run by trained horticultural therapists who tailor horticultural programs to meet the needs of many different kinds of people.

Horticultural therapy has been around in many forms for a very long time. For ages, people have used gardens and gardening for quiet pleasure, introspection, and contentment as well as fresh air and exercise. It is reported that even early Egyptian doctors prescribed a stroll through the garden for disturbed patients. More recently, horticultural therapy has been formalized in treatment programs, and now it is even possible to obtain a degree in horticultural therapy from many universities.

Cleveland Botanical Garden

11030 East Blvd., Cleveland, 44106; 721-1600

Two part-time horticultural therapists consult with health and human service agencies here to develop new programs. They conduct 10-session spring and fall workshops for the Golden Age Centers of Greater Cleveland and offer seasonal workshops at the Cleveland Botanical Garden and at selected institutions, including the Sight Center, Camp Cheerful, Health Hill, Eliza Jennings Home, Rainbow Babies and Children's Hospital, and many others.

Holden Arboretum

9500 Sperry Rd., Kirtland, 44060; 946-4400

At Holden, a single, full-time horticultural therapist concentrates on training therapists at certain nursing homes or rehabilitation centers. "I customize my programs to fit into their existing treatment programs. They learn to use horticulture as a motivational and rehabilitation program within the existing institution," said Karen Haas. To a lesser extent, she may work directly with patients at a particular institution on a regular basis over an extended period of time.

Holden Arboretum has held horticultural therapy workshops at Sea World's All-Access Garden. (Photo courtesy of Sea World.)

Garden Libraries

Gardening is popular among readers, and reading is popular among gardeners. Consequently, you can find many gardening resources at area lending or reference libraries. In addition to popular books, many libraries also have gardening magazines, videos, and, in certain cases, catalogs and antique books.

Cleveland Museum of Natural History Library
Wade Oval, Cleveland, 44106; 231-4600

This noncirculating library has a large collection of botanical and native plant magazines, journals, and books. They also have a few books on gardening with native plants.

Cleveland Public Library
Main Branch, 325 Superior Ave., Cleveland, 44114; 623-2800;
see the phone book for branch libraries

For gardeners, the Cleveland Public Library has a large collection of gardening books, including 62 gardening dictionaries, 32 books of garden fiction, and 44 books on the gardens of England, many of which were written in the late 1800s and early 1900s. In the special collections section, you can see herbals, culinary guides, and botanical prints collected since 1869. Go back even further in time by looking at the older herbals and journals in the rare book section (which are not available for borrowing). You'll find modern gardening books in the science and technology section of the library.

Cuyahoga County Public Library
see the phone book for a complete listing of branches

Among the many branches of the Cuyahoga County Public Library system you can find most of the better gardening books and magazines. If your local branch doesn't have what you need, you can have books or magazines sent from other branches.

Cleveland Botanical Garden Eleanor Squire Library
11030 East Blvd., Cleveland, 44016; 721-1600; closed Mondays

This 15,000-volume library of gardening, landscape architecture, flower arranging, children's, and teaching books is one of the largest of its kind in the country. Books circulate to members for three weeks at a time; nonmembers may use the books for reference in the library. There are 200 different garden-oriented magazines and 750 rare historical books (accessible by appointment). You can find over a thousand nursery and garden supply catalogs, over a hundred videos, and a file of speakers who can talk to groups on horticultural and related subjects. The library also publishes a newsletter, *Off the Shelf.*

Gardenview Horticultural Park Library

16711 Pearl Rd., Rte. 42, Strongsville, 44136; by appointment only; 238-6653

This strictly reference library is open to Gardenview members by appointment. It contains over four thousand volumes, especially British classics and monographs on special items, including roses, primroses, magnolias, rhododendrons, and azaleas. Most are for advanced gardeners.

Herb Society of America

9019 Kirtland-Chardon Rd., Mentor 44094; 256-0514; call for open hours

This is the national headquarters of the Herb Society of America, where a small staff keeps a library of about six hundred herb-related books. The library is open for reference only, and available for use only with HSA staff supervision.

Holden Arboretum

9500 Sperry Rd., Kirtland, 44060; 946-4400; admission fee for nonmembers; closed Mondays

The Arboretum library, open for reference only, holds about 6,300 horticulture-related books. It also has 1,200 volumes of rare books that are available for research by appointment only. You will also find 125 magazines, vertical files, a collection of color slides, and three videos— "A Flying Piece of the Sky" (about bluebirds), "In Wonder of Trees," and "The Sugar Bush"—that can be leased by schools or community groups.

Gardening Publications

If you are focusing on one particular kind of plant and have trouble finding books that are detailed enough at a library, check with a plant society in that field. Some have small libraries that their members may use; others can refer you to their favorite publications. You also may want to subscribe to a magazine on the subject; many provide month after month of ideas and inspiration. If you want to browse a bit yourself, write for catalogs or subscription information from gardening publishers. Some of the better ones are:

Books

- Goosefoot Acres Press, P.O. Box 18016, Cleveland Hts., 44118; 932-2145; books by local author Peter Gail on edible weeds and Amish lifestyles
- Rodale Press, 33 E. Minor St., Emmaus, PA 18098
- Storey Communications, Schoolhouse Rd., Pownal, VT 05261
- Timber Press, 9999 S.W. Wilshire, Portland, OR 97225-9962

Magazines

- *Fine Gardening*, P.O. Box 355, Newtown, CT 06470
- *Flower and Garden*, 4251 Pennsylvania Ave., Kansas City, MO 64111
- *Horticulture*, 98 N. Washington St., Boston, MA 02114
- *National Gardening*, 180 Flynn Ave., Burlington, VT 05401
- *Organic Gardening*, 33 E. Minor St., Emmaus, PA 18098

Other Periodicals

- *North Coast Garden*, Alan Hirt's consumer guide to gardening; P.O. Box 351, Valley City, 44280; $17 for 10 issues per year.
- *Ohio Gardening*, Cuyahoga County Cooperative Extension Service, 3200 W 65th St., Cleveland, 44102; 631-1890.
- Many clubs, plant societies, and professional groups have regular newsletters. (See individual listings in chapter 7.)

Other Answer Sources

Sometimes answers to specific questions are as close as your telephone. If you can get through to the experts answering these popular telephone hotlines and newspaper columns, you may find a free solution.

Cleveland Botanical Garden

Gardening Information: 721-0400

Staff horticulturists answer garden questions 9 a.m. to noon and 1 to 4 p.m. Tuesday and Thursday, and 1 to 4 p.m. Saturdays.

Cooperative Extension Services

Ohio Cooperative Extension Service, Ohio State University

Cuyahoga County: 631-1890

Master Gardeners answer gardening questions from 9 a.m. to noon Mondays and from 1 to 4 p.m. on Thursdays.

For prerecorded seasonal gardening tips, call the Home and Garden Teletip (631-1895).

Other County Extension Services set different schedules for answering questions. Call them for more information:

Geauga: 834-4656
Lake: 357-2582
Lorain: 322-0127
Medina: 725-4911
Summit: 497-1611

Ohio State University Cooperative Extension Service Plant and Pest Diagnostic Clinic

OSU, 110 Kottman Hall, 2021 Coffey Rd., Columbus, 43210; (614) 292-5006

Pest and disease diagnostic services are available. For a $5 fee you (or the local cooperative extension service) can send plant or pest samples for identification. Disease identification costs $12. Hard-to-identify plant viruses cost an additional $15 to $50.

Ohio State University Research Extension Analytical Laboratory

1680 Madison Ave., Wooster, 44691; 263-3760

Soil sample analysis: obtain test kits from local County Extension Service office.

The Plain Dealer

1801 Superior Ave., Cleveland, 44114

Some questions submitted in writing are answered by Jack Kerrigan, county extension agent, in a regular Saturday column.

Sun Newspapers

5510 Cloverleaf Rd., Cleveland, 44125

Some questions submitted in writing are answered in "The Green Scene" column.

Special Events: Festivals, Fairs, and Shows

You can have fun, find unique plants or crafts, and learn a little by attending some of the special events put on by garden centers, clubs, nurseries, and rural community organizations. The list of special events that follows is by no means comprehensive; it only includes some of best-attended or most regular events. There are many other festivals that you will discover if you watch ads and entertainment previews in the local newspapers, especially during the growing season.

To profit the most from special events, take a little time to look closely at the booths, crafts, and plants. Read the labels on plants and jot down the cultivar names of the ones you like. Note how a craftsman has braided lavender stalks together, made a cornhusk doll out of an ear of field corn, or turned apples into fritters. These are all things you can do yourself, if you are provided with a few tips from the artisan whose work you are admiring or if you are willing to read a book on the subject.

Apple Butter Festival

Burton; 834-4204

In early October, it's time to celebrate the apple season at Burton's Century Village. You'll see how to make old fashioned apple butter, apple fritters, and other apple dishes. You'll also see plenty of crafts and antiques.

Chagrin Falls Herb and Flower Festival
Chagrin Valley Chamber of Commerce; 247-6607; free

Drop by this day-long event held one weekend in May. Wander though charming Chagrin Falls and stop under the big tent in Riverside Park to browse through displays of landscapers, herbalists, flower arrangers, and more.

Cleveland Botanical Garden Winter Holiday Show
11303 East Blvd., Cleveland, 44106; December; free admittance; 721-1600

As a preview to the winter holidays, the Botanical Garden fills its halls with plants, both traditional and unusual, plus flower arrangements, collectibles, and props—towns, woods, ponds—whatever will depict the theme for the year. For example, in 1994, the Botanical Garden recreated a fairy tale world with Jack's beanstalk reaching up into the clouds and a gingerbread house you could walk through. The work is done, in large part, by a volunteer committee with a staff coordinator. It's great fun for everyone and costs nothing to see. (Also see Floralscape.)

Floralscape
Cleveland Convention Center; late February or early March; entry fee; 721-1695

The Cleveland Botanical Garden runs this premier horticultural festival, which is similar to the world-famous Philadelphia Flower Show. You'll see fabulous landscaped gardens, which occupy more than half of the show space. Recently, one garden was so big it earned the title of Nation's Largest Indoor Garden. It featured a waterfall, reflecting pool, nearly 100 trees, over 1,000 perennials and 2,000 flowering bulbs.

Beyond the gardens are usually displays of bonsai, flower arranging, and house plants, as well as booths of nurseries and garden suppliers. Floralscape also attracts top national and international guest speakers, free with the price of admission.

Fowler's Mill Harvest Festival
Chardon; 286-2024

On the second weekend in October, you can take a drive into the country east of Cleveland to see the beautiful fall foliage. Stop at Alpine Valley ski area to ride the chair lift and enjoy the scenery. Go on to Fowler's Mill to take hayrides, see shows, and demonstrations of pioneer skills.

"Hale" to Spring
Hale Farm and Village, 2686 Oak Hill Rd., Bath; 666-3711; admission fee

Kick off the growing season with a fun-filled day of planting demonstrations, herb and garden lectures, an herb sale, and tours of historic Hale Village.

Huntsburg Pumpkin Festival
15 mi. east of Chester Township; held one weekend in early Oct.

This annual pumpkin festival features pumpkin baked goods, a pumpkin show, totem poles of pumpkins, squash and gourds, carved pumpkins, pumpkin pottery, old-fashioned games, pony rides, entertainment, and a Fun Run.

Lake County Farmpark
8800 Chardon Rd., Kirtland, 44094; 1-(800) 366-3276

Special events at Lake County Farmpark include Threshing Days in July, Bud Day in September, a Fall Harvest in September, and Cornucopia (about corn) in October.

National Herb Week Celebration
Contact Kathleen Gips, 247-5014

The week before Mother's Day is the International Herb Association's National Herb Week. Kathleen Gips of the Village Herb Shop in Chagrin Falls coordinates events in this area. They often include lectures, teas, garden tours, and special herbal menus at participating restaurants.

National Home and Garden Show
IX Center; early March; entry fee; contact Terry Drohan, 464-4850

The National Home and Garden Show features over 30 display gardens, each of which is dedicated to local celebrities. The garden themes often tie into a local arts organization. For example, in 1995, the theme was Monet's garden at Giverny, France—a fabulous panorama of plant colors and textures crafted by Monet's own hand. Monet's garden was recreated with the help of students at the Cleveland Institute of Art. The gardens in 1996 will be devoted to a British theme.

Beyond the gardens, you'll find the Boulevard of Dreams, a street of landscaped homes, plus a large home improvement area, lawn and garden retailers, and arts and crafts booths. The show is easily accessible to wheelchairs.

Plant Discovery Day
Wooster, contact Ken Cochran, 263-3761

Wander through fields of May blooming trees and shrubs at Secrest Arboretum and stop in at the plant sale, rare plant auction, and many demonstrations and activities.

Quailcrest Fall Herb Fair
2810 Armstrong Rd., Wooster, 44691; first Sunday after Labor Day; 345-6722

Take the scenic drive to Quailcrest Farm the first Saturday after Labor Day to see the lovely gardens and booths of 60 artists and gift exhibitors. There's also food and music.

Richardson's Greenhouse and Farm Market Fall Festival
375 Tuxedo Ave., Brooklyn Heights, 44131; one weekend in October; 661-7818

This festival includes arts and crafts, farm animals, prizes, and special events for children.

SpringFest
Fellows Riverside Gardens; 816 Glenwood Ave, Youngstown; 743-7275

Come see this garden glow with spring bulbs on Mothers Day weekend. You'll also be treated to music, entertainment, and a plant sale.

Sunnybrook Farm Fall Herb Fair
9448 Mayfield Rd., Chesterland, 44026; one weekend in September; 729-7232

Come for talks and demonstrations, about twenty booths of gifts and crafts created by artists and specialists, contests, games, and food.

Western Reserve Herb Society Fair
The Cleveland Botanical Garden, 11030 East Blvd., Cleveland, 44106; one Saturday early in October; 721-1600

This popular fundraising fair offers a wide variety of herbal products, decorations, and foods as well as herb-related demonstrations.

Wooster Garden Festival
Wooster; contact Ken Cochran, 263-3761

This event will be held again in 1997 at Secrest Arboretum and the Agricultural Technical Institute. Visit to wander through all the area gardens—and there are plenty!—talk to garden experts, and see a variety of exhibits including model train gardening, kite stunt flying, outdoor bread baking, and garden artists.

World's Largest Gourd Show
One weekend in early autumn at Morrow County Fairgrounds, Mount Gilead; (419) 946-3302; admission fee

If you want to try something really different, go to this huge show to see mountains of gourds—made into lights, dolls, bowls, wind chimes, hats—plus other food and festivities. It's all put together by the Ohio Gourd Society, P.O. Box 274, Mt. Gilead, OH 43338; (419) 362-OHIO.

Zoo Blooms
Cleveland Metroparks Zoo, 3900 Brookside Park Dr. 44109

This day-long festival, held in mid-July, features tours of the wonderful zoo gardens and landscaping along with a variety of gardening lectures.

Home and Garden Tours

Northeast Ohio has many lovely residential gardens, each with a story to tell about landscaping, soil preparation, plant growth, and troubleshooting. One of the best ways to find out the whys and hows behind a garden is to take garden tours organized by communities, plant societies, or garden clubs. Some of these are listed here.

Brecksville Nature Center
Cleveland Metroparks; 526-1012
You can take free guided prairie walks June to September. Tour dates and times are noted in the Metropark's Emerald Necklace Newsletter.

Chagrin Falls Preservation Historic Garden Tour
192 E. Washington St, Chagrin Falls 44022; 247-8319
On Father's Day, this group holds a fund raising tour of many interesting gardens in the Chagrin area.

Chippewa Garden Club Home and Garden Tour
7411 Old Quarry Ln., Brecksville, 44141
This Brecksville-based club often sponsors a biannual weekend home and garden tour that helps finance community projects and scholarships.

Cleveland Botanical Garden
11030 East Blvd., Cleveland, 44106; 721-1600
The Cleveland Botanical Garden offers periodic tours of local gardens, gardens within a day's drive, and sometimes gardens in other countries.

Cleveland Rose Society
Contact Jim Wickert, 696-5729
If you like roses, see if you can tag along when the society visits some of the members' gardens in full bloom.

Cuyahoga County Cooperative Extension Services
3200 W. 65th St., Cleveland; 44102; 631-1890
You can tour the Extension's vegetable, herb, and perennial gardens from 10 a.m. to noon Thursdays and have your questions answered by Master Gardeners.

Dahlia Society of Ohio

Contact Monica Rini, 461-4190

The Dahlia Society sometimes allows guests to join their annual summer garden tour and see glorious dahlias blooming at the homes of Dahlia Society members.

Growing Arts Tour

Contact the North Ridgeville Visitor's Bureau; 327-3737

On a Saturday in late April, you can take a self guided tour of the former greenhouse capital of Ohio which now features a variety of green industry businesses. Your stops will treat you to special sales, talks, tours, and prizes.

Hudson Garden Club House and Garden Pilgrimage

P.O. Box 651, Hudson, 44236

This active and experienced club puts on one of the most popular home and garden tours.

Northern Ohio Perennial Society

Contact Eva Sands, 371-3363, or Betty McRainey, 732-9155

This plant society often tours members' gardens during the summer.

Medina County Fall Foliage Tour

Contact the Medina County Convention and Visitors Bureau, 124 W. Lafayette Rd., Medina, 44256; 722-5502

This October outing features farms, gardens, and museums in rural Medina County.

CHAPTER 9

Learning from Other Gardens

Like home-decorating enthusiasts who tour beautiful homes or attend real estate open houses just to see what fabulous places really look like inside, people who garden like to see what other people are doing with *their* gardens. Fortunately for us, northeast Ohio boasts a great number and wide variety of public and semipublic gardens. This chapter introduces many of this area's best gardens, particularly those in which you can enjoy the sights and also learn a few things that will help you with your own garden.

For example, if you are curious about how to keep weeds down in perennial beds, each of twenty perennial gardens listed here may have a unique way to tackle weeds. If you are thinking about adding an Oriental influence to your landscape, sample the Japanese gardens at the Cleveland Botanical Garden and Stan Hywet Hall. If you love the fragrance of flowering lilacs or crab apples or enjoy the sight of big sweeps of spring bulbs, immerse yourself in them at the Cleveland Museum of Art and Lake View Cemetery. For different perspectives on English gardening, try Gardenview Horticultural Park and Claystone. Still other gardens will give you ideas for different ways to grow indoor plants, herbs, wildflowers, edibles, roses, and trees.

There are hundreds of wonderful home landscapes and gardens in northeast Ohio that are fun to pass by and ogle from the street or, better yet, tour with a plant society or during a community fund raiser. The gardens listed here are generally open to the public during certain hours and months, though a few will open their gates by advance appointment only.

The gardens range in scale from modest to grandiose and feature many different themes, types of plants, and garden layouts. Each has particular strengths. Some shine in spring or peak in fall; others change focus throughout the seasons.

I have divided the garden areas into those where you can drop in unannounced and those where you will need advance appointments. They are listed in alphabetical order by garden name. For more details about the organizations behind the gardens, associated educational activities, or attached nursery areas, follow the cross-references to other chapters.

Gardens Open to the Public

Brecksville Nature Center, Metroparks
Brecksville Reservation, Chippewa Creek Drive, Brecksville; 526-1012

Behind a spring wildflower garden you will find a unique two-acre prairie area. It's not a true garden but a re-created ecosystem (a system of interacting living things and nonliving environment) similar to that which grew in this area centuries ago when weather conditions were drier. You can observe the prairie close-up from a walking path that cuts through it or scan it from the observation deck above. In late summer, this prairie is spectacular with its towering grasses and flowers, and since prairie wildflowers such as coneflower and blazing-star have an important place in gardens, you might see something here that will give you ideas for home.

Naturalist Karl Smith, aided by staff and volunteers, collected seeds for all the plants here from within Ohio (even though similar seeds can be bought from nurseries in prairie states to the west). They are adamant about keeping the prairie a pure-as-possible replica of local history. Smith has included Ohio species of goldenrod, lilies, mountain mint, spiderwort, giant sunflowers, boneset, butterfly weed, and cordgrass.

"Unlike a garden, we make no attempt to control the animals—they have free interaction. So the area is heavily browsed by deer, groundhogs, rabbits. Voles, at one point, cut most of the blazing star flowering stalks off at ground level. Caterpillars eat the greenery, then turn into butterflies that visit the flowers. But we do attempt to control the plants, to maintain the area as a prairie." Smith keeps woody trees and shrubs from invading the Brecksville Reservation prairie by burning it annually.

Cahoon Memorial Rose Garden

Cahoon Memorial Park, Cahoon and Lake roads, Bay Village; for tours, call Elizabeth Preedy, 835-3617

This charming collection of roses is situated in Bay Village's Cahoon Park, within sight of Lake Erie. A white picket fence encloses a traditional garden; inside, a thousand rosebushes throw out lots of bright color, even in the rain. On the perimeter of the garden, roses ramble up along the fence; inside, the beds form circles surrounding a central sundial memorial.

"This is a traditional design, used by the Incas and other cultures because it has a pattern similar to the sun. There is a central circle and paths that radiate out from it like the rays of the sun. The other curving beds complement the central circle, which in this case is a memorial to World War II, Korean and Vietnam War veterans," said Frank Aleksandrowicz, the garden's volunteer designer who cared for the rose garden for eight years. In addition to the circular layout, a triangular bed surrounds the bulky base of the flagpole and lateral strips of roses run east to west at the south end of the garden.

Cahoon Memorial Rose Garden is an American Rose Society display garden, so it always has some of the best new varieties on display. Debbie Sutherland, curator, said this garden houses over a hundred different varieties of miniatures, hybrid teas, floribundas, grandifloras, shrub roses, new David Austin English roses, rugosa roses, and old garden roses—in short, almost anything a rose grower could want to see.

"When I was planning the garden," said designer Aleksandrowicz, "I tried to find historic English rose types that were repeat bloomers [most historic roses bloom only once in spring] so that the whole garden keeps flowering all summer. It seems to me that this is important for a public rose garden. You want people to come back in June, July, August, and September and say each time, 'Hey, this is nice', because there is so much happening."

"When all the roses bloom, their scent is so wonderful—it out-smells anything else around," said Sutherland. "People just love the place, but for different reasons. One woman comes out to photograph monarch butterflies only on cloudy days. Another person videotapes the garden and puts it to music. Some people come up to get ideas for their own garden. A lot of folks stopped by in 1992 to see if we were having as much trouble with black spot [a fungus disease of roses] as they were at home. One man came by specifically to see 'Dolly Parton', a very temperamental hybrid tea rose, which I sprayed weekly and still couldn't keep clean."

Cleveland Botanical Garden

11030 East Blvd., University Circle, Cleveland, 44106; 721-1600; self-guided tour brochures avail.; free admittance; garden always open

The Cleveland Botanical Garden is an educational institution with display gardens designed on a smaller scale, making it easy to walk through and enjoy or to take new ideas home from. It is also frequently the site of wedding parties lined up waiting for their turn to take wedding photos, artists capturing scenes with paint or photographs, and occasional parties that spill out onto the grounds.

You can learn about good gardening practices from the example the grounds set. Note how the formal clipped hedges are narrower at the top so that no part of the plant is shaded. Look closely at the perennial gardens where green L-shaped English link-stakes hold up floppy plants. "You can hook any number of these stakes together and loop them around a plant, preferably before, but even after, the stem flops," horticulturist Robin Siktberg said.

Check out how mulch is layered around trees that are growing in the lawn. "We put bark mulch around the trees to keep down mower damage and give the tree roots a small space where they are not competing with grass," Siktberg said. "But we only put mulch on two inches deep and don't touch the trunk."

You also will see many excellent plants that are not used enough in our area. Some are labeled, but label-snatching seems to be a popular sport in that neighborhood and labels frequently disappear. A few plants that grow on these grounds may not be hardy enough to survive long if you plant them further from the lake.

For more information on the gardens, ask at the front desk for self-guiding tour brochures. For the history of the Cleveland Botanical Garden, see their book, *Fifty Years of Growing and Serving: 1930 to 1980.*

Following are some of the specific garden areas within the grounds of the Cleveland Botanical Garden:

Western Reserve Herb Society Garden

This large herb garden, one of the finest in the country, was designed by landscape architect Elsetta Barnes in 1964. It includes a Tudor knot garden (a formal garden with clipped herbs that form intricate, interwoven geometric patterns), as well as culinary, medicinal, dye, fragrance, trial, and historic rose sections. Between brick walkways, the herb beds interweave flowers, foliage, and specimen plants to create a tapestry of colors and textures.

"It seemed reasonable for the garden to cover the interests of our members, which, on inquiry, I discovered were all aspects of herb gardening. I could not picture one large garden including such a mixture of plantings, and thus evolved the functional groupings," Barnes said.

What you won't know, unless you visit the garden on Tuesday or Thursday mornings when Herb Society volunteers are working there, is the amount of labor and love that goes into keeping everything just-so in this garden. Before the garden was developed, there were doubts about whether a volunteer organization could finance and maintain a garden of this scale. Now, after nearly thirty years, the industrious Herb

Society has it heavily endowed, mostly from the proceeds of annual autumn herb fairs. How the Herb Society and their garden have risen from modest beginnings to national acclaim is documented in *A History of the Western Reserve Unit of the Herb Society of America: 1942–1992*, written by Elizabeth Scher and Jenifer Richter and published by the Western Reserve Herb Society for the Unit's fiftieth anniversary.

Mary Ann Sears Swetland Rose Garden

This garden replicates a formal Roman rose garden enclosed in a clipped evergreen border. A series of angular rose beds, each devoted to a different color of rose, surround an octagonal marble fountain. The garden seems simple and serene; this is by careful design. It replaced an older, unmaintained rose garden that was full of brambles and weeds—no one wanted that to happen again.

Evans Reading Garden

The Evans Reading Garden serves as an extension of the large Cleveland Botanical Garden library. It invites visitors to stop with a book under a lengthy vine-covered pergola/summerhouse or on benches situated in shady nooks. It is also a place to find unusual plants such as Alleghany pachysandra, Himalayan sarcococca, and Russian arborvitae, some of which were collected on the worldwide travels of the garden's sponsor, Betty Evans.

Japanese Garden

This garden, a naturalistic miniature mountainscape, is downhill from the Reading Garden. Walk through a wrought-iron gate along a stone path to a wisteria-draped trellis, a tea garden, and a dry waterfall torrent created of rocks and clipped shrubbery. Covering the slopes and surrounding the tea garden are Oriental plants such as dwarf Mugo pine, Japanese holly and maple, and evergreen azalea. This garden was designed by David Slawson, former Clevelander and author of *Secret Teachings in the Art of Japanese Gardens* (1987, Kodansha International, Tokyo).

Wildflower Garden

To the west of the Japanese Garden is the most recent addition to these grounds. For many years before it was actually developed into a garden, the late John Milchalko, former commissioner of shade trees for the city of Cleveland, dumped tons of leaves there, making the soil rich and fertile. Milchalko helped spearhead volunteer efforts to relocate wildflowers that were on construction sites to the safety of the ravine. The Cleveland Botanical Garden continued where the volunteer efforts left off when the city leased them the property in 1987.

Over the past ten years, the ravine has been converted from a brush-covered no man's land into a woodland glade woven with paths, seats, and flowers. Native wildflowers such as wild columbine, trillium, and Solomon's-seal, and wildflower-like species from other countries, such as Siberian bugloss, Bethlehem sage, and Lenten rose spread in abundance up and down the ravine slopes. For more details on this garden, you can purchase a trail guide inside the building.

The Interior

If you tire of being outdoors, view the grounds from the glass-walled building, which houses activities, the extensive library, and occasional educational or art displays. The building also holds garden shows, including Floralscape, a horticultural festival at the Convention Center, and a winter holiday show.

Perennials grow beneath white birch trees at the Cleveland Botanical Garden. (Photo courtesy of the Cleveland Botanical Garden.)

Cleveland Metroparks

For a directory and map describing the Metroparks, call 351-6300

The park system circling greater Cleveland is primarily a place for natural scenery and recreation, but it also includes a few gardens well worth visiting. Herb and wildflower gardens cluster near several nature centers, combining the outdoors with facilities for discovering more about plants and how people and animals interact with them. The following Metroparks facilities are described elsewhere within this section's alphabetical listing:

• Brecksville Nature Center
• Cleveland Metroparks Zoo
• Cleveland Metroparks Zoo RainForest
• Garfield Park Nature Center
• Rocky River Nature Center
• Sanctuary Marsh Nature Center

Cleveland Metroparks Zoo

3900 Brookside Park Dr., Cleveland, 44109; 661-6500; admission fee; discount for members of the Cleveland Zoological Society

Like many zoological parks nationwide, the Cleveland Zoo has expanded its horticultural exhibits, which now include over two thousand plant species and make the zoo a prettier place to visit and a more comfortable home for the animals. The zoo staff also plans to label the plants in most areas over the next couple of years. "Recently I've been hearing visitors comparing our landscaping to other zoos, which shows people are noticing what we are doing," said Don Krock, assistant park manager in charge of horticulture and service maintenance.

Take a moment as you walk through the zoo to look at the display gardens situated at strategic locations around the park. Specialty gardens highlight conifers, ornamental grasses, and annual and perennial plants. An alpine rock garden occupies a slope near the seal and polar bear corner of the zoo. Krock is experimenting with new hardy plants around the Outback Railroad area, where kids like to go to see kangaroos boxing. Although the small display greenhouse overlooking the giraffe yard is often overlooked, you should stop in there to find wonderful cacti, tropicals, orchids, and seasonal flowers. An animal flower garden outside the greenhouse is devoted entirely to plants with animal-related names like tiger marigold and hen-and-chickens.

Other gardens depict the flora of an animal's homeland. One such garden surrounds the three-quarter-acre outdoor gorilla enclosure. Inside the enclosure, landscaping simulates a gorilla's natural habitat with tropical forest-type plants—bamboos, grasses, and trees (hot-wired to keep gorillas from climbing them). To give visitors an even better feeling for the wild areas where gorillas play, the walkway nearby is heavily landscaped to simulate a tropical rain forest. Of course this isn't the tropics, so Krock has substituted plants that he hopes will be hardy, including:

• Big-leaved magnolias (*Magnolia tripetala* and *Magnolia macrophylla*), with three-foot-long leaves and spring flowers
• Catalpa (*Catalpa bignonioides*), which has rounded leaves eight inches long and showy clusters of white flowers
• Empress tree (*Paulownia tomentosa*), which is not reliably hardy but so far has survived three winters at the zoo. Although this tree may

die back to the ground during a harsh winter, it can resprout and grow 20 feet in one year. It has huge heart-shaped leaves twice the size of a catalpa
  • Italian arum (*Arum italicum*), an unusual perennial with long arrowhead-shaped leaves that are evergreen in winter but die down in summer
  • Plume poppy (*Macleaya cordata*), a fast-spreading perennial that can reach eight feet high, and bearing lush plumed flowers and eight-inch-long, lobed leaves that are furry white beneath
  • Giant reed (*Arundodonax*), an ornamental grass that can tower up to 18 feet high and fill out into massive clumps

The landscaping surrounding the paddocks for the African plains animals looks very much like African savanna, right out of a Tarzan movie. All around the animals of China exhibit, next to the gorillas, you'll see plants from northern Asia that give you a better idea of where these animals originated.

If animals are grazing on the landscaping, Krock must be sure the plants are not toxic to any primates or ungulates. You will see that the tree canopies end just inches away from the big male giraffe's outstretched neck. But baby cheetahs are harder to keep away from the plants. "Baby cheetahs, who have a lot of extra energy, will pick a different clump of ornamental grass every day and chew it down to the ground. Fortunately, the grasses do resprout," Krock says.

In the bird house, a number of exhibits include plants in the bird enclosures. "Birds chew on the leaves and fly onto the branches, so they can be hard on plants. But they also take care of the small pest problems by eating white fly, aphids, scale, and spider mites. We never have to spray," Krock said.

Cleveland Metroparks Zoo RainForest
3900 Brookside Park Dr., Cleveland, 44109; 661-6500; admission fee; tickets avail. at the gate or from Ticketmaster, 241-5555

This exhibit is the Metropark's jewel—for plants as well as animals. It re-creates the ever-diminishing rain forest areas of the world where a wealth of plant and animal species are threatened with extinction. The RainForest exhibit also represents horticultural pioneering at its best. It contains 10,000 live plants of 360 different varieties, including common and rare tropicals, orchids, bromeliads (a group of plants that grow on trees for support), cocoa trees, and vanilla vines.

"There is no other exhibit like this large-scale combination of live plants and animals within a 15-state area," Krock said. "The RainForest is a unique experience the public has never had a chance to see before. We are using high-tech graphics, Walt Disney effects, and fiber optics so lightning will flash and rain will fall beside the walks. In most areas, light levels will be fairly high so the plants should grow for five to six years before we have to replace them or they get too tall for the 35-foot roof. We use biological controls for pest problems, like beneficial insects [that prey upon or parasitize plant pests] and spot-spraying with non-toxic Bt [a bacterial disease of caterpillars], light horticultural oil [a nontoxic petroleum oil that coats and kills pests], or Safer's insecticidal soap [nontoxic soap made of fatty acids that kill soft-bodied insects]. (For more information on natural pest control, see Rodale's *Chemical-Free Yard and Garden*, 1991, Rodale Press, Emmaus, PA.)

You can also identify the plants; the exhibit resembles an overgrown ruin area throughout which a researcher went tagging plants with their common and botanical names. Volunteers can explain about rain forest plants of particular economic importance, such as fruits, woods, and fibers.

The plants are a combination of ornamental tropicals (such as black olive and fig trees used commonly for interior plantscaping) and unique flowering specimens (such as orchids that are rotated in and out of the exhibit as they come in and out of bloom). In the southeast corner, where butterflies emerge from their cocoons, you'll find nectar-producing plants such as passion vine and Egyptian star, which require extra light from overhead lamps. The floor plants grow in a peat-based growers' mix, not true soil, and those growing on the wall are rooted in carpet fiber and fed nutrients through a computerized watering and fertilizer system. It's an amazing assortment of plants and techniques brought together in an extraordinary exhibit.

Look at the landscape outdoors, too for a blend of hardy and, in season, tropical plants that create a dense tropical atmosphere.

Chagrin Valley Herb Society Garden

Geauga County Public Library, Bainbridge Branch, 17222 Snyder Rd., Chagrin Falls, 44023; 543-5611; tours by reservation

Just outside the Geauga County Public library entrance you will find a small herb garden that is charming. Take a few minutes to look closely. This garden, designed by Kathy Catani and planted and maintained by the Chagrin Valley Herb Society. It is the first phase of what is hoped will be a larger garden project. Phase two will feature a roofed teahouse surrounded by a garden for all seasons.

The garden beds employ geometric patterns, a traditional way to design herb gardens. One bed is planted to resemble a wagon wheel, with spokes dividing the area into four quadrants devoted to different kinds of herbs and flowers. Another bed is filled with mints; free-ranging silver variegated pineapple mint—which spreads with abandon—fills the entire bed except in strategic locations where green-leafed mints remain in clumps.

The garden abounds with unusual herbs, including Florence fennel, chamomile, horehound, and angelica, and also fragrant plants such as scented geraniums. Especially attractive is the silver and blue bed, which combines plants with silver foliage—such as 'Silver Mound' artemisia, silver santolina, silver lamb's-ears, and dusty-miller—with blue-flowered plants, such as blue ageratum, salvia, lavender, and comfrey. A literary garden centered on an herbal knot includes herbs mentioned in poetry, the Bible, and Shakespeare.

"The idea for the herb garden actually came first, and then the Chagrin Valley Herb Society formed to create and work in it," said Kathy Catani, garden founder. "We now have about forty active members participating. One of the members is a librarian who knew nothing about gardening but seemed to be the one we always conferred with about the garden. Now she goes out and pulls weeds at lunch and has put in a couple of herb gardens at her own home. After a while, we made her an honorary member."

Gardenview Horticultural Park
16711 Pearl Rd., Rte. 42, Strongsville, 44136; 238-6653; non-members can visit on Saturdays and Sundays; admission fee charged for nonmembers

Gardenview Horticultural Park, a surprising, tranquil garden hidden in a commercial area of Strongsville, contains expansive English cottage gardens and traditional perennial borders unlike any other garden in this area. The six acres of artistic gardens, through which you can wander on winding paths, back up to ten additional acres devoted to an arboretum of crab apples and spring bulbs.

The garden has been the lifelong creation of Henry Ross, who has bartered and traded for an astonishing number of rare plants and has single-handedly developed and maintained the garden. Ross has a special touch with plants; his gardens combine some of the area's most creative annual displays, which change every year. Especially impressive past combinations have included:

- Large white flowering tobacco plants with modern compact white flowering cultivars at their feet
- Tropical five-foot-tall cannas with golden variegated leaves, orange flowers, and red buds with burgundy-leaf coleus, red-plumed cockscomb, and purple-stemmed ornamental kale
- Ruby-stemmed Swiss chard with pink double-flowered impatiens

Some areas of this park have a calculated impromptu look. In one undeveloped meadow off the main path, wonderful leafless flower stalks of light orchid lycoris (*Lycoris squamigera*) flowers bloom beautifully without any obvious sign of human intervention. They stand out—a bold color amid autumn grasses.

In the midst of these colorful displays you will find rare plants that nurseries across the United States have come to covet. Look for hybrid

Lenten roses (Ross has the largest collection of *Helleborus* in the country). They begin to bloom in mid-February. You'll also see a great assortment of variegated, golden, and silver-leafed plants, including hostas, variegated comfrey and variegated Siberian bugloss (*Brunnera macrophylla*). There are also simply unusual plants such as deciduous ginger, bear's-breeches, and Italian arum.

Of the garden, Ross writes, "Gardenview was designed as, and is, not only a magnificent example of glorious 'real gardens'; but an inspiration to those visiting it. Containing primarily very rare, uncommon and unusual plants, it is made up of about thirty individual gardens, . . . all informal and casual, fitting together into one picture, like pieces of a puzzle. Its purpose is not only to provide pleasure to those viewing it, but to inspire them to 'go home and do likewise'. It provides not only numerous examples of planting combinations; but layout ideas as well. It is a 'real gardeners' garden and not an extravaganza for the general non-gardening public. It is also intended to make people realize that ornamental 'real' gardening is a pleasure and a joy and to inspire people to create and enjoy 'real gardens' and to abandon the idea of wanting— and settling for—a low-maintenance landscaped area made up of green lumps which require little or preferably NO care; because they have been brainwashed into believing that real gardening is unpleasant work and should be avoided."

In his philosophy and in his life's work, Ross displays a European perspective that proves enlightening as you peruse the grounds of Gardenview.

Cleveland Museum of Art, Fine Arts Garden and Interior
11150 East Blvd., University Circle, Cleveland, 44106; 421-7340; free admittance

You find traces of gardens where you least expect to see them. Such is the case with the Cleveland Museum of Art. The Art Museum is located at one end of the Fine Arts Garden, a strolling area designed in the early 1900s by the landscape architecture firm of S. Olmsted Brothers of Brookline, Massachusetts. Garden areas circle a lagoon and include intriguing European-style pleached sycamore trees, which are pruned to have a flat-topped, interwoven, ceiling-like look. The general layout and the pleached trees remain from Olmsted's original garden and create an elegant setting for the museum building. Most of the garden has been cleared to make it a safer place to stroll—90 percent of the original shrubs have been taken out, and the remaining trees have had their lower branches removed so they do not create hiding places. Still, the Fine Arts Garden remains an oasis of greenery in the middle of the city.

Near the garden and elsewhere around the museum are about a dozen American elms, the few survivors of an attack of Dutch elm disease several decades ago. Also, there are interesting collections of cherry and crab apple trees, some quite rare, but it's difficult to tell one from another because they aren't labeled. Regardless, May and June are wonderful times to visit, as the bulbs and flowering trees produce an abundance of flowers.

Inside the museum, you'll find many flowers and conservatory plants that complement the season and the art displays. One week a month in the north lobby, you'll find a large flower arrangement crafted by volunteers from the Women's Council of the Cleveland Museum of Art. Elsewhere, plants are used to help guard the artwork.

"Plants keep the public back away from the exhibits. They hide the mechanics of the displays and guide the public through the right corridors," said Leon Santamary, former museum horticulturist. "Sometimes plants become part of the show. I tried to match the spirit of each show with the appropriate plant—like papyrus for the Egyptian exhibit, exotic cacti for the Picasso exhibit, bamboos and palms for Japanese exhibits."

Another special feature you will see from time to time are lavish pots of flowering orchids—*Cymbidium* orchids from November to February, and smaller botanical species in the summer. "We're unique from other art museums because we have our own greenhouse and can maintain a large collection of orchids—all of which have been donated to us by people in the area," Santamary said. The horticultural staff rejuvenates the plant collection by taking cuttings when the older plants begin to take a beating. They use cold frames for forcing bulbs into bloom.

In the heart of the museum, a garden court stretches up 25 feet high and provides a home for large tropical palms, fig trees, and rubber trees—huge old specimens that have seen decades come and go inside the museum.

Cleveland Museum of Natural History
Wade Oval, Cleveland, 44106; 231-4600; admission fee; garden tours avail. with advance reservation

As at the zoo, the link here between animals and plants is a natural. At the Museum of Natural History, native plants are cultivated in open courtyards within the museum. One garden is in a woodland; the other is open and in sun. Both include plants from different habitats (environments of different types of soil, watering, or light in which certain plants usually live).

Jim Bissell, curator of botany, said, "We created these gardens for minimal maintenance and now find that a lot of people come to see them because they are gardens that you can leave pretty much alone. It's funny how well accepted that idea is today. When we started these gardens 20 years ago, people used to complain because they thought we had run out of money and hadn't finished."

The first garden you'll see upon entering the main lobby is the

Thelma and Kent Smith Environmental Courtyard, which is a riot of color in late summer as the prairie species take over. If you look closely at plant labels, you will find unusual native species from the northern hardwood forest, such as yellow birch (*Betula lutea*) and mountain maple (*Acer spicatum*). You'll also find more common plants that you may have heard about but never knew what they looked like, including elderberry (a fruit), goldenseal (a medicinal plant), and horsetail (*Equisetum hyemale*), the pioneer source of scouring brushes. Some of the species here are interesting simply to watch grow and develop.

"We found a neat phenomenon in the prairie area where big bluestem and Indian grass grows. Grasses are supposed to be wind pollinated but we saw that when the flowers are covered with dew before the sun hits them in the morning, the bees will pollinate them like crazy. They carry away pollen by the bucketload," Bissell said.

The second garden, located off the dinosaur gallery, is the Perkins Wildlife Memorial and Woods Garden. Most of the plants are clustered within a circular path that leads past animal cages. Because the area is shaded, its main display comes in spring. One section exhibits bog plants such as the very early blooming, heat-generating skunk cabbage and golden-flowered marsh marigold. Another is devoted to mixed mesophytic forest, with sugar maple, beech, oak, black cherry, witch hazel, sassafras, and tulip trees, and spring-blooming trilliums, Virginia bluebells, liverworts, and violets. A third section is devoted to such plants as Kentucky coffee tree, Chinquapin oak, bladdernut, trilliums, wild hyacinth, and trout lily.

Eastman Reading Garden

Cleveland Public Library, 325 Superior Ave., Cleveland, 44114; 623-2800 (Because of library construction, the garden will be closed from October 1993 until summer 1997)

A couple blocks east of Public Square (which in itself is worth a wander through to see the informally pruned taxus hedges, fountain, and flowering trees) is a garden in which you can truly relax. It's the Eastman Reading Garden, part of the main branch of the Cleveland Public Library. Because it is enclosed in an encircling wall of greenery with tall buildings looming on either side, the garden feels especially peaceful and secluded given its proximity to bustling traffic.

The garden was established in 1937, converted from an unkempt city park to a place for outdoor reading. It was stocked with racks of books and magazines during library hours. The open-air access to the library collection didn't last long, though, because there was no way to control traffic flow through the area. In 1959, civic leaders took the garden in another direction by landscaping it with flowering trees and ivy, adding ornamental gates, a sundial, and wall fountain. The garden was renovated again in 1982 and decked out in new paving, raised beds for sweet-gum shade trees, a new fountain, and crab apples 'Dorothea' and 'Redbud'. The gates are still in place and are open from 9 a.m. to 5 p.m. from spring through fall.

Garfield Park Nature Center, Metroparks

Garfield Park Reservation, 11350 Broadway Ave., Garfield Hts., 44125; 341-3152

This Reservation has one of the largest cultivated gardens in the Metropark system. The spring wildflower garden is a must-see, but you also can walk down a garden path clothed on either side in hummingbird and butterfly flowers. The creatures fly back and forth across the walk as they feed. Relax by the central waterfall fountain and pool, then check out the herb garden, a composting display, and a developing pioneer plant garden (with plants that early American settlers used. An old field garden of naturalized and native plants such as Queen Anne's Lace, Teasil, goldenrod, and asters shows how to leave a unique wild space in your garden.

Because this collection of gardens is so large, the nature center is always looking for volunteers to help maintain them. Volunteers are recognized at a garden party in early May. Call 341-3152 for more information.

Goldsmith Garden at Hale Farm

2626 Oak Hill Rd., Bath, 44210; 575-9137; open Wednesday to Sunday, May to October and during December; admission fee

The Goldsmith Garden at the Western Reserve Historical Society's Hale Farm and Village can take you back to the pioneer era when people were much more reliant on their gardens than today. Pioneer gardens provided fruit, vegetables, flowers, medicine, cloth dyes, and fragrances, all of which you will see in sections of this elaborate garden. To supplement garden varieties, a field behind is devoted to an apple orchard and to large field crops, including potatoes, squash, and corn.

Western Reserve Historical Society volunteer Kathleen Van Devere designed the Goldsmith Garden using an 1830s garden plan and pre-1850s diaries, journals, and manuscripts. As was typical in that era, the garden is enclosed with a tall stockade fence in the back and picket fence in the front, both essential for keeping out marauding animals. Like the Cahoon Memorial Rose Garden, the Goldsmith Garden has a round central focal point, which was a spring-fed water source in the original 1830s plan. Unlike the rose garden, however, the beds here are four feet wide, rectangular, and raised—a layout popular among modern intensive gardeners because its center can be reached from either side without stepping into the bed and compressing the soil. According to research, early garden designers also were concerned with other issues we ponder today, such as providing for a succession of bloom (a sequence of flowers to bloom through the summer), easy-to-grow flowers (quite similar to our low-maintenance emphasis), and flowers that bloom for a longer period of time.

Van Devere said that people tend to be pleasantly surprised because the garden is so sophisticated for a village of this size. But that's the way higher-income families of that time gardened. If you want to see how families in the lower economic scale gardened, look at the kitchen garden growing by the Saltbox. They are rows of things put in the ground. Early gardeners had a surprising diversity of plants available to them. Historical society literature lists 41 cultivars of apple trees available. Among the vegetables and herbs early pioneers in this area grew were sweet potatoes, cucumbers, turnips, peas, caraway seeds, cabbage, lettuce, beans (five kinds, including tropical castor oil, which is not a true bean at all), asparagus, rhubarb, artichoke, gourds, turnips (or large radishes), four kinds of squash, three kinds of corn (including black, popcorn, and broomcorn, which was used to make fibrous brooms), six kinds of potatoes, rutabaga, onion, pepper, tomato, peppergrass, broccoli, carrots, cauliflower, beets, purple eggplant, parsley, sage, savory, sweet marjoram, and hops.

Among flowers, diversity is again amazing. Early settlers had 60 kinds of verbena, chrysanthemums, spiderwort (*Tradescantia*), peonies, dahlias, irises, carnations, pinks, sunflowers, an assortment of bulbs, and azaleas. Determining the exact species or cultivars grown a century ago, though, is a difficult proposition.

For more information on the Hale Farm, look for *The Jonathan Hale Farm: A Chronicle of the Cuyahoga Valley* (by John J. Horton, Publication 116 of the Western Reserve Historical Society). For more information on historic cultivars, contact the Seed Saver's Exchange, a nonprofit organization devoted to trading and preserving old-fashioned plants, at Rural Route 3, Box 239, Decorah, IA 52101.

The Goldsmith Garden depicts gardens from 150 years ago.
(Photo courtesy of Hale Farm and Village.)

Haymaker Parkway

Rte. 59 from Longmere St. to Willow St. in Kent; organized by the Kent Environmental Council; pick up brochures at Kent City Hall, 678-8105, or Chamber of Commerce, 673-9855; for more information, call Mary Hewitt, 678-8105 or Joan Sturtevant, 626-3953

The State Route 59 Bypass in Kent, a one-mile stretch called Haymaker Parkway, has become home for a network of gardens—mixed beds of perennials, ground covers, and shrubs with hundreds of shade and evergreen trees. The result of grassroots networking, it's worth a visit when you are in the neighborhood. The project was undertaken by the Kent Environmental Council in 1985. Ten years of fundraising efforts and volunteer labor were completed in 1994. More than half of the plantings were given in memory or recognition of local residents.

Eight large perennial beds and many smaller beds, ornamental grasses, flowering shrubs and trees, and shade and evergreen trees stretch along the parkway. The landscape design, by Dr. Joan Sturtevant, co-owner of Gateway Gardens, makes the area a visual delight any time of the year. The city of Kent maintains the parkway.

One of the most unusual planting areas is at the front and side of city hall. It includes over three thousand bulbs and seven kinds of ornamental grasses. There also are drifts of popular perennials such as Salvia 'East Friesland', lobelia, pinks (*Dianthus* species), bergenia, and lilyturf (*Liriope* species) interplanted with twelve cultivars of heather and five kinds of junipers. Near the front walk to city hall are over eighty old-fashioned roses, a thousand bulbs, and more mixed plantings of perennials, trees, and shrubs.

Among the woody plants, look for more unusual specimens such as the smoke tree, Japanese pagoda tree (*Sophora japonica*), purple and tricolor beech, tree lilacs, sapphire berry (*Symplocos paniculata*), fragrant epaulette tree (*Pterostyrax hispidus*), and false spirea (*Sorbaria sorbifolia*).

Hiram Community Gardens: Hurd Memorial Garden

corner of Hayden and Bancroft streets in Hiram; garden tours avail. by advance reservation with Jamie Barrow, P.O. Box 402, Hiram, 44234

One of the best public gardens in this area is not large, but every inch of it is beautifully used. The Hurd Memorial Garden on the campus of Hiram College is a Victorian garden—a Perennial Plant Association Honor Award winner—that was designed by Valerie Strong.

"The garden was created because the old Hurd house had been torn down against the wishes of the community. To placate them, Jamie Barrow [a local garden enthusiast] who had organized the installation and maintenance of other Hiram gardens, decided to turn the property into a garden. It was dedicated to the Hurd family, two generations of doctors who were in Hiram from the late 1800s to about 1960. Now that the garden is maturing, it has made up for a whole lot of bad feelings. Hiram has a lot of gardens, but most are contemplative rather than display," Strong said.

As was common in Victorian times, Strong divided the long, narrow corner lot that the garden occupies into two gardens: a medicinal garden on the north end, and a yellow garden in the center. You can enter through a vine-covered arbor and walk looping trails that open up to exciting new views around each turn. There are Victorian plants such as bayberry, spirea, lilacs, catmint, phlox, sunflower, purple loosestrife, ornamental grasses, and cleome; some of the best of popular new cultivars of older plants such as coneflower 'Goldsturm', threadleaf coreopsis 'Moonbeam', and sedum 'Autumn Joy'; and some unique specimens such as a cut-leaf sumac and weeping mulberry (also popular in Victorian times). Secluded benches scattered throughout invite you to rest. Strong tends to group each type of perennial plant and many of the shrubs in masses so that they make a big impact. The garden is well groomed and full of color throughout the seasons, even in winter, when the ornamental grasses stand golden against the snow.

In the medicinal garden, beds swirl around a Victorian urn; a crescent of foundation stones saved from an early Hiram building and old Victorian lampposts extend along the walk. "The garden is arranged so it is closed off by shrubbery from the street, which makes it seem private even though it's public. It is surrounded by a fence that is a replica of the perching fence that enclosed the original campus. Couples used to sit there on the top board—a modern-day drive-in," said Strong.

If you join up with a garden tour, you can also see eight other, smaller, gardens around Hiram: Copper Beech, Bonney Castle, Pendleton, Century House, Missionary Garden, Mahan House, Hadsell Piney Woods, and Horticulture Garden. (These have been featured in an American Greetings calendar.)

A Victorian urn makes a creative container garden and focal point at the Hurd Memorial Garden in Hiram. (Photo courtesy of Hiram Public Gardens.)

The Holden Arboretum
9500 Sperry Rd., Kirtland, 440940; 946-4400; admission fee for non-members; closed Mondays

The Holden Arboretum's 3,100 acres of land make it one of the largest arboreta in the country and a great asset for our community. You can get a feel for the expanse of all this land by driving to the arboretum on the newly rerouted Sperry Road, a replacement for the old pothole-ridden gravel road. The new road winds through rolling landscape that the old road kept hidden.

"We had always been so close to the old road that we never considered that we could back off from it until we had a master plan designed by a Pittsburgh landscape architect. He said we had to get rid of that straight line, and picked a new route that gives a wonderful view of the landscape through the east branch of the Chagrin Valley to the top of Little Mountain. It really shows the vastness of the area," said Holden Arboretum director Eliot Paine.

If you focus your sightseeing, you can see the garden areas of the Arboretum in a single visit. Look for the following:

Myrtle S. Holden Wildflower Garden

This five-acre garden of Ohio plants starts beneath a high canopy of sugar maples and stretches out of the woods into rockery, prairie, fen, and bog plantings. The collection includes over five hundred species, most of which the Arboretum staff have propagated in Holden's greenhouses.

The plants, which grow in natural groupings along winding trails, pack the woodland with color from April to May. The prairie takes over in summer. The bog garden is especially interesting because the plants, including pitcher plants that catch and consume insects, grow on top of acidic water covered with a layer of sphagnum moss. A fen is a similar boggy area, but with alkaline water and a different set of plants. The rockery area contains species that grow naturally in dunes, sand, or rock areas—including endangered plants like the Lakeside daisy, one of the rarest plants in Ohio. The plants are labeled with different colored tags according to how rare they are.

"The whole thrust of this garden is to model habitat communities— to duplicate soil, moisture, and light conditions—in which these plants naturally grow. We don't expect to save endangered species by planting them in our garden, but we teach people about them and learn the basics of their biology that land managers may some day need. We also send the seeds and spores to the Federal Seed Repository, where they are maintained and preserved for the future," Brian Parsons, garden curator, said.

Display Garden Landscape Collection

This area just south of the visitor's center is more of a working and idea area than a beautiful garden, but in it you will see some of the better landscape plants for our region. "We do have collections of single items like viburnums, lilacs, and a new daylily area, but we also are trying to show how different plants will grow together and how to combine various textures and colors," said Jim Mack, superintendent of grounds. For example, one grouping uses a paperbark maple with a backdrop of lilacs to show how well the peeling cinnamon-colored bark shows up against a curtain of green.

Rhododendron Garden

This three-acre collection of rhododendrons, artfully arranged beneath ancient trees, including a 350-year old white oak and a red oak 100 years its junior, is well worth hiking to in late May and early June. Some of the rhododendrons are over fifty years old; others are new hybrids developed by local breeders, including Peter Girard, Dr. David Leach, the late Anthony Shammarello, and the late Paul Bosley. This garden also features famous earlier types, such as Dexter rhododendrons (Massachusetts, 1920s), Ghent Hybrid azaleas (Belgium, early 1800s), and Knap Hill azaleas (England, 1870s). These rhododendrons and azaleas flower prolifically amid related companions of heather, heath, mountain laurel, mountain andromeda, blueberries, and leucothoe.

Holden Arboretum has an interesting hedge collection.
(Photo by Paul Huling, courtesy of Holden Arboretum.)

Judson Retirement Community, Judson Park Garden

2181 Ambleside Rd.; 791-2990; always open

A new garden has replaced a parking lot here. It's designed to engage residents and visitors of all ages in experiencing and enjoying the outdoors. The garden is made up of three sections. There's a waterfall park with two ponds and close up observation areas suitable for wheelchair access. Masses of perennials and plots for residents to plant cluster nearby. The second section is a garden lawn for playing croquet or bocce. The third section, which is still in the planning stages, will be a horseshoe pit and putting green.

Judson Retirement Community, Judson Manor Rooftop Garden
Judson Manor: 1890 E. 107th, 44106; 721-1234; open by appointment

Judson Manor residents can grow flowers and vegetables in raised beds on the rooftop. "What makes this garden very special is that while you're enjoying the garden itself, you can also view the city skyline and the waterfront," said Kelly Hendricks, of the Judson staff.

The garden at Judson Retirement Community's Judson Park is set up for easy wheelchair access. (Photo courtesy of Judson Retirement Community.)

Lantern Court
9203 Kirtland-Chardon Rd., Kirtland, 44094; gardens open Wednesdays; tours on some Sundays; pay admission at the main Holden Arboretum building; house can be reserved for meetings by nonprofit organizations

This lovely 25-acre garden, on the former estate of Warren and Maud Corning, was built in the early 1930s. The gardens were originally designed by local landscape architect Donald Gray, but have been expanded and refined over the years. Mr. Corning was an avid plant collector and some of his original plantings remain, including daffodils, tree peonies, primroses, pines, hemlocks, oaks, and a weeping willow. Tom Yates, the garden superintendent for the last twenty years, has done his share of seeking out new cultivars and unusual plants for the gardens, adding to the start Corning made.

As you enter the grounds, which are around the corner from the Arboretum entrance, you will see the Corning formal garden. Its terraced rose beds and geometrical cutting gardens stretch between a hemlock hedge, clipped yews, and a long English-style perennial border. The small details, such as tiny blue lobelia plants flowering between the steps that link rose and cutting gardens, are charming.

Along the drive and across the front of the property, flowing island beds of spring flowering bulbs, perennials, and flowering shrubs are molded to the contour of the slope. The woods creep along the drive on the front (west) side of the house close to a small arcade-like orangery (an early greenhouse used to grow citrus trees). Nearby, a shallow boggy ravine is filled with plants that like wet feet. Look for rare species such as pitcher plants, Western skunk cabbage, and exotic primroses. Beside the ravine runs a shaded primrose walk and rock garden with dwarf conifers, heather, and small alpine plants.

Switch gears by taking a path through informal gardens. It lies east of the house and will lead you through a wildflower- and hosta-planted woodland behind the house to a fern garden and steep hemlock-clothed ravine with a dramatic waterfall.

Lake County Farmpark
8800 Chardon Rd., Kirtland, 44094; (800) 366-FARM; admission fee

Lake County Farmpark combines an emphasis on animals with the accompanying agricultural practices (haymaking, grain harvesting, threshing), gardens of old-fashioned vegetables (dragon tongue beans, broomcorn, grain amaranth, and coriander), and fruit orchards and berry fields.

"We have blueberries, strawberries, grapes, and raspberries that you can eat by invitation during regular tours. We also let schoolchildren sample the honey straight from the honeycomb in our apiary. We pass the honey around and, when everyone has their mouth full, I ask them if they know how honey is made. A lot of full-mouthed kids are shocked to learn bees take in the nectar, and then regurgitate it to make honey," says Tim Malinich, horticulture specialist.

If you look closely or ask nearby gardeners, you can learn about experimental mulching, training, and soil amending techniques that are in use.

In 1992, Lake County Farmpark added a new horticultural center in their Planter's Overlook area. It includes a hydroponics exhibit, which was growing 20-foot-high tomato vines at one point. You can see smaller models of commercial and do-it-yourself hydroponics kits that you may want to try at home. Kids can get involved in a variety of hands-on projects such as planting corn and potatoes in spring and picking them in the fall. Other exhibits explaining how plants grow and develop and where food comes from.

Lake Erie Nature and Science Center

28728 Wolf Rd., Bay Village, 44140; 871-2900

This privately operated nature center devoted to wildlife in the Metropark's Huntington Reservation has a small nature garden developed by its women's board. You can stroll through the garden to see native wildflowers and non-natives that can attract wildlife to home landscapes. (The gardens will be under renovation until 1996 to let in more sunlight and combine formal and informal plantings.) "One of our big drawing cards is that families with young children can come here and see the whole facility in an hour, and then go do whatever they have to do that particular day," said Larry Richardson, director.

The Nature and Science Center also offers wildflower walks in the surrounding 108-acre park, tree-identification programs, and other plant-oriented field studies or classes. They have a spring plant sale called the Spring Thing, and offer annual and perennial plants and wildflowers, some of which are local.

Lake View Cemetery

12316 Euclid Ave., East Cleveland/Cleveland Heights, 44106; 421-2665; self-guided tour avail. at office

This cemetery, full of statues and monuments (including the burial place of President James Garfield), is also is a 285-acre arboretum. Originally developed in 1869 as a Victorian landscape park, its layout is true to those times: winding drives curve through a large park and over sloped ground that moves from the low-lying sandy areas toward the lake to the clay ridge in Cleveland Heights.

Like a museum, the grounds hold horticultural history and ancient trees—500 of which are labeled so you can appreciate them better. Because Lake View Cemetery was established during an era of extensive plant exploration in the Orient, it is a treasure-house of big Oriental species and other unusual woody plants, including:

- Rare Chinese species, such as paper bark maple (*Acer griseum*), Chinese toon (*Cedrela sinensis*), hupeh evodia (*Evodia hupehensis*), and Chinese maackia (*Maackia chinensis*)
- Tree giants like the 100-year-old Sargent's weeping hemlock (*Tsuga canadensis* 'Sargentii'), a Moses Cleaveland American beech, and tulip trees and white oaks
- Unusual trees, including a cut-leaf weeping sugar maple, double-flowered dogwood, and big-leaf magnolias
- Loads of beautiful flowering trees, such as redbud, buckeyes, crab apples and magnolias
- Over 100,000 bulbs on three-acre Daffodil Hill

Mary Elizabeth Garden, Lake County Nursery, Inc.

5052 South Ridge Rd. [Rte. 84], Perry, 44081; 259-5571;
for more information contact Maria Pettorini

The Mary Elizabeth Garden, named after the wife of Felix Zampini, the founder of Lake County Nursery, Inc., is a one-acre garden featuring over five hundred types of herbs and flowers grown by this wholesale nursery. Paths wind past thousands of spring bulbs, shade gardens of ferns and hostas, unusual conifers, perennial flowers, a waterfall and sunken garden, and many of the nursery's own cultivars.

Moldovan's Gardens

Steve Moldovan, 38830 Detroit Rd., Avon, 44011; 934-4993; open to the public during flowering season from May to August, but the peak of daylily bloom is July

Behind what appears to be an ordinary white house on the outskirts of Avon stretches a four-acre garden, a beautiful display area and breeding ground for hostas and daylilies developed by Steve Moldovan. Neat freeform garden beds sweep down the gentle incline of the long and relatively narrow yard. Here and there, masses of daylilies interweave with other perennials, including bellflowers, peonies, periwinkle, and pink-flowered lungwort, as well as annual flowers and dahlias.

The sunny beds are broken by specimen plants such as dwarf Japanese maple, roses, large oaks, magnolias, and small groves of maple trees. There are seats and sculpture interspersed throughout the main part of the garden, which stands out from the surrounding lawns and fields of corn and soybean. Also, an intriguing secret garden section lies just downhill from a reflecting pool and rock garden. Enter it through an opening in a wild bamboo thicket and find thousands of seedlings planted beyond.

Shady nooks provide the setting for Moldovan's hostas, a perennial grown primarily for its interesting leaves. Hostas also bloom, often in midsummer, sending up spikes of white or lavender flowers that can be fragrant. One hosta, called 'Corduroy', is especially eye-catching; its leaves are each over a foot long, making the plant more than four feet wide and high, and it holds up especially well into early September, when other hosta are fading.

You can see subtle signs that the area is a working garden. All the plants are labeled with aluminum tags and some of the seedpods are tagged as well.

North Chagrin Nature Center, Metroparks

North Chagrin Reservation, Buttermilk Falls Parkway, Mayfield Village, 44094; 473-3370

There is an herb garden outside the nature center doorway and a nearby garden of wildflowers that bloom in the spring and change throughout the seasons. A small garden of hummingbird flowers and bird-feeding shrubs stands outside the window where you can watch the animals at work during both summer and winter.

Oberlin College Campus

Oberlin, Lorain County; self-guided garden tour brochures avail. at the Oberlin College Inn, North Main St.; 775-1111

A necklace of perennial gardens and mixed beds of woody plants stretches across the Oberlin College campus. It's an excellent display to check out in midsummer when the campus is quiet, according to William Salo, manager of grounds.

You can learn while you stroll if you buy a tour brochure, which tells the history of the college campus and points out examples of microclimates and hardiness variations. Because the campus was founded in 1833, it features wonderful big trees—some planted over 150 years ago. They're most notable in Tappan Square, the site of many early college buildings. A campus brochure notes, "Early settlers cut down the native trees, creating a field of stumps, and the area was for a time known as Stumpyville. Later the Square was enclosed by a hedgerow of Osage Orange, which remained until the 1880s." Since the original clearing of the Square, tree planting has become an annual event led, in early years, by ". . . students from the East, whose life had not been a constant warfare with trees."

The largest group of perennial gardens surrounds the Oberlin College Inn, where about a hundred different varieties of bulbs and flowers spread through eight gardens. Near the Allen Memorial Art Museum, you'll find a formal herb garden developed with a symmetrical display of evergreen herbs for winter color, and other herbs that shine in summer.

Oldest Stone House

Lakewood Park, Bell and Lake avenues, Lakewood; 221-7343

In the small enclosed area surrounding the Oldest Stone House, you can browse through an herb garden, the working and display site of the Oldest Stone House Herb Society. The L-shaped garden houses about fifty different kinds of herbs that the society harvests for their herbal projects. It ends in a rockport, where historical tombstones are interplanted with traditional herbs that represented loss or were used for embalming, such as santolina, lilies-of-the-valley, foxglove, southernwood, artemisia, and costmary.

"Overall, this garden is similar to the casual doorstep garden of an early dwelling in this area," said Sandy Koozer, curator of the Lakewood Historical Society.

Rockefeller Park Greenhouse

750 E. 88th St., Cleveland, 44108; 664-3103; free admittance; open daily; guided tours avail. with four-week advance reservation

The Rockefeller Park Greenhouse, a working greenhouse for the city of Cleveland and, more recently, a public display garden, is attracting more visitors than ever before. It is a fun place to go, and it's free (though in some places not beautifully maintained because of city staff cuts). You can reach the greenhouse by driving north from Chester Avenue on Martin Luther King Jr. Drive through what remains (very little, unfortunately) of the Cultural Gardens. Look for the many new plantings along MLK—there are 90,000 day lilies, 69,000 daffodils, and other assorted perennials. the hillside near the Greenhouse sports a new tiered perennial planter.

At the greenhouse, four acres of outdoor gardens stretch north and south of the greenhouse range and parking lot. To the south, beyond a gazebo, are a mixture of different gardens (many donated by local organizations) that are collectively called the Peace Garden. There you can see interesting displays of globe artichokes, new annual cultivars, dahlias, and irises.

"Irises grow so much better here in the rich loose soil and more moderate climate. We're only about a quarter-mile from the lake," said iris breeder Tony Willott. "It's like a different world from where I live in Beachwood."

Four persimmon trees—two male, two female—bear a crop unusual in this area. "We had two trees that never fruited. Then two ladies from Seven Hills came in and said they had persimmon trees that flowered but never fruited. Since you need both male and female trees to have a crop, they donated their trees to us. Ever since then, we've had tons of fruit around the first fall frost," said Chris Jagelewski, horticulturist maintenance foreman.

To the north of the parking lot is a formal lawn area, the English Mall, that is backed by a wonderful rock-sculpted Japanese garden that you may have seen without knowing it—it is a frequent site of television interviews. Below the greenhouse is the unique Betty Ott Talking Garden for the Blind, which contains plants that appeal to senses other than sight and offers a taped explanation of each area. It was renovated in 1992 by The Women's City Club and has spurred interest in the development of similar gardens elsewhere in the United States.

Inside the greenhouse you'll find a world of tropical plants, orchids, cacti, fountains, and changing displays of lavishly massed flowers. The greenhouses are the remains of the old orchid growing range built by nineteenth-century philanthropist William J. Gordon. Around the turn of the century, John D. Rockefeller bought the property and added onto the greenhouse ranges. When Rockefeller quarreled with the city about unpaid taxes, he moved out of the area and left the greenhouse to the city. It became a working nursery, supplying other city parks with flowers and trees. In 1960 a tropical showroom and some of the outside gardens were added, and it began to attract visitors.

To keep up the present displays, Don Slogar, manager, encourages volunteer groups to help with planting or maintenance. Slogar has also helped start the Friends of the Cleveland Greenhouse, a nonprofit group that helps raise funds to support greenhouse activities .

"We can't justify the Greenhouse's existence by beauty alone. This has to be a people place, and it has become one. We have dozens of people here every day, from toddlers to seniors," said Slogar.

It's always tropical inside Rockefeller Park Greenhouse.
(Photo courtesy of Rockefeller Park Greenhouse.)

Rocky River Nature Center, Metroparks
Rocky River Reservation, 24000 Valley Parkway, North Olmsted, 44070; 734-6660

You will find three gardens here. One is devoted to flowers that attract butterflies and hummingbirds in summer. Another, the Ron Hauser Memorial Wildflower Garden, peaks in April and May but also contains a few summer-blooming native plants such as columbine, cardinal flower, blue lobelia, and closed gentian that stretch the blooming season. The third, a small herb garden, features plants that area settlers relied on for medicine, cooking, and hiding the odors of overly ripe meat and overly ripe people. Among the herbs you'll see here are sage, once used to help people digest greasy meats; chamomile, used then and now as a yellow dye, for tea, and as a hair rinse for blondes; and wormwood, strewn on dirt floors to repel fleas.

Sea World of Ohio
1100 Sea World Dr., Aurora, 44202; 562-8101; admission fee

Sea World of Ohio, a 90-acre marine-life park, features some of the prettiest grounds in northeast Ohio. The park is situated on a natural glacial lake amid rolling hills. Rushing streambeds, patterned paving stones, and artistic floral displays are well suited to the clean, high-quality park setting.

Rob McCartney, Sea World of Ohio's manager of horticulture, believes landscaping is meant to entertain. "There is a purpose behind every plant, tree, and flower. This applies to anything that goes in the ground, whether it's a marigold or maple," says McCartney. "With this philosophy, we try to re-create a feeling, a 'micro' environment for each attraction."

For instance, Shamu Stadium is enhanced by plantings from the Pacific Northwest, where killer whales are found. At Shark Encounter, guests are greeted by rather jagged limestone boulders, spikes of yucca, prickly junipers, fragrant spruce, saw-tooth oak, and red Japanese blood grass, which conjure up images of sharp teeth among splashing waters.

Sea World of Ohio is devoted to meeting the needs of all its guests. So they created an Access-for-All Garden for people with or without disabilities (see chapter 4 for details).

If you have any questions as you stroll the park, ask horticultural staff members in the bright green shirts.

Plants set the stage for fun at Sea World.   (Photo courtesy of Sea World.)

Shaker Lakes Regional Nature Center
2600 South Park Blvd., Shaker Heights, 44120; 321-5935

When you drive into the parking lot of this nature center, you are greeted by a spectacular boardwalk that traverses a wetland area. Wander along this "All People's Trail" (accessible to all abilities) to see interesting marsh plants, blackbirds, water birds, muskrats, and other wildlife. the three-mile Stearns trail is more rugged and loops around the woods.

Although less obvious, a wildflower garden is located to the east of the Nature Center building. This mature garden was started about twenty-five years ago by members of the Shaker Lakes Garden Club, who still maintain the area. "One of our biggest battles now is keeping out unwanted plants like periwinkle, pachysandra, and goutweed. We spend a lot of time pulling things out," said Linda Johnson, Nature Center volunteer and board member.

The Nature Center also offers environmental education classes for children and a spring plant sale.

Silver Creek Farm

7097 Allyn Rd., P.O. Box 254, Hiram, 44234; 562-4381; tours, group talks, and slide shows avail.

Although this is not a show garden, you may enjoy seeing how an organic market garden operates. Silver Creek Farm, operated by Ted and Molly Bartlett, is certified organic by the Ohio Ecological Food and Farm Association, which means the produce is grown in a chemical-free environment and in a manner that safeguards the land. The Bartletts own 125 acres, much of which is woodlands held in a land trust. The fields are devoted to blueberries, squash, greens, peas, peppers, herbs, eggplant, beets, broccoli, garlic, and heirloom tomatoes.

You may have to walk past several fallow fields to reach the growing area. Although weeds can be seen between the raised, plastic-mulched beds, these are evidence that no herbicides touch the land. And the crops grow beautifully. The key, according to Molly Bartlett, is building the soil with livestock manure, creating a proper environment for beneficial bugs that eat other pests, and rotating crops so that different plant families follow in different spots, eliminating pest buildup.

"We use our own barnyard manure that has no livestock chemicals in it. It's very different from stable manures," said Bartlett. "Sometimes we grow companions together that benefit each other, like leeks with tomatoes. Earlier in spring we once had to dust the eggplants with diatomaceous earth (microscopical, prickly, sandlike particles harvested from marine algae), and that stopped most bugs; and we use Bt for cabbage loopers. I think if you could cover everything with Reemay (a brand of floating woven row covers) you could eliminate most problems, especially on young plants of cucumbers and watermelons."

The Bartletts encourage visitors to come for Farm Market, every Saturday, 10 a.m. to 4 p.m., from Mother's Day until New Year's Day. They kick off the spring season on Mother's Day by selling seedlings of heirloom tomatoes (herb, vegetable, and flower seedlings and other specialty items are sold all summer long), offering sheep-shearing demonstrations, and harvesting exotic Oriental shiitake mushrooms, which they cultivate in their woods. They also have craft items—sheep skins, yarns, sweaters, maple syrup—and other gifts for sale all season long. You can also find their produce at the Food Co-op in University Circle, the Baricelli Inn, Parker's in Ohio City, and at other restaurants and grocery stores selling organic produce. Call and ask about their community-supported agriculture program.

Stan Hywet Hall

714 N. Portage Path, Akron, 44303; 836-5533; admission fee; grounds tour avail. with advance reservation

If you want to visit a garden that will impress and inspire, go to Stan Hywet Hall in Akron, the former estate of F. A. Seiberling, co-founder of Goodyear Tire and Rubber Company. The 70-acre landscape was developed beginning in 1911 by landscape architect Warren Manning, who helped design New York's Central Park. Although the gardens have changed over the years, the Stan Hywet Hall Board of Trustees is in the process of restoring the gardens to their original design.

The most recent renovation is the Walled English Garden, restored to its 1930 glory, an elaborate flowery design originally prepared by Ellen Shipman. Her garden included 1,500 flowers and bulbs flowering in white, pale yellow, pink, rose, blue, and lavender within a sunken brick-walled area.

Shipman was a genius at coordinating all these plants. The design is perfect. The rectangular garden includes a large reflecting pool and a statue with a fountain, both surrounded by walks and garden beds. In late summer, every bed blazes with tall airy asters and anemones, delphiniums, glads, phlox, and lower growing sedum and forget-me-not— all in full bloom without signs of late summer fatigue. This is possible, said garden volunteer Kathleen Van Devere, because plants are moved in and out of the garden following Shipman's plan. Signs of spring bloomers remain in the foliage of peonies, Siberian bugloss, and coral-bells, which form strong edging lines that complement the brick walks and unify the garden.

It's easy to imagine the garden 70 years ago with women in swirling long dresses and gentlemen in suits tipping their hats during a garden party, or Gertrude Seiberling, wife of F.A. Seiberling and mother of six surviving children, taking a cup of tea out there in the peaceful surroundings. A poem by the lower entrance reads:

> A garden is a lovesome
> Thing God wot
>   Rose Plot
>   Fringed Pool
>   Fern'd Grot
> The veriest school of peace and yet the
> fool contends that God is not God! In Gardens!
>   When the eve is cool?
> Nay but I have a sign tis very sure God walks in mine.

A lot of labor is required to maintain this garden; part of the work is supplied by Akron Garden Club volunteers on Monday and Friday mornings. The other gardens spread out from the grandiose Tudor Revival mansion built early in this century. As you enter through the main gate, you will see Manning's idea of a welcome: the great meadow lawn, which provides a foreground to distant views and a quiet informal space without the blaze of color and hard formal lines that make up a summer garden.

Manning sectioned the estate into individual areas. When you park, you will see the huge cutting gardens, now larger than Manning originally planned. They supply flowers for arrangements created in the manor house by volunteer flower arrangers. You will see massive beds of peonies, eucalyptus, zinnias, ageratum, snaps, coneflowers, lisianthus, and sunflowers.

Closer to the house is a superb rose garden enclosed in a perfectly clipped taxus hedge. On the north end of the cutting garden are the working and display greenhouses. Walk from the greenhouses through an arbor to the birch allée, a wonderful 550-foot-long tunnel formed under a canopy of interlacing white bark birches. At one end lies the manor house, a treasure in itself. At the other is a teahouse overlooking the Cuyahoga Valley. From there, rustic stone steps lead down to a water-filled quarry and a marvelous Japanese garden (which is scheduled for restoration). Wander the trails along the creek and by all means do walk over the steeply arching Japanese bridges that cross and recross the creek. You will eventually come to a shady area, where lies the traditional Japanese garden, which is serene, quiet, secluded. Here you will find offset stone walks and steps (which look like they are the work of nature rather than a careful plan), stone lanterns, gracefully manicured evergreens, trickling water, bamboo, and many other beautiful details.

To the south of this wonderful garden is a naturalistic dell riddled with trails and a sycamore-rhododendron allée that leads back to the manor. The huge sycamores are, unfortunately, stricken with Ceratocystis canker, which is evident in the deterioration of their trunks. Determining how to replace these sycamores without disturbing the rhododendrons is presently being debated, said director John Miller.

On the east side of the manor you will find another garden that has been restored to its original form. This is the blue and gold breakfast garden, Manning's contribution. This small garden lies between brick walks that lead up to a sculpture fountain, a copy of the fifteenth-century Italian, *Boy and Dolphin*. The beds are planted with old-fashioned flowers such as bugleweed, bellflower, morning glory, hosta, squill, violets, iris, narcissus, foxglove, columbine, and lungwort. This garden is just outside the manor's breakfast room and has been restored to resemble an earlier era, from old photos and the recollections of Irene Seiberling Harrison, the last of the Seiberling family who in 1992 was 102 years old.

"The Breakfast Room faced east, so the sun shone through the French doors in the morning. During the summer, Mother would open the doors and open the room out into the garden. We would all look past the doors, and the blue fringe of morning glory that crept up the edge of each, to the sunlit planting and the darling fountain. The drip of water from the fountain added to the serenity of the moment," Harrison said.

If you are not in a rush to get home, drive back along Riverview Road or Akron Peninsula Road through the lovely natural areas of the Cuyahoga Valley National Recreation Area.

The terrace overlooking the Cuyahoga Valley is just one of many grand sights at Stan Hywet. (Photo courtesy of Stan Hywet Hall.)

Sunnybrook Farms
9448 Mayfield Rd., Chesterland, 44026; 729-7232; guided tours avail. by advance reservation

Some of the gardens surrounding Sunnybrook Farms in Chesterland are worth a drive to visit, even if you are not planning to buy anything. When you pull into the nursery at Sunnybrook, you will see a narrow rock garden perched on a high retaining wall beside the greenhouse. In it you will find a nice combination of herbs and alpine plants, a good source of inspiration for your own rock garden. The herb gardens that were maintained west of the driveway in past years, however, are now closed and are likely to remain unattended for some time.

Most fun here is walking down the drive that passes by the garden center area and plastic tunnel greenhouses. Tall evergreen trees and shrubs form a dense wooded area that is honeycombed with narrow paths and is home to epimedium, ferns, and hundreds of different kinds of hostas. The walks crisscross the dark shady garden and meander past interesting woody specimen plants such as variegated pachysandra,

Pieris japonica, and mammoth taxus shrubs. When you exit the garden, follow the stone lane back toward the greenhouses; it passes a field of sheep, some of whom may come visit you if you call to them.

Gardens Open by Appointment

The following gardens welcome visitors, but only by prior arrangement with the garden caretakers.

Claystone Farm

Newbury; open for group tours by appointment only; contact Don Vanderbrook, 371-0164

This is the working, experimental, and display garden of nationally known floral designer Don Vanderbrook and his partner Tony Badalamenti. The garden, which stretches across a hillside, has a formal English layout. Main walks run up and down the hill; smaller paths cross perpendicular, creating many rectangular beds between them. Boxwood hedges, clipped hollies, and trellised espalied fruit trees also define areas of the garden.

Masses of flowers ramble across the beds; many are excellent for cutting. Some, such as foxglove, poppies, columbines, and salvias, scatter their seed and pop up where they will, giving a spontaneous look to the otherwise structured garden. Vanderbrook collects flower species and varieties from the Royal Horticultural Society, British flower designers, and other unusual sources that he tests for hardiness and usefulness as cut flowers. As a result, he often has exotic bloomers on display. Other plants have come from large parties he has decorated; flowering cherries were left after a cherry blossom festival in Washington, D.C.; bamboo remained after it was used to cast shadows on Japanese screens. His most recent garden is devoted to the new shrub roses developed by English breeder David Austin—they have been given much press in horticultural magazines in America.

Gilmour Academy Restored Tudor Garden

Corner of SOM Center and Cedar roads, Gates Mills, 44040; groups welcome with advance reservations; contact development director Jean Buchannan; 473-8001

Entering the Gilmour campus past brick walls and down a winding road to a historic Tudor house, is a little like entering a different time. But blue tennis courts and groups of jeans-clad students bring you back real fast. Behind the Tudor house is one of the few Warren Manning gardens that remain in Cleveland. (For more on Manning, see the Stan Hywet Hall entry in this chapter). "This is the original house of Francis Drury, a Cleveland industrialist who helped develop the oil stove. It was on Euclid Avenue Mansion Row, where the Drury Theater is now. When the family retired to Gates Mills, Drury had the home reproduced, and moved the garden there, including its original lighting and furnishings," said Jean Buchannan, director of institutional advancement and development.

Actually, not much of the garden remains except the skeleton, but that is due to change, says Buchannan. Gilmour is raising funds for restoration of the home and gardens.

The rectangular sunken garden surrounds a reflecting pool and blends with nearby Tudor architecture, although the massive retaining walls are unsettled at present and in need of major repair. Huge vining hydrangeas climb over the walls, and towering arborvitaes loom in each corner; these are the only original plants remaining. Where flowers used to cluster, pachysandra, sheared taxus, and lawn have taken over. Buchannan envisions returning a greater abundance of flowers as the restoration proceeds. She hopes to use the garden more for school ceremonies, weddings, and other special events, and that perhaps it will again become a living classroom.

"We used to give boys academy appointments—you might have called them detentions—that they spent weeding in the garden. A lot of them ended up learning much about plants and being inspired. One of those boys went on to become the assistant director of The Greater Cleveland Garden Center," Buchannan said.

Gwinn

Bratenahl, open by reservation only to nonprofit organizations for meetings, programs, seminars, retreats; for more info, contact University Circle Incorporated, 791-3900

Built in 1907 for William Gwinn Mather, a leading turn-of-the-century industrialist, the Gwinn estate is now used as a conference center. The grounds feature a historical landscape and an elegant home. Unfortunately, it's not open for public visits. But if you get a chance to attend a meeting on the grounds, take it. You will see the work of well-known early landscape architects Charles Platt, Warren Manning, and Ellen Shipman, who collaborated on the property for several decades. The landscape today is not maintained with total historical accuracy, but it retains the original layout, focusing on the wonderful views of Lake Erie and combining natural and formal plantings.

The blending of natural with formal, found in both Gwinn's garden and the Mather home, resulted from using a team of two designers, each of whom proposed a different approach. Charles Platt, an architect and landscape architect, proposed laying out the property using modernized classic Italian designs, which he had written about in *Italian Gardens* (1893, Harper, New York, NY). His influence was felt in the architecture of the home and formal garden, and in the linking of indoor and outdoor spaces. In contrast, Warren Manning enjoyed designing naturalistic gardens, which take up much of the property and enhance the views. He used a large number of native American plants in a style now called "emerging American."

In addition to Manning and Platt, in the late 1930s Ellen Shipman came to Gwinn to create a new planting plan in the existing formal flower gardens. These had been set off from a parklike expanse of lawn and from the lake shoreline by a garden wall and pergola to the north and by a teahouse to the south. As was typical of Shipman gardens, the plan was complex—almost astonishingly so by modern standards—and required high maintenance. Today, her elaborate plans have been simplified but still use the original plant list and color scheme of soft blue and yellow, creamy white, and soft pink. Gwinn gardeners custom-grow many unusual varieties of perennials in the original working greenhouse, which also supplies cut flowers for the house. Fifty years ago, the greenhouse also grew grapes and nectarines for the table.

Mooreland Estate, Inc
Lakeland Community College, 7800 Clocktower Dr., Kirtland, 44094; 953-7306; public events held once a month starting in spring; admission fee

The turn of the century was a lavish time for estate gardens in the Cleveland area—several, including Stan Hywet, Gwinn, Lantern Court, and Quail Hollow, have been maintained or are being restored. Another to include among the once-greats now coming back in grand style is the Mooreland Estate.

The garden is connected to an Edwardian home, a retreat for industrialist Edward Moore and his family. The estate once included 2,000 acres, which were sold to Lakeland College in 1968. The home was deserted from 1982 to 1989, but since then has been under ongoing restoration by volunteers. The gardens include mature privet hedges, wisteria-covered pergolas, dogwoods, and spectacular rhododendrons—one of which now is two stories high.

A rose garden that once had 3,000 roses still has 1,000; more are on the way. It is enclosed in a rectangular rose-edged privet hedge; enter through a gate in the hedge or beneath the wisteria pergola. The main garden surrounds a fountain and is bordered by a ring of white roses, another ring of pink roses, and then four crescents of multicolored roses.

Elsewhere, a formal green garden of periwinkle, ivy, rhododendrons, and yews spreads out from a reflecting pool; this garden replaced the estate tennis courts in 1928. A formal garden features symmetrically patterned beds of annual and perennial flowers. Daffodils line paths, and a new grove of apple trees is getting off to a strong start.

Roemer Display Garden
North of Roemer Nursery, 2310 Green Rd., North Madison, 44057; 428-5178 or (800) 955-5178; avail. for tours of 15–30 people by reservation

This one-and-a-half-acre garden is a class act, pretty and full of unusual plants that will awe a horticultural collector. You'll walk along winding brick walks and turf paths, which sometimes widen to show you a broad view over a large section of the garden or narrow so that you look closely at a small collection of plants nearby. The paths branch out into areas you can crisscross to find the plants that interest you most.

Interesting plants abound here. You'll see weeping, creeping, and cascading forms, golden hemlocks, and beech trees with purple leaves edged in pink. There is a water garden, unusual garden seats—one is made of a big slab of stone—and such spectacles as a huge old clump of roots that now support a community of alpine plants.

Carolyn Stroombeek, who devised and now manages the garden, uses it to test new plants and has found some exceptional selections that Roemer Nursery sells to the nursery trade. Most notable is Schmidt's boxwood, which is exceptionally hardy, staying healthy despite cold winters that kill other kinds of boxwood back to the ground. Another recent Roemer introduction is a variegated evonymous called 'Sunny Lane'.

Farther Afield

Here a few special gardens that may require more travel time for some but are well worth a trip.

Fellows Riverside Gardens and The Garden Center

Mill Creek Metropolitan Park District, 816 Glenwood Ave., Youngstown, 44502; 743-7275; or for The Garden Center; 123 McKinley Ave., Youngstown, 44509; 792-7961; Gardens open free year round; Garden Center has limited hours that change depending on the season.

Just as Cleveland has the Emerald Necklace, Youngstown has a wonderful green belt of parks that stretch along rolling hill beside Mill Creek. In addition to lovely natural scenery and historic sites, you'll enjoy Fellows Riverside Gardens, a conglomerate of many different gardens. Although it has plants of interest through all seasons, it is most spectacular in spring when more than 40,000 bulbs and scores of flowering shrubs and trees proclaim the coming of a new growing season.

A formal garden features patterned parterres of bulbs and flowering trees and later annual flowers. Nearby is a shade garden with spring bulbs and perennials that make the most of early season sunshine, and perennials that grow well in summer shade. Around the corner, you come to a perennial border walk and climbing rose *allée*, featuring over 65 cultivars of perennials ideally suited to our climate. The roses and trellises were renovated in 1994; check the labels to find the names of old favorites and good new roses. At the end of the walks is an English bower and sitting area.

Stop at the formal rose garden to look over the 44-acre Lake Glacier before wandering through beds of over 1300 roses, set off by clipped evergreen hedges. You'll pass through an informal herb garden and on to a Victorian gazebo surrounded by old-fashioned flowers such as roses, irises, peonies, and daylilies. In the spring, be sure to wander over to the Schmidt Rhododendron Collection, five beds of rhododendrons, azaleas, viburnums, and spring-flowering bulbs.

Further on, around the perimeter of the garden is a rock garden filled with dwarf and unusual plants and interesting ornamental grasses. Winding paths bring you up close so you can view and appreciate them. Keep going to the Great Terrace, for an awesome view of downtown Youngstown. Then enjoy equally majestic beech trees, including weeping beeches, tricolor, and copper beeches. Head back through the Long Mall, edged on both sides by plants that bloom in sequence through the growing season.

While you're in the neighborhood, stop in at the neighboring Fred W. Green Memorial Garden Center, home to a variety of horticultural workshops and plant shows. The building is owned by the park system but operated by the Garden Forum of Greater Youngstown. It includes a library, gift shop, and display areas.

Franklin Park Conservatory

1777 E. Broad St., Columbus, 43203; (614) 645-8733; open Tuesday through Sunday, except Thanksgiving and Christmas; admission fee

One of the most exciting gardens I've ever seen is indoors at the Franklin Park Conservatory. This spectacular facility was renovated and enlarged to its present colossal size for Ameriflora, an international garden exhibition held in Columbus in 1992. The conservatory re-creates many different climates from around the world and includes thriving specimens of fabulous tropical plants. There's a steamy tropical cloud forest, a cool Himalayan mountaintop, a Pacific Island water garden, an arid desert, and a tropical rain forest. You'll also see an ancient bonsai garden and a tree-fern forest.

The last time I visited, the conservatory was even more fun. A nearby art school had incorporated a display of dinosaur statues amid the greenery. Imagine seeing a little dinosaur peeking out from beneath a tree fern—I had as much fun as my kids did. We also enjoyed the gift shop and the delicious food at the snack bar.

Just outside the conservatory is a huge and impressive formal display of annual flowers surrounding a fountain—like something you might see at a palace in France. There also are more than 20 acres of park and gardens, some of which remain from Ameriflora.

Kingwood Center

900 Park Ave. West, Mansfield, 44906; (419) 522-0211; self-guided tour brochures avail.; group tours by advance reservation

This spectacular 27-acre garden (with 20 additional acres of woods) is the former estate of C. K. King, once president and chairman of Ohio Brass. He left his estate to a trust that now operates Kingwood Center. Because the grounds are free, open dawn to dusk, and full of colorful flowers and impressive formal gardens, Kingwood Center has become a popular horticultural center for local residents. It also attracts gardeners from all over the country who want to see new plants or new planting combinations.

There are massive displays of spring bulbs, including 55,000 tulips and a lawn carpeted with crocuses, a herb garden, formal and informal flower beds, an orangery of unusual indoor plants, and acres of trial gardens for All America Selections (an organization that tests new seed-grown cultivars in gardens across the country and gives awards to outstanding newcomers). There is also a new two-acre terrace garden with woody plants, flowers, and ornamental grasses.

The brilliant swirling annual beds are remarkable. One recent color combination was 'Celebrity Blue' and 'Celebrity Hot Pink' petunias with 'Lavender Lady' globe amaranth and purple *Verbena bonariensis*. Some of the strange and astonishing annuals displayed here have been the swollen, hotdog-shaped crimson flowers of 'Ritz Rocket' amaranth, the tiny plumes of 'Flamingo Feather' cockscomb, tiny, furry tail-like flowers of a miniature chenile plant (*Acalypha repens*), and eight-foot tall purple 'Dwarf Red Spire' castor beans.

"Not many places have as extensive collections as we do that also are put in interesting garden settings. When people want to look at plants, they come to see us because we have just about everything in the better cultivars of peonies, roses, daylilies, iris, and hostas," said Bill Collins, education coordinator.

In the perennial garden are some intriguing and quite unusual specimens, including *Bletilla*, a hardy orchid, bronze-leaf *Ligularia dentata* 'Dark Beauty', and fleece flower (*Polygonum* x 'Border Jewel'). You can find similar "jewels" of the plant world by browsing through the many other garden areas here, which are so extensive and well laid out that you may want to park your car in several different locations around the grounds so you can take it all in during a single afternoon.

Malabar Farm State Park

4050 Bromfield Rd., Lucas, 44843; (419) 892-2784; open all year; admission fee

Malabar Farm State Park, which is off of I-71 and State Route 603 near Bellville, will introduce you to agriculture as you may never have seen it before. This is a state park that preserves the farm and large country home of Louis Bromfield, Pulitzer Prize-winning author and conservationist.

Plant lovers can enjoy mature woods, carpeted with wild flowers in spring, and fields of farm crops. Come for special events such as the maple syrup festival, draft horse plowing competitions, Arbor Day, trail day, farm field day, or craft festivals. While you're there, tour the mansion and take a wagon all the way around the farm. Stay for lunch, picnics, fishing, or camping.

Ohio State University Research and Development Center
Historic Rose Garden and Secrest Arboretum
1680 Madison Ave., Wooster, 44691; 263-3700

This arboretum, named for Edmund Secrest, the first state forester, is a working area where Ohio State University staff and students evaluate new and old plants. You can see magnificent mature specimens of rhododendrons, azaleas, crabapples, hollies, trees, shrubs, and evergreens, including fifty kinds of arborvitae and a hundred kinds of taxus. Some of these were planted as long ago as 1909. Come in May for crabapple viewing; in mid- to late-May for the rhododendrons and azaleas.

Here, you'll also see:

The Garden of Roses of Legend and Romance
Of special interest to lovers of historic roses, this garden is in peak bloom in early June. This two-and-a-half-acre garden includes about five hundred varieties of roses of antiquity, legend, and romance, including old moss, species, damask, eglanteria, scotch, cabbage, alba, foetida, bourbon, gallica roses along with old climbers, ramblers, and other roses.

Agricultural Technical Institute's Horticultural Gardens
The nearby ATI Horticultural Gardens (1328 Dover Rd., Wooster, 44691; 264-3911) feature gardens of herbs, perennials, English roses, espalied pyracantha, perennials, a greenhouse-conservatory, and an All America Display Garden of annuals.

Quail Hollow State Park
13340 Congress Lake Ave., N.E., Hartville, 44632; 877-6652; grounds open daily dawn to 11 p.m.; house 1 to 5 p.m.; group tours avail. with advance registration

In the 1920s, a family hunting cabin owned by railroad tycoon Harry Bartlett Stewart was expanded into a large, Greek revival country retreat. This historic manor is the centerpiece of Quail Hollow State Park.

The manor presided over 720 acres of land, part of which was landscaped by Warren Manning, one of the greatest American landscape architects of the time. Manning was a man of many talents. Just as he had done with Stan Hywet Hall in Akron, he created long views with rolling lawn framed scenically by trees and shrubs. Then, behind the house, he created a series of landscape rooms, intimate and detailed gardens for close-up observation.

"The garden rooms are mostly deteriorated now," said Carol Kern, chairman of the gardens, "but remnants of an old walled English garden and a few others still remain."

Meanwhile, newer gardens have emerged. Kern and other members of the Quail Hollow Herb Society are in the process of installing a large herb garden where the sunken croquet court used to be. "When we were excavating the site originally, we kept pulling up old wickets," Kern said.

The herb garden is surrounded by a low wall and is sunken slightly below the lawn. It is divided into beds of different shapes and interconnecting walks. The center of the garden has a square bed; nearby are two half-moon-shaped beds, and adjoining them are rectangular beds. Each bed is planted with a different theme. The herb society has already established beds devoted to everlasting flowers (for dried arrangements), scented geraniums, fragrant plants, silver plants, and one bed just for experimenting. They will soon tackle the remaining gardens, planned to feature Native American, culinary, dye, and medicinal herbs.

Quailcrest Farm
2810 Armstrong Rd., Wooster, 44691; 345-6722

This wonderful nursery garden is small in comparison to its neighbor, Kingwood Center, but it is well maintained, comfortable, and full of good ideas and interesting plants. Thirty-five display and trial gardens surround the house, and there are nursery areas set within the beautiful velvety-green lawn. Discover an unusual toad lily in a shade garden, a passion flower vining on an arbor in the herb garden, and curly-leaved parsley used as a frilly edging for a mixed shrub and flower garden. Several color combinations are particularly striking in fall, a time many other gardens are failing: a drift of 'Purple Palace' coralbells nestled in front of crimson-flowered sedum 'Autumn Joy', and, in another garden, crimson snapdragons at the feet of the red berries of a cranberry viburnum bush.

Roscoe Village
440 N. Whitewoman St., Coshocton, Ohio 43812; (614) 622-9310

Roscoe Village features historic inns, museums, and shops typical of a mid-1800s port on the Ohio and Erie Canal; it also has charming plantings and gardens well worth a second look. Just as if you stepped back a century and a half into the past, you'll find many of the foundation plantings rich in perennials—good durable flowers such as hosta, lady's mantle, iris, poppy, peony, and ferns.

Some gardens show what the folks from that era grew to be somewhat self-sufficient. The garden beside the 1840s home of Dr. Mario

Johnson features medicinal, culinary, and decorative herbs and old-fashioned vegetables. (The Roscoe Village Herb Society has recently created a knot garden of green and silver santolina there.) The weaver's garden by the Village Craft Center contains dye herbs that color fibers used for weaving.

The Buckeye Garden, named for a large Ohio buckeye tree that blew over in 1990, now houses a thriving red buckeye, a shrub or small tree with red flowers in spring, and a new Ohio buckeye, which will take some time to reach large size. The garden also features perennials in beds divided by gravel and brick walks (some of the brick is salvaged from the original road in Roscoe), and stone walls built with antique foundation stones. Plans are under way to build a pergola.

A new showcase garden is devoted to Frances Montgomery, a Roscoe Village co-founder who passed away in 1989. It features some of Montgomery's favorite plants. She loved to garden and was frequently seen around the grounds pruning, dividing, and lending a hand as needed.

Montgomery had some strong opinions about how gardens should look. She liked the sandstone that had been stockpiled along the canal, so the new garden features stone walks and walls. She didn't like fountains, so a naturalistic waterfall adds the music of water to the garden. And she enjoyed good, solid plants such as English ivy, hemlocks, spruces, spirea, hollies, hydrangea, and viburnum (which are loved as much today as in the past). They have become the stars of the new garden.

In one of Montgomery's favorite books, *100 Great Garden Plants* by William H. Frederick, Jr., she learned about plants that reached Ohio canal towns in the 1800s, the era Roscoe Village depicts. These included plants such as the pagoda tree (*Sophora japonica* 'Regent') and Chinese dogwood (*Cornus kousa*), which you can also see on the grounds.

Otto Schoepfle Arboretum
11106 Market St., Birmingham; (800) 526-7275; staffed 8 a.m. to 4 p.m. weekdays; tours avail. with advance reservation

This arboretum, one of Lorain County's best-kept secrets, was the home of Otto Schoepfle (who died in 1992), former chairman of the board and garden columnist of the *Elyria Chronicle Telegram*. He has developed 22 acres of gardens adjoining 50 acres of woods and meadows along the Vermilion River. Schoepfle has donated the arboretum to the Lorain County Metroparks, which now helps maintain the gardens.

The arboretum is formally designed in the front, then changes to naturalistic plantings and, ultimately, to native woodlots. It features clipped hedges, unusual beech trees, a harem of mature American hollies (one male with 15 females), perennial borders, a pine grove with rhododendrons, and astilbe and hosta collections.

"There is a European influence, which Mr. Schoepfle brought back from his travels. And there is something of interest at all times, including winter, when you can see the shedding bark of stewartia, the bright colors of red twig dogwood, the curving stems of contorted filberts, and the evergreen topiary," said Joel Loufman, horticulturist. Fortunately, most everything is labeled so you can learn while you wander.

Zoar Village
Rte. 212, 3 mi. off I-77, Zoar; 874-3211

Zoar Village was founded in the 1800s by a cult of religious separatists. They built their cabins, started subsistence farming, then created a two-acre garden in the center of town. They surrounded a central planting of trees and shrubs with circular beds of flowers, an impressive sight today and certainly a phenomenon in pioneer times. Beside the garden is one of the first greenhouses in Ohio, which was used to house houseplants of wealthy Clevelanders during the winter.

Unfortunately, the future of the 18-acre Zoar Village State Memorial is uncertain because of Ohio Historical Society budget cuts.

Atriums and Indoor Plantings

When the weather becomes too hot or cold to enjoy outdoor gardens, you might try browsing through some of the local atriums. Many of the larger and newer office buildings include an area of skylights and greenery, often accompanied by water. Malls, too, often have plenty of greenery and can be wonderful places to walk for exercise and to experience a touch of the tropics in the winter. Many of the mall owners compete to put up the most lavish indoor plant displays—and you can be the beneficiary even if you don't buy a thing. The pace tends to pick up closer to Christmas, says Mary Blaha from Interior Green, an interior plantscaping company, as many offices and malls call in their plantscapers to add flowering plants, Christmas trees (though most are silk), and other festive decorations. Here are a few enjoyable atriums in town:

BP America Building
Public Square, Cleveland

This large atrium area has warm and quiet landscaping that features a few large trees and a fountain.

The Arcade
401 Euclid Ave., Cleveland

Simple vines soften this busy five-story arcade with high glass ceiling. It's not a horticultural showplace, but window boxes of green vines (which include durable grape ivy) stand out amid the shopping bustle. The Arcade puts on an especially ornate Christmas greens display.

Tower City Center
Public Square, Cleveland

 Plantings are not the dominant factor here; fountains, towering glass ceilings, and endless balconies of shops are. But take a closer look at the cast-iron plants, such as Chinese evergreens, which look good even though they grow on the balconies, where light levels are quite low.

Areas to Drive Through

 The following are not gardens but attractive growing areas to drive through and view from your car:

Exceptional Cleveland Street Trees
 When you are in Cleveland, you may want to drive through some of the streets lined with especially interesting trees—a few of which are cultivars found or developed here in Cleveland. Some of these are:

- Callery pears along Ferndale Avenue, where the cultivar 'Cleveland Select' was originally discovered. 'Cleveland Select' trees also line West 172nd Street south of Puritas.
- Norway maples on Parkhurst Drive, where the cultivar 'Cleveland' was discovered. 'Cleveland' Norway maples line Brooklawn Avenue.
- 'Bowhall' maples stretch along Mayview Road.
- 'Briotii' hybrid horse chestnuts bloom bright red on West 58th Street.
- Korean evodia along Cortland Dr. off West 140th Street.
- Japanese tree lilacs produce fragrant white flowers in late June and early July on Fairville Avenue off Rocky River Drive.

Avon Greenhouse District
 You can find a number of nurseries and greenhouses around Avon. From Detroit Road, travel south on Stony Ridge.

Forest Hill Historic District
From intersection of Mayfield and Lee roads, north on Lee Rd., East on Brewster Rd. in East Cleveland and Cleveland Heights

 This area was developed by John D. Rockefeller, Jr. in the 1920s. It is rich in interesting homes surrounded by great mature plantings. Drive by slowly and enjoy the cool shade trees, interesting specimen plants, and relaxing atmosphere.

Lake County Nurseries and Greenhouses
State Routes 20 and 84, and nearby areas from Heisley Rd. to Madison in Lake County

Despite a gradual decline in the number of growers, you will still find many nurseries, greenhouses, and garden centers clustered in this part of Lake County. If you are looking for new plants, you can find just about anything along this route.

The fertile soils and mild lake-effect weather here is perfect for nursery crops, orchards, and grapes, which you will find in abundance. This area once was called the Nursery Capital of the United States, a title now shared by warmer areas like Florida and California.

Schaaf Road / Brooklyn Greenhouse District
This area of fertile sandy soils once housed market gardens and was later a center for a thriving greenhouse industry. Although most of the greenhouse ranges have given way to industry and housing, you can still see an impressive collection of ranges, many of which are wholesale only. Drop in on the few businesses that welcome retail customers. Look for Richardson's Greenhouse, Rosby Brothers, and, on nearby Jennings Road, Christensen Greenhouse.

West Shoreway in Cleveland
off West Shoreway by W. 49th St. exit

What was recently a nine-acre dumping place for old concrete, kitchen sinks, and granite blocks has become a meadow of little bluestem, blazing-star, and black-eyed Susan. And, by 1995, Cleveland landscape architect Judith Vargo expects the land to have matured into a prairie of ten species. "This is the first time the city has done this kind of prairie planting instead of planting turf grass (which gets boring after a while). We liked the idea that the prairie is intended to be self-maintaining," said Vargo.

Ohio Wineries

Since the 1850s, when Nicholas Longworth planted vines in the hills overlooking Cincinnati, Ohio has been a state dedicated to the art of winemaking. His vision was expanded by German immigrants who settled Lake Erie's beautiful "Wine Islands." After Prohibition, dozens of families rebuilt cellars along the shores of Lake Erie from Toledo to Conneaut. In the 1970s, the fourth generation of winemakers planted grapes across the state—along country lanes, amid rolling hills, and nestled in river valleys. The established wineries expanded both acreage and facilities.

Today's Ohio wine industry is proud to be nationally recognized as a producer of premium vintages. In wine competitions across the country, in challenges against vintages from around the world, Ohio wines are surprising experts with their quality and great style.

The following northeast Ohio wineries have vineyards, welcome walk-in visitors, and give tours.

Buccia Vineyards
518 Gore Rd., Conneaut, OH 44303; 593-5976

Chalet Debonne Vineyards
7743 Doty Rd., Madison, OH 44057; 466-3485

Ferrante Winery and Ristorante
5585 Rte. 307, Geneva, OH 44041; 466-8466

Firelands Winery
917 Bardshar Rd., Sandusky, OH 44870; (800) 548-WINE

John Christ Winery
32421 Walker Rd., Avon Lake, OH 44012; 933-9672

Klingshirn Winery
33050 Webber Rd., Avon Lake, OH 44012; 933-6666

Lonz Winery
Middle Bass Island, OH 43438; (419) 285-5411

Markko Vineyard
R.D. 2, South Ridge Rd., Conneaut, OH 44030; 593-3197

The Winery at Wolf Creek
2637 South Cleveland-Mass. Rd., Norton, OH 44203; 666-9285

For more information on Ohio wine and wineries, contact The Wines of Ohio, 822 North Tote Rd., Austinburg, OH 44010; (800) 227-6972.

Index

More Good Books About
CLEVELAND

If you enjoyed *The Cleveland Garden Handbook*, you'll want to know about these other fine Cleveland guidebooks and giftbooks . . .

■ **Neil Zurcher's Favorite One Tank Trips**
At Last! Northeast Ohio's favorite TV traveler shares his favorite getaways in a book. This guide shows how to take delightful mini-vacations close to home. Describes hundreds of unusual, surprising, and nearby attractions.
$12.95 softcover • 208 pages • 5½" x 8½"

■ **Cleveland On Foot** by Patience and Harry Cameron
Follow the hikes and walks in this guide and discover Greater Cleveland's historic neighborhoods, distinctive suburbs, glorious Metroparks, and surrounding nature preserves (and get some great exercise, too!) Step-by-step directions & maps.
$12.95 softcover • 264 pages • 5½" x 8½"

■ **Cleveland Discovery Guide** by Jennifer Stoffel and Stephen Phillips
The best family recreation in Greater Cleveland—in a handy guidebook. Written by parents, for parents; offers detailed descriptions, suggested ages, prices, and more. An idea book for how to share more "quality time" close to home.
$12.95 softcover • 208 pages • 5½" x 8½"

■ **Cleveland Golfer's Bible** by John H. Tidyman
Describes in detail every golf course, driving range, and practice facility in Greater Cleveland. Includes descriptions, prices, ratings, locator maps.
$12.95 softcover • 240 pages • 5½" x 8½"

■ **Cleveland: A Portrait of the City** by Jonathan Wayne
105 brilliant color photographs capture Greater Cleveland in all seasons, showcasing familiar landmarks and uncovering surprising hidden details. Descriptive notes provide historical background. A handsome hardcover giftbook.
$35.00 hardcover • 96 pages • 8½" x 10½"

Available at Your Local Bookstore.

These and other Gray & Co. books are regularly stocked at most Cleveland-area bookstores and can be special-ordered through any bookstore in the U.S.

For information, call:

Gray & Company, Publishers
11000 Cedar Avenue • Cleveland, Ohio 44106
(216) 721-2665